THE GENERATION OF POWER

The Generation of Power

THE HISTORY OF DNEPROSTROI

ANNE D. RASSWEILER

New York   Oxford
OXFORD UNIVERSITY PRESS
1988

Oxford University Press

Oxford   New York   Toronto
Delhi   Bombay   Calcutta   Madras   Karachi
Petaling Jaya   Singapore   Hong Kong   Tokyo
Nairobi   Dar es Salaam   Cape Town
Melbourne   Auckland

and associated companies in
Berlin   Ibadan

Library of Congress Cataloging-in-Publication Data
Rassweiler, Anne Dickason.
The generation of power.
Includes index.
1. Hydroelectric power plants—Dnieper River—Design and
construction—History. 2. Earth dams—Dnieper River—Design and
construction—History. 3. Dnieper River Valley—History.
4. Dneprostroi (Project) I. Title.
TK1486.D6R37 1988   333.91′4   88-1543
ISBN 0-19-505166-1

1 3 5 7 9 8 6 4 2

Printed in the United States of America
on acid-free paper

TO JOHN

ACKNOWLEDGMENTS

The great dam on the Dnepr River, the Vladimir Il'ich Lenin Dam, was built by many thousands of unsung heroes. This book acknowledges the immense labor of those men and women workers who built the dam, the locks, the power station, and subsidiary installations. I thank those Dneprostroevtsi with whom I had the privilege to speak about their experiences during the work.

It is a pleasure to acknowledge the support of the International Research and Exchanges Board and the Fulbright-Hays Fellowship Program. IREX made possible the research on which this book rests. I am also particularly grateful to the support of the Kennan Institute for Advanced Russian Studies of the Wilson Center, Smithsonian Institution. I thank the staffs of Firestone Library at Princeton University, particularly Zdenek David and Oreste Pelech, and the staffs of the Library of Congress, New York Public Library, Moscow State University, the Museum of the Revolution (Moscow), Kiev University, INION, the Lenin Library, and the Library of the Academy of Sciences in Kiev. My special thanks go to my advisor at Moscow University, Vladimir Zinov'evich Drobizhev, who gave generously of his time and advice and helped me locate scarce sources. The late Elizabeth Cooper Hardin graciously gave me letters from her father, Hugh L. Cooper, to her mother, Frances Cooper; Frances Cooper's diaries; pictures; and other mementoes of Col. and Mrs. Cooper's life in the Soviet Union.

This study grew out of a dissertation completed at Princeton University, where S. Frederick Starr gave inspiration and useful recommendations at the start of this project and repeatedly thereafter. Stephen F. Cohen made very important suggestions as dissertation supervisor, for which I thank him greatly. I also thank Cyril Black and Moshe Lewin for reading numerous versions of the manuscript and for their suggestions. Adele Lindenmeyr played a crucial role as friend and critic, encouraging, correcting, and encouraging again. Lynne Viola made excellent recommendations after a close and careful reading, and I have done my best to carry them out. I also thank Kendall Bailes and Richard Burgi for their suggestions, and Jean MacDonald for her ready and skilled bibliographic assistance. I thank the editorial staff of Oxford University Press for their careful reading of the manuscript and for their attention to the myriad details involved in the production of this book, especially Nancy Lane, senior editor; Peter Kracht; and Wendy Warren Keebler.

I have incorporated into this book material which previously appeared as "Soviet Labor Policy in the First Five-Year Plan: The Dneprostroi Experience," in the *Slavic Review* 42, no. 2 (1983).

My family provided the sane background and laughter for these years of work. I thank particularly my mother, Katherine M. Dickason, for her encouragement; my children, Janet, Dick, Jay, and Michael, for their confidence that the dam book would be finished; Mrs. Hairston for her special contributions; and John, to whom this book is dedicated.

CONTENTS

THE GENERATION OF POWER

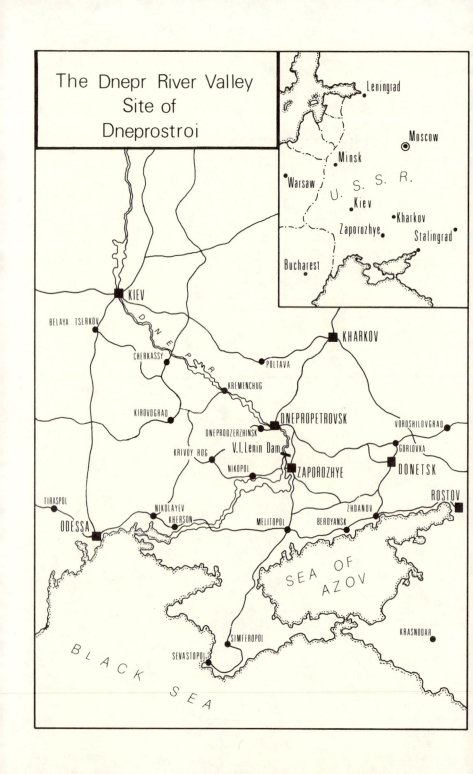

The Dnepr River Valley
Site of
Dneprostroi

Introduction

COMMUNISM IS SOVIET POWER AND THE
ELECTRIFICATION OF THE WHOLE COUNTRY!

The familiar slogan shone brilliantly in ten-foot-high letters, proudly celebrating the successful completion of the Dneprostroi dam and generation of power. The sixty-thousand Dneprostroi workers, technical and engineering personnel, the crowds of visiting dignitaries, and the foreign guests attending the formal opening had reason to be pleased. The giant dam, larger than any in Europe, equipped with equally giant generators, harnessed the turbulent river's energy and transformed it, according to the chief engineer, into "hundreds of thousands of kilowatt energy. . . . The Dnepr is bridled, the Dnepr is conquered, the Dnepr must henceforth serve the people building a new life."[1] As V. M. Mikhailov, deputy chief, said at the opening ceremony,

> Today the homeland of soviets celebrates the victory over the Dnepr. Here a structure has been created, never before been seen in history. Dneprostroi is the mighty foundation of socialist construction. Only the October Revolution made possible the construction of such a giant. The proletariat of the USSR through the Dneprostroevtsi has shown what the Bolsheviks can do![2]

Moreover, wrote the central trade unions' press correspondent, A. Khublarov, it took Soviet power to implement a project originally planned under the tsar but never built: "It was built by enthusiasts, by shock troops for whom labor became in truth a matter of heroism and honor." The project was their school in technology; there they "mastered foreign techniques and improved them."[3]

The celebration marked the successful conclusion of Dneprostroi, the earliest large project of the first Five-Year Plan. It was the forerunner of the giant construction projects, centers for the forced industrialization drive of the early 1930s.

The construction project, the *stroika*, was the funnel for workers into industry and, therefore, the common environment for them and new worker-recruits during the first Five-Year Plan. Dneprostroi, begun in

3

1927, was followed by Magnitostroi (1930), Traktorstroi (1930), Kuznetskstroi (1930), and the Stalingrad Factory (1931), to mention only a few of
the most well-known giant construction sites. In 1932, at the end of the first
Five-Year Plan, more than 3.1 million workers were employed in construction and even more in enterprises where construction and production went
hand in hand. These projects were well known in their day to Soviet citizens
through daily press coverage of their needs, their difficulties, and their
record-breaking accomplishments. They were also known through novels,
plays, and movies. A major novel, *Energiia* by F. Gladkov, and the important sound film *Ivan* by A. Dovchenko featured Dneprostroi. Hundreds of
documentary films and shorts were produced about socialist construction
in these years.[4] Social transformation and the "reconstruction of a new
Soviet man" were important themes in these works.[5] Dneprostroi was
known to U.S. citizens as well; it was featured at the Soviet pavilion of the
World's Fair in New York City in 1939. Margaret Bourke-White did a series
of photographs featuring industrial construction for *Life* magazine, and
John Scott wrote his memoirs of the heroic battle for construction at
Magnitogorsk in *Behind the Urals.*

The Dneprostroi project stood out from the others; it was the first and
the symbol of the first Five-Year Plan. It was daring in conception. With
one dam, the author of the project, I. G. Aleksandrov, proposed to
harness the Dnepr River and produce eight hundred thousand horsepower. This power would supply energy for industrial and agricultural
development, and for popular use. Three locks would open the river to
the Black Sea and make fifteen hundred kilometers navigable. Moreover,
in a time of general economic hardship, Dneprostroi promised employment in construction and in the new productive facilities. And, not least
important, Aleksandrov's design introduced mechanization into construction work, promising lower costs in the future and more efficient use
of resources.

The decision makers who supported Dneprostroi and its successor
industrial projects shaped the policies governing their construction. They
inaugurated a new period in Soviet history, founding the system we know
today. The period of the first Five-Year Plan is quite rightly regarded as
critical in the history of the Soviet Union.

Until lately, it was the restricted preserve of economists and political
scientists, but recently scholars have reexamined broad historical issues
and raised anew questions of social and cultural change. This study of
Dneprostroi is the only study in English of a construction site. It gives a
complex picture of industrialization, including the premises underlying
the policies, their implementation, and, more importantly, the extempo-

raneous nature of the industrial development. It focuses on the experience of the work force and the organizations designed to lead the workers and interact with them. It examines traditional interpretations of Soviet industrialization, raises additional questions, and suggests new interpretations.

For example, the very idea of the Dnepr dam was developed from projects dating back to Peter the Great. Many goals—the introduction of new industries and the improvement of manufacturing and mining, of transportation, and of communication—were held by the Bolsheviks' imperial predecessors as well as by the Bolsheviks themselves. Some authors claim that the imperial heritage was decisive in the Bolsheviks' first stages of planning; the first planners and plans came from the old tsarist bureaucracy. In the cases of Dneprostroi, the Turk-Sib Railroad, the Volga-Don Canal, Magnitostroi, and Kuznetskstroi, it is well documented that these projects had imperial precedents. In order to explain the link between the imperial and Bolshevik industrialization plans, however, one must ask why the Bolsheviks chose these particular projects. Did the Bolsheviks reformulate or redefine their predecessors' projects in a significant way?

An important theme in the history of the Soviet Union's industrialization is economic backwardness relative to Europe and the United States. The Bolshevik revolutionaries anticipated that the revolution and the victory of socialism would promote the development of the economy, industrialization and rising living standards. But until the material base for socialism was built, what sort of socialism could there be? At what pace could changes be introduced by the party and the proletariat? Who was to pay the costs of industrialization? During War Communism, the peasants bore the cost of the state's formation through forced requisitioning. But when Lenin promoted the *Electrification Plan* of 1920 and the New Economic Policy of 1921, he supported the idea of development based on the cooperation of peasant and working classes.

In 1924, when the economy began to recover from its low point during the Civil War, party and nonparty economists debated alternative paths to economic development and their political consequences.[6] The Bukharinites supported a program providing for a balanced rate of development based on a controlled market economy. Stephen F. Cohen and Moshe Lewin argue that this was a real alternative to the path taken.[7] It was supported by a majority in the lower echelons of the party, the trade union organizations, and skilled workers, argues Roy Medvedev.[8] But the debate ended in 1928 with the victory of Stalin and the Stalinist faction. The policies of forced industrialization and collectivization were adopted. Where did the Stalinist faction find its support, and what circumstances favored supporters of rapid industrialization? How important, for instance, were regional ambitions or foreign military threats?

Recent interpretations of the developments during the first Five-Year Plan have taken two main approaches. One has emphasized the exploitation of the workers and the peasants by the party elite throughout the years of the first two five-year plans. In explaining the evolution of labor policies and laws that bound the workers to jobs, Robert Conquest and Solomon Schwarz emphasize the personal responsibility of Stalin, who demanded rapid expansion of industrialization and brooked no questioning of his views.[9] To obey him and to protect their political futures, his officials used tough, fast-acting policies to produce quick, visible results. Theodore Von Laue ascribes Soviet labor policy to a late developer's need for strong central control in conditions of global economic and military competition, and he deemphasizes the role of Stalin, the Communist party, and ideology.[10] Roger Pethybridge, too, sees the gradual expansion of labor rules as part of the growth of bureaucracy, which he ties to a history of political authoritarianism and social backwardness.[11]

These authors describe a linear development of ever harsher proscriptions and penalties, and they attribute greater coherence to the process than was actually there and greater effectiveness to the laws than they actually had. They view the process from the viewpoint of the capital, disregard the competing ideas among the leaders, and ignore the local level where policies had to be executed and were often changed or ignored. They treat the first Five-Year Plan as an integral part of the Stalinist period, which came to be characterized by a harsh purge atmosphere, forced labor, and careerist party members. In fact, however, these characteristics were not dominant in the years from 1927 to 1932.

In a second approach, some historians portray the events and the controversies of the 1920s and early 1930s as issues in which leadership politics were reflected but did not yet dominate.[12] They introduce new topics. Lewin analyzes the growing chaos in a society whose old structure was destroyed by revolution and civil war and whose structure in the period of the new economic policy (NEP) was shattered and then reshaped by revolution from above. Lewin emphasizes the flux in the initial years of industrialization.[13]

John Barber examines the changing characteristics of the working class during the first Five-Year Plan period and the variety of conflicting social and cultural attitudes within it.[14] He discusses the resistance of both workers and managers to state policy and emphasizes the internal dynamic of working-class development, historical connections, and local circumstances (including, of course, collectivization). Kendall Bailes investigates the formation of the technical intelligentsia—the structure of the group, its influence in society, and, particularly, its interaction with the Communist party.[15] In this second approach, circumstances peculiar to the period from 1928 to 1932 shaped its development; personalities, institutions, social dynamics, and the context of the action are as important as the dominating figure of Stalin.

While both Soviet and Western historians stress the importance of the Communist party in the industrialization process, the Western interpretation emphasizes the importance of Politburo economic decisions and party-sanctioned force in compelling their execution. Whereas Soviet scholars emphasize the leading role of local party organizations in industrial construction, only a few Western historians have investigated closely the party role at the local level. With evidence from his study of the Smolensk archive of this period, Nicholas Werth supports the view that the party activist was taught that it was his duty to lead in production tasks.[16] And Sheila Fitzpatrick emphasizes the special efforts of the Bolshevik party to promote members of the working class into positions of authority and responsibility.[17] But one must ask how critical was the role of the party in the execution of plans on the *stroiki*. This study will examine how the local party organizations defined their tasks and carried them out.

At Dneprostroi and the other giant projects that were modeled on it, policies were initially designed to encourage the development of a sense of community, of responsibility, particularly in work and civic organizations, and cultural self-development. But it was soon demonstrated that these policies were not necessarily compatible with the production goals of the work sites. How did the priorities of the leaders evolve when their plans met realities? How congruent was the goal of industrialization with that of building socialism?

Chronicle

Tens of thousands of workers streamed to the Dneprostroi site in the first years of construction, looking for jobs, education, and new careers. At first, they wielded picks and shovels and carried bricks, mortar, and railroad ties. They built railroad spurs, barracks, and warehouses. They lived in temporary barracks and tents and ate rough food. Their numbers rose and fell reflecting the seasons—the breakup of the ice in the spring and the call of farm work, the planting and harvesting months of April and August, the onset of freezing weather.

At the end of the first year, machinery, most of it foreign and much of it previously unknown in the Soviet Union, arrived from the United States and Germany, and some came from other parts of the Soviet Union. Foreign instructors, Soviet engineering and technical personnel, and worker brigades assembled and gingerly operated the new excavators, cranes, pneumatic drills, and automatic dump cars. Schools were organized—literacy schools for the many unable to read; technical study circles in practical skills; and courses in construction, electrical and mechanical engineering, and other technical subjects.

By the end of the first building season, much preparatory work had been done: forty kilometers of railroad track had been laid for the transport of fill and rock away from the site, and timber, concrete, and iron and steel for new construction. A temporary dam, to block one third of the river on the right side, was nearly finished, and a second one, for the left, was partly built as well.

Workers also constructed a temporary power station, administration building, saw mill, and compressed-air factory. Work was begun on a large mechanical workshop, woodworking shop, concrete and rock-crushing factories, a summer theater, and a mechanized cafeteria designed to serve six thousand meals and to cook food for branch cafeterias. Workers built eight brick houses for the American village, supplied with water and sewers, and 152 two-family brick dwellings in three villages. There were also barracks, 62 of a permanent type, 25 with central heating, and 147 temporary barracks and two bathhouses.

The workers were supplied with food, goods, and services by the administration, cooperatives, and trade unions. Groups of workers who had come together lived together and had their food prepared by their own cooks. State supply centers were supplemented by free-market bazaars where local produce and some manufactured goods were sold. Workers could trade their belongings there as well as materials stolen from the site. Medical services included a hospital and two mobile clinics. There was a library with eighteen thousand books and two bookmobiles, propaganda centers, called "red corners," and a club which sponsored cultural and propaganda activities of all kinds.

Many workers left the site because of the winter cold and the demands of spring sowing, and the site's population shrank to sixty-five hundred from its September high of thirteen thousand. Little work could be done in the freezing temperatures. In the spring, the administration hired few new workers until the ice broke up and the passage of the spring floods made it possible to work again on the temporary dams, known as coffer dams. Once the right and left work sectors were fully enclosed by coffer dams, workers pumped the water out and prepared the ground for the dam foundations—clearing off loose fill and blasting soft rock down to the granite suitable for the dam's underwater foundations or footings. This work continued through the summers of 1928 and 1929, on both the right and left sides of the river.

Supplementary work in 1928 included the completion of the rock-crushing and concrete-mixing plants. Many machines were introduced onto the site, and workers were urged to learn to use them. It proved to be difficult to plan their use and to operate and maintain them efficiently. Much work continued to be done by hand.

As will be discussed in later chapters, much housing was built, but it could not keep up with demand. Many workers lived in tents, even in winter. A cafeteria opened but worked poorly. The majority of workers continued to supply their own meals. Food, goods, and services were in increasingly short supply. The poor living conditions contributed to growing labor turnover.

Most of the preparatory work for the dam was complete by the time of the spring floods in April 1929. After the flood waters subsided, the work site enclosed by the coffer dams was pumped dry. Concrete work for the body of the dam and the foundations and piers for the water gates was started. The schedule required this work to be complete on the left side so that the river, now flowing through the central channel, could be diverted over the completed foundations on the left side. The central coffer dam then had to be set in place before the spring floods of 1930. Shock-troop volunteers helped with concreting. Enough was accomplished. The river was diverted over the left foundations even though the strengthening of the underwater granite base was not then finished. During the winter of 1929–30, the middle-channel coffer dam was finished. Excavation work began in the central channel and continued in the powerhouse and lock areas.

Louis Puls, assistant to Colonel Hugh Cooper, the American consultant for the project, wrote:

> *1930.* The battle was on. The call went out for volunteers to assist in the rock excavation and they the *oudarnikies*, worked faithfully. Young boys and girls, students, as well as the office workers and kitchen help were seen in the hole continually, day and night. As the excavation was carried forward, the concrete work advanced from both ends, and thus the battle was carried on. . . . When the rock excavation work was complete the call went out for volunteers for the placing of concrete. Again the call was answered, and it was a common sight to see girls wearing men's pants and boots shovelling concrete and doing other miscellaneous work.

> On Dec. 4th, 1930, the objective of the workers' counter plan had been accomplished and before the season's work came to an end on Dec. 28th, 517,000 cubic meters [of concrete] had been placed in Dneprostroy, thus establishing a world record.[18]

The tempo of work quickened, but productivity did not. Thousands of workers continued to be employed in spite of the increased mechanization. Further, because of the abominable food and housing and low morale in the work force, turnover continued to be high and even reached new heights. By the end of 1930, all foundation work for the dam was complete. Concrete work was thirty-nine percent complete. Excavation work for the locks bypassing the dam was ninety percent complete, and concreting started. In the powerhouse, turbine emplacement was well under way, and steel work for the superstructure to house the generators was begun.

Very little was done during the winter of 1930–31. Food was very short; housing, fuel, and medical services were inadequate. In addition, the weather was cold and the site very icy. Dam work in the spring was delayed by the abnormally high flood waters. Work continued, however, in the powerhouse and lock areas and even started early because of the mild spring weather. Gate emplacement went slowly; the piers were not well aligned because of poor workmanship. Exceptionally mild weather that winter permitted continued concrete work in the dam, "especially in January [1932] when the alarm was given and the *oudarnikies* again took hold."[19] The final buckets were poured on March 28, 1932, "with fitting ceremony."

The year 1931 saw the arrival and erection of the first turbines and generators. Concrete work and excavation were continued in the locks and approaches to them. Work there was delayed, however, as equipment was loaned to Zavodstroi, one of the factories being built to utilize Dneprostroi's power.

In 1932, the chief emphasis was placed on the power-producing units. By January, five turbines and three generators were installed. On May 7, 1932, the first power was produced. Five units were finished and tested during the summer. Work continued on the locks and on the cranes used to control the spillway gates. The power plant opened on October 10, 1932. By this time, 3.5 million cubic meters of earth and rock had been excavated, and more than one million cubic meters of concrete had been poured in the dam, powerhouse, and lock structures. Forty-seven sluice gates were mounted between piers; nine turbines and generators were put in place. With the installation of the ninth generator in 1939, generating capacity reached five hundred sixty thousand kilowatts. During the years before the German invasion of 1941, the power station produced 16.7 million kilowatts of electric power. The first instrumental steel was produced in 1932, a regular steel factory began to operate in 1933, and a coke factory, iron works, and aluminum complex were added in rapid succession. At the same time, the countryside benefited from greater supplies of electricity and irrigation, and the new locks, opened in 1933, carried increased freight. The population of Zaporozh'e, the nearest large town, grew from fifty-six thousand in 1926 to two hundred eighty-nine thousand in 1939.

Similar chronologies of construction, start-up, and expansion can be written for the other giants of the first Five-Year Plan—Magnitostroi, Kuznetskstroi, Traktorstroi, the Stalingrad tractor factory, just to mention a few. Dneprostroi was the forerunner of these great enterprises. Policies worked out at Dneprostroi were implemented at the other sites in the early 1930s, and in the later years of the first Five-Year Plan all the sites shared in the convulsions caused by the forced tempo of collectivization and industrialization. By studying Dneprostroi, we can learn about the evolving goals linked with industrialization and measure progress toward these goals during the first Five-Year Plan.

1

"Electrification Is the Second Party Plan"

The century of steam—the century of the bourgeoisie
The century of electricity—the century of socialism
Gleb M. Krzhizhanovskii, February 1920

The importance of the Dneprostroi project in the earliest years of the Soviet Union can only be understood in the context of Bolshevik commitment to "Electrification—the second party plan."[1] The first party plan was the establishment of proletarian dictatorship and its evolution to communism—the political plan explained by Nikolai Bukharin and Evgeni A. Preobrazhenskii in *The ABC of Communism.*[2] The second, economic plan was the *Electrification Plan* presented by Lenin to the Eighth Congress of Soviets in December 1920. At that time, he asked his colleagues in the party to give the plan high priority, announcing that "Communism is Soviet power and the electrification of the whole country!"[3]

Dneprostroi was one of a number of projects featured in the plan and thereby associated with these most publicized ideas and most popular slogans of Lenin. Because of the scale of investment required, the technical difficulty of the construction, and especially the conception of economic reconstruction, Dneprostroi presented a difficult challenge to the Soviet industrializers. At the same time, it had particular promise as "a powerful lever for the socialist construction of the USSR."[4]

In his support of the electrification plan, Lenin expressed visionary, even utopian, ideas. In order to understand his enthusiasm and the support he won for the plan, it is necessary to examine Lenin's vision. What did he expect of electrification? To what extent was his vision shaped by the events of the moment and to what extent by his ideas about the future development of the economy and Soviet society?

Lenin set the direction of the *Electrification Plan*, but there were many other contributors as well. Most of them were engineers with practical experience in the field, and they brought specific knowledge of problems and projects with them. They produced the rationale for the Dnepr project and others like it, sometimes reflecting continuity between the imperial period and the Soviet one, and sometimes a very real change. Lenin's popularity ensured general support for the electrification plan, but some of his followers criticized it vociferously. Others refused to take it seriously, including Stalin, who ignored it for months.[5] Engineers, economists (Bolsheviks and those outside the party), and political leaders argued over the plan and the individual projects in it. The *Electrification Plan* clearly influenced the further development of Soviet economy and society and helped define the direction of "building socialism."

Lenin's Vision

When Lenin said, "Electrification is the second party plan" and "Communism is Soviet power and electrification of the whole country," he meant more than expansion of power production and its utilization in the mechanization of communication, transportation, and industrial production. There is much evidence in Lenin's early writings that he saw great advantages to the introduction and application of electric power in homely tasks. He foresaw the transformation of farming and rural life as man escaped the limitations imposed by nature. In "The Agrarian Question and the Critics of Marx" in 1901, he reported on the successful application of mechanical devices.[6] Better than steam, "electricity was more divisible, distributable over a broad territory and it ran machines more correctly and more quietly."[7] Lenin anticipated higher production as a result of application of electricity to milking, threshing, and milling. Later, in 1902, he added the electric plow to this list of the special benefits to be derived from electrification.[8] Electricity would also speed and reduce the cost of transporting agricultural goods and make possible the expansion of irrigation systems.

Lenin wrote in 1913 that the worker's day could be shortened as his work became more productive. The electrification of all factories and railroads would make conditions of work more hygienic; deliver millions of workers from smoke, dust, and dirt; and speed up the transformation of dirty, loathesome workshops into clean, light laboratories worthy of human beings.[9] Further, "electrical lighting and heating would free millions of 'house slaves' from the necessity of spending three quarters of their lives in a filthy kitchen."[10]

And in the *Electrification Plan* itself, the introductory pages offered the citizens of the Soviet Union a vision of a new world.[11] Electrification would serve to free agriculture from the whims of nature. Irrigation, night lighting, soil electrolysis, soil heating, and industrial fertilizers would make agriculture less dependent on weather and soil conditions. As the mechanization of agriculture was seen as a function of size, it was anticipated that farms would be worked as large units with tractors and electric plows supplanting animate labor. At the same time, factory work would be made fast and automatic. Electricity was cleaner, safer, and simpler to use than other forms of energy, and its hardware was light and durable. It facilitated the mechanization of work, especially lifting, loading, and pumping. Electricity supplied direct, easily divisible power which was constant, reliable, and applicable to many processes. It permitted the use of second-class fuels and a greater flexibility in the location of industry. In transportation, electricity could replace coal and obviate the necessity of carrying quantities of fuel to be burned in transit.

Beyond these practical applications of electricity and, moreover, because of them, Lenin anticipated the coming transformation of the Soviet Union:

> We must show the peasantry the organization of industry on a contemporary, most advanced technical level, on the basis of electricity which links the city with the countryside, makes an end to the difference between city and countryside, makes it possible to raise the cultural level of the countryside, [and] to vanquish backwardness, darkness, poverty, illness and "running wild," even in the most remote corners.[12]

He argued that the electrification plan was of paramount importance as a weapon in the battle against the remnants of capitalism in the countryside. Inefficient, small-scale farms would be superseded by technologically superior, large, mechanized farms:

> Anyone who has carefully observed life in the countryside, as compared with life in the cities, knows that we have not torn up the roots of capitalism and have not undermined the foundation, the basis of the internal enemy. The latter depends on small-scale production, and there is only one way of undermining it, namely, to place the economy of the country, including agriculture, on a new technical basis, that of modern large-scale production. Only electricity provides that basis.[13]

Electricity would also serve to facilitate the cultural transformation of the population. Lenin recounted how he and his wife, Krupskaia, had attended the opening of a local power station at Kashino, near Moscow. There, in a peasant's speech, he heard an echo of his own thoughts. The peasant welcomed electricity, saying that previously peasants had been in darkness and now they had light, "artificial light which would lighten our peasant darkness."[14] Lenin drew a lesson from these words. What was "artificial," he said, was that peasants and workers had lived for so long in such darkness and poverty, oppressed by landowners and capitalists. And this darkness would be terminated by electrification. Each electric power station would serve as a center of culture. Of course, it would supply the energy for the light bulbs which permitted study after darkness fell. But beyond that, copies of the *Electrification Plan* would be kept both at power stations and in the schools, to be the inspiration and practical instruction book for all workers and peasants, who would learn what tasks stood before them and the schedule for their completion. The electrification plan would provide them with the opportunity to learn to participate in the reconstruction of the economy and in its development:

> And comrades, you can and must compare on the spot, work over, check out the existing situation, make sure that in each school, in each circle discussing what is communism, the answer is not only that which is written in the program of the party, but that you also speak about how to get out of the condition of darkness.[15]

In sum, Lenin believed that social revolution and development would inevitably follow technological change. His concern was to hurry it, particularly in the countryside which would otherwise restrain Russia's development.

Communism, Lenin had said in February 1920, presupposes Soviet power as the political organ which gives the masses the possibility of "checking all matters" through their elected councils.[16] But only "cultured, conscious, educated workers" could carry out such a function.[17] Since such workers were so few in number under the present conditions, it was the party's duty, as the leader of the masses and their avant-garde, to direct all its energies and labors to executing the electrification plan and to involve workers in both its political and economic aspects.[18] In giving the party members such an assignment, Lenin did in fact raise the *Electrification Plan* to the status of the "second party plan," second only to the political plan of the party outlined in *The ABC of Communism*.[19]

In his enthusiastic endorsement of electrification as a catalyst for change, Lenin was expressing a conviction common to his generation. Henry Adams had thrilled to the humming of the dynamo at the Paris World Fair in 1900.[20] After the turn of the century, popular and scientific journals regularly carried news of the marvelous applications of electricity. Americans talked about the new era to be ushered in by rural electrification with the same enthusiasm as Lenin had in writing about the Soviet countryside.[21] Observers worldwide looked to science as a progressive force. Some even argued that electricity would make war so technically perfect and destructive that it would become unthinkable as an arm of policy.

Science was regarded as a progressive force by the majority of writers because it enabled humans to exercise control over nature and to exploit natural resources. Material gains achieved through science and technology encouraged observers to believe that with reason and more scientific discovery all material difficulties could be solved and social problems resolved.

Lenin's specific interpretations of the past and of future developments were particularly influenced by Marx and Engels's materialistic views and their interpretations of the role of science and technology. In the Marxian analysis, man's life is conditioned by his struggle with nature. Technology is his means of substituting machines for human labor, inanimate for animate power.[22] It has a basically progressive role, for it changes the nature of work and, with this, the characteristics of the working class. Advances in technology had enabled man to participate in a wide range of work processes and required that he continuously expand his knowledge to keep up with science and its applications.[23] Engels saw that because of technology even the peasant might come to share in the knowledge revolution occurring in the urban centers.[24] Marx and Engels welcomed man's opportunity to undergo a wide range of work-related experiences, noting that his creative powers would have a freer scope.

The technology that Marx and Engels were discussing was the technology of steam power. It was only toward the end of his life that Marx commented on electricity. He was interested in electricity in agriculture[25] and realized that one of the most important breakthroughs was in its successful transmission, demonstrated by Marcel Duprès's experiment in 1882.[26] According to Wilhelm Liebknecht, Marx foresaw a great change on seeing an electric locomotive:

> [N]atural science is preparing a new revolution. The reign of the greatness of steam is overturned . . . in its place there will be an immeasurably more revolutionary force—the electrical spark. . . . Political revolution is the inevitable consequence of economic revolution, since the second is only the expression of the first.[27]

Engels also prophesized a revolutionary role for electricity. In 1883, he wrote in a letter of the "colossal" revolution to be expected of electricity:

Steam machinery taught us to transform heat into mechanical action, but the use of electricity opens for us the way for the transformation of all types of energy—heat, mechanical energy, electricity, magnetism, light—one into the other and back again and apply them to industry. . . . [Dupres's transmission experiments] free industry from almost all limits laid down by local fuels, make possible the use also of the most distant water power, and if in the beginning they are useful only for *towns*, in the end they will become the most powerful lever for the removal of the antithesis between town and country.[28]

Lenin was in full accord with the Marxian emphasis on the importance of technology. He argued in 1908, in *Materialism and Empiro-criticism*, that man translated his experience of the world into a concrete mode of handling it. Through his tools, Lenin reasoned, man affected his environment.[29] As man was in turn affected by his surroundings, Lenin was saying, in effect, that man could contribute significantly to his own fate. He could use his knowledge to change his material-technical environment and thereby create a radically new sociopolitical situation.[30]

Mankind could also use knowledge to guide economic development along rational and scientifically devised lines. Central planning of all means of production was a basic tenet of socialism. A scientific plan would permit the most rational allocation of resources and just distribution of products. The *Electrification Plan* was an important sketch of a single, national plan, according to Lenin.[31] He saw its introduction to the Congress in December 1920 as the dawn of a new epoch "when politics would become less and less important, when there would be less talk, less often of politics, and engineers and agronomists would talk more."[32] Here Lenin was arguing as he had in *State and Revolution* (1917). There he had asserted that the management of the economy could be done by workers taking turns in administration, making choices informed by facts. Lenin was either uncharacteristically naive in thinking that "facts" or "scientists" could be absolutely correct and uninfluenced by politics, or so engrossed and enthused by his subject that he ignored the unreality of his own suggestions. Nevertheless, his faith in the progressive role of science was characteristic of his era, in Russia and the Western world.

The Origins of the Plan

The force of Lenin's argument lay in the fact that the plan he promoted was the first single plan for the reconstruction of the economy. Moreover, it paid attention to problems that had been troublesome since imperial times, namely, the shortages of fuel and transportation and the generally low level of labor productivity. Lenin was also addressing the sore needs of the moment. The economy, already strained by three years of foreign war, had suffered further deterioration during the years of civil war and foreign invasion. The policies implemented in the ensuing period were designed to mobilize all resources to meet immediate military and political imperatives. No surpluses existed for the maintenance or expansion of future productive capacity. Short of fuel, raw materials, and labor, many factories closed and cities emptied. Production in all types of industry declined steadily; it nearly ceased in heavy industry by 1920, and in manufactured goods it was only 12.9 percent of production in 1913.[33]

In December 1919, the civil war was nearly won, and Soviet leaders could give more attention to the development of the economy. Shortages of food and fuel loomed large to responsible leaders. It was actually a fuel crisis in the capital that was the immediate cause of Lenin's enthusiastic promotion of electricity. In the midst of the crisis, Lenin received a note from Gleb M. Krzhizhanovskii, an engineer, friend of Lenin, and member of the Bolshevik party serving in the electrical trust of the Supreme Economic Council.[34]

In Krzhizhanovskii's work, Lenin found a new approach to industrial reconstruction.[35] Electrification was the key to technical progress, and in combination "with the organization of work in a socialist way (agriculture and industry) it would give the fastest and surest basis for the reconstruction of industry."[36] Lenin asked Krzhizhanovskii to prepare a plan for the electrification of all Russia—agriculture and industry—to present immediately in the press. He emphasized that the plan should not be presented as a technical matter for scientists but as a job for the proletariat, a program that would "captivate the masses." He suggested the inclusion of concrete tasks, the estimated date of completion, and maps showing the specific stations and transmission lines, the future power net. Lenin's purpose, confidence, and energy pulsed through his letters. "Call me," he wrote, "on receiving this letter," pressing Krzhizhanovskii to immediate action.[37]

Krzhizhanovskii responded to Lenin's appeal with a plan which was published as a brochure and in *Pravda*. Lenin introduced it to a combined session of the state executive committee and the Council of People's Commissars on February 2, 1920. There he dwelt on the significance of electrification as a stimulus for industrial reconstruction and for overcoming "that backwardness, that fragmentation, dispersion, the darkness of the countryside which is the chief cause of all the stagnation, backwardness, and oppression to this day."[38] He suggested that a commission of scientists and technologists work out a plan for electrification. Accordingly, GOELRO, the State Commission for the Electrification of Russia, was formed and given two months for its task.[39]

The Electrification Commission

There already existed a multitude of committees and plans from which GOELRO could pick and choose. The administration and reconstitution of existing energy production plants were the responsibilities of the electricity department of the Supreme Economic Council. Reporting to it was the Commission to Study Russia's Power Resources, formed January 1918, with branches throughout the country.[40] In addition to these commissions, individual trusts (*glavki*) had their own electrical subcommittees, such as the Committee for the Application of Electricity to Agriculture.

In the spring of 1918, a new council, the Electrotechnical Council, had been formed on the initiative of Leonid Krasin, a Bolshevik and member of the Supreme Economic Council's presidium. This council was responsible for overseeing matters of theory and science. It also gave attention to problems in the electrical industry, especially to the establishment of norms and the standardization of materials and machines.[41] On April 10, 1918, the council reported that cheap energy was necessary for the revitalization of the economy. It recommended central power stations, especially those using water power and low-quality fuels.[42] Later in the same year, A. G. Kogan, a deputy chief of the council, presented a plan for the general electrification of industry and transport and the development of resources.[43]

Representatives of the Electrotechnical Council and subcommittees concerned with electrical matters agreed that there should be greater coordination in their work. Activated by Lenin's interest, they formally resolved that all commissions, departments, and groups working on electrification should be brought together and their work coordinated by GOELRO, which would report to the Supreme Economic Council.[44] Members of the new commission had to be confirmed by the Council of People's Commissars, recognition of the importance of the work they were entrusted to do. Their goal was the survey of resources and a practical plan for their utilization, "which meant a start was being made on the creation of a state plan for the country's economy."[45]

Who were the members of GOELRO? How did they view their task? That task, of course, was shaped by Lenin's vision and the specific assignment: electrification as the basis for economic development. This was not to be simply a plan for the reconstruction of the economy but a plan to transform its base and to create a foundation appropriate for building socialism. The composition of the commission reflected Lenin's particular faith in science and practical solutions; the members were all professional engineers and professors in science and technology. Krzhizhanovskii, the only Bolshevik, was elected chairman; deputy chairman was A. I. Eisman, assisted by A. G. Kogan and B. I. Ugrimov and their deputies, N. N. Vashkov and N. P. Sinel'nikov. The committee had nine members, five deputies, and two secretaries.[46] Other specialists assisted GOELRO in working out specific plans. Altogether there were 180 authors and consultants.[47]

Constraints of time complicated the tasks of the planners. They were given only two months—later extended to ten—to complete the plan. Under these circumstances, haste was essential, and the use of existing plans and projects recommended itself to them. On the other hand, they were exhorted not only to revive but to reconstruct the economy, considering new technology. To some planners, it seemed nonsensical to create a detailed, integrated, national plan in a period of economic breakdown.[48] To others, including Ivan Gavrilovich Aleksandrov, the designer of Dneprostroi, it was only proper that they should plan boldly. He developed a plan for the whole South Russia region and spoke dramatically about the coming of an economic revolution at the heart of which was regional development. According to him, it was necessary to create energy centers and plan all types of enterprises to work in combination with them.[49]

Projects for Economic Development in the Imperial Period

Aleksandrov's plan did not emerge full-blown in the work of a few months. On the contrary, he, Krzhizhanovskii, and other members of GOELRO had done developmental work in the imperial ministries and in business before the revolution, and they carried their projects with them. Some of these projects had their roots in even earlier periods. They addressed basic transportation and resource utilization problems of interest to the central ministries, regional governments, and manufacturing and commercial interests. Soviet planning, therefore, reflected this continuity with the imperial period.

The Dneprostroi project had its earliest roots in eighteenth-century transportation projects to improve navigation. Both Peter I and Catherine II, as well as their successors, were interested in developing transportation to facilitate the southern transfer to troops and to move coal and grain north from the Ukraine.[50] Unfortunately, the potential of the Dnepr waterway as a north-south route and passage to the Black Sea was blocked by ninety kilometers of dangerous rapids.

In the 1890s, new incentives caused the state to reexamine the possibilities of bypassing the Dnepr rapids. The central Russian government became particularly interested in the area of southern Russia because of its growing productivity. Foreign exchange earned by the export of grain and other agricultural products was vital for the financing of Russia's imports and support of its credit abroad. It is not surprising, therefore, to find the government increasingly concerned about the handling and transport of grain.[51]

Members of the Association of Industry and Trade, a prominent organization for businessmen, published numerous articles between 1906 and 1917 criticizing the transportation system of the empire.[52] They argued that the high cost of transportation was a severe constraint on the development of Russian trade and kept domestic products from competing with foreign ones. In addition, they blamed the poorly developed transportation system for periodic fuel crises, inefficient handling of grain, and lack of development and integration of potentially rich provinces—the Urals, Turkestan, and Siberia. They wrote that the improvement of the railway system continued to be vital, but, because it was not keeping up with Russia's needs, they suggested that cheap water transportation, especially in conjunction with railroad construction, was worth developing.[53] The association recommended the speediest accomplishment of work on the Dnepr rapids and the construction of the Volga-Don canal, improvement of navigation on secondary rivers, and the permission for private initiative "in those circumstances when the Treasury could not itself provide means."[54] The Dnepr waterway was included on this list because the area through which it flowed had increasing imperial importance. Coal and metal products produced in the south of Russia were needed in the factories of St. Petersburg, and grain needed to be moved south to ports for export to foreign markets where it could earn foreign exchange. A few businessmen even promoted projects such as the Dnepr waterway as measures to help the agricultural sector earn cash which could then be used to buy manufactured goods, thereby stimulating the internal market.

The Dnepr cataracts were suddenly transformed from a liability into an asset when electric power technology began to make rapid progress at the turn of the century. The successful transmission of power over distance in 1891 stimulated new interest in water power, or "white coal," and second-class fuels such as peat, brown coal, and shale oil. Water flowed over the Dnepr rapids at an average rate of fifty-five thousand cubic feet per second. This flow represented a potential of more than one million horsepower when translated into electricity. For a nation that was beginning to identify the deficiencies that made it backward in comparison to its neighbors, here was a resource of great importance, a great natural reserve of inanimate energy. Although at the turn of the century electric power was little developed in Russia, many Russians shared the world's growing fascination with electricity.[55] Some were convinced that energy production and consumption were an index of civilization.[56] One engineer whose writings influenced Lenin argued that cheap electricity should be considered a necessity because it raised productivity and improved living conditions, and he urged his readers to demand this improvement, both in the countryside and in the city.[57]

Plans for the Dnepr

The Dnepr attracted commercial interests seeking to develop water transportation and hydroelectric power production. As early as 1898, an Englishman named Perry, descendent of the Perry who had explored the Dnepr for Peter I, bid for a ninety-nine-year lease to develop the waterway. According to one author, the landowners were successful antagonists to this plan.[58] Another applicant was an English stock company which planned to build both locks and an electric power station. Supported by the Ministry of Finance, discussed by the Council of Ministers, the concession was rejected because of the strong protest of the riverbank landlords.[59] In addition, according to a report of the Chicago *Daily News*, "a local press campaign contributed to the defeat of a British investment in the dam."[60] An American named Targen bid in 1900 to build a number of electric stations, and there was a German bid as well.[61]

Among the most elaborate of the foreign investment plans presented at this time was a scheme proposed by a Belgian engineer, Gustav Dufosse.[62] He suggested uniting Kherson on the Black Sea and Riga on the Baltic with a large sea canal between the Dnepr and the West Dvina, using the water of the latter to deepen the former. A similar project was submitted by a Russian engineer named Rukteshel', but in 1905 a special committee of the Ministry of Ways of Communication turned down these proposals. While acknowledging the military significance of a viable route from the Baltic to the Black Sea, the committee objected to the proposals because of their cost, technical difficulties, and political problems.[63]

The Ministry of Ways of Communication financed new studies in 1905 and 1910, and one, by Rozov and Iurgevich from Kiev, was approved by the engineering council of the ministry.[64] No action was taken, however, for the demands of railway construction still dominated the ministry's budget. There were also legal problems relating to rights of eminent domain and local objections to the flooding of villages.

In 1912 and again in 1914, a private financial consortium was put together by A. I. Putilov and A. A. Davydov, Russian investors who had the support of Dnepr landowners. Their primary interest was in the production of electric power, but their designs included navigational features as well. One of their plans introduced a new element, the irrigation of the steppes from dam reserves. The proposals were rejected, but the objections to it were not made clear.[65] The ministry had a project of its own which the technical council had already passed, so it is probable that it rejected the private proposal because it competed with that of the government. It is possible that those holding land on the river, including the tsar's brother, Mikhail Aleksandrovich, lobbied against the concession and the loss of their lands. Opposition probably also came from competing energy suppliers—Produgol', the southern coal monopoly, and Ugletok, a new electric and gas stock company. Finally, there were technical criticisms of the project. The claims of electrical productivity were questioned, as were the flood-control measures, dam structure, and the navigability of the shallow waterway.[66]

In 1914, proponents of improving the Dnepr waterway and further investigating the project for production of electric power mustered support in the Duma, the elected legislature created in the wake of the 1905 revolution. The Duma approved the assignment of two hundred thousand rubles to the project in the current year and three million rubles for construction work in 1915.[67] This draft law was struck down by the State Council, the upper chamber of the legislature, whose consent was necessary before a law was passed.[68] Conservative landowners were well represented in the State Council, and it is likely that their opposition was decisive. The outbreak of war delayed resolution of this conflict.

National Planning

Bolshevik planners incorporated the Dnepr waterway and hydroelectric power project together with other transportation and energy-producing projects into the *Electrification Plan*. Already in the 1900s, there was interest in national planning as a means for improving the economy.

Many people in the imperial government, professions, and businesses were concerned with the empire's poverty and technological backwardness. Their plans emphasized a national, balanced approach to economic development. At the same time, individuals and industrial and regional interests competed with one another for investment funds and special developmental rights. In 1905, the expanded interest in economic planning was overshadowed by war and political revolt. Civic matters dominated public and private discussion then and in succeeding years. Nevertheless, some plans and individual projects continued to receive institutional support and public financing.

Among those most active in the search to improve industrial development was V. I. Grinevetskii (1871–1919), professor of engineering at the Moscow Higher Technical School and member of the Imperial Russian Technical Society. He urged the professional engineering and scientific organizations "to assume the task of preparing a national economic plan," because, he said, the government bureaucracy lacked competence and vision, and businessmen lacked objectivity and a macroeconomic viewpoint.[69] He composed a plan for the rational economic development of Russia,[70] published only in 1919, which summarized projects discussed by the Imperial Russian Technical Society, the Association of Industry and Trade, the imperial ministries, and other organizations.[71]

Grinevetskii strongly supported the construction of large, regional electrical power stations and the use of local, inexpensive fuels. He recommended harnessing the Volkhov, Dnepr, and Svir rivers for the production of electric power. After fuel, Grinevetskii argued, it was critical to improve transportation. He supported new railroad construction as a stimulus for ancillary industries, as had been done in the days of Sergei Witte, and as an integrator of Russia's far-flung regions and markets. Waterway improvement was supported to meet the need for low-cost transport for bulk goods not dependent on speed. Finally, he emphasized the importance of increasing the production of metals, especially in southern Russia, "in close unity with the Ukraine." He expected to have to finance this construction with investment from abroad in the form of limited concessions.[72]

Grinevetskii's work was studied by Bolshevik and other socialist economists associated with Lenin's planning commission for GOELRO. The fruit of their work was published in the plan and presented by Lenin and Krzhizhanovskii to the Eighth Congress of Soviets in 1920. The map of the proposed development was presented to delegates in a dramatic manner. More than twenty-six hundred delegates from all parts of the new republic, dressed in their worn coats, boots, and fur hats, gathered in the unheated Bolshoi Theater. Krzhizhanovskii threw a switch (some say all the lights in Moscow were off to guarantee the power for the show) and brought to life the bright dream of the future—thirty electric centers to be developed in the next ten years. The half-frozen delegates cheered the vision and went home full of enthusiasm for it.

Publicizing the plan and teaching about electrification gave party members and Congress delegates something positive to focus on, a future bright with optimism and some special tasks to fulfill. Lenin requested booklets in a popular style and suggested the use of a special car with movie apparatus which could drive around the country, illustrating the idea of electrification.[73] More extravagantly, he suggested the building of a small electrical plant which would acquaint the populace with the benefits of electrification and so win their support.[74] He very practically suggested that electric lights be widely installed: "We must advertise electricity. How? Not only with words but by example. . . . For this we must now work out a plan of lighting *every* house in the RSFSR with electricity."[75]

Lenin also suggested to the Bolshevik pamphleteer I. I. Skvortsov-Stepanov that he write something to popularize electrification. Skvortsov-Stepanov attempted to bring knowledge of electricity, its principles, and uses to a large audience, especially to workers. He explained that it is man's task to draw sustenance from nature, to use natural sources of energy.[76] Looking at agriculture, he wrote that it was "impossible to build communism on the basis of old agricultural technology."[77] Only with electrification could industrial and agricultural processes be mechanized and rationalized.

Lenin wrote to Skvortsov-Stepanov:

> so now I am delighted with this book. It is a model of how a Russian savage should be taught from the very beginning, but taught not merely "half science" but the whole subject.[78]

In his preface to the second edition of the book in 1922, Lenin warmly recommended the work to all Communists. "If all our literary marxists . . . sat down in front of such texts . . . we would not have experienced this disgrace, that after having won political power almost five years ago . . . the old bourgeois scholars teach (more truly, corrupt) the young with old bourgeois rubbish."[79] He pointed out that the *Electrification Plan*, which he had requested be deposited in every county library, had not been studied. He recommended that Skvortsov-Stepanov's book be distributed and mastered by all.[80]

Opposition to the GOELRO Plan

The GOELRO plan was not met with enthusiasm everywhere. Opposition existed on a variety of grounds. While Lenin looked to technology for the resolution of social and economic problems, other Bolsheviks objected to his reliance on engineers and what they identified as simple technical solutions to complex, many-faceted problems. Y. Larin, N. Osinskii, and L. Kritsman, advocates of comprehensive, centralized planning, objected that no coordination of national and enterprise goals and resources had been undertaken. Kritsman complained that the plan was no plan, just material for one. Larin wrote that the plan was not economic, that it was only a narrowly technical blueprint, unrealistically based on the 1916 economic situation, not the present. Osinskii agreed and stated that an economic plan should be written by economists.[81] V. Miliutin attacked the GOELRO plan for incorrect methodology. It "mechanically" linked the future economy to prewar conditions.[82]

Both L. Trotsky and A. Rykov spoke critically of the plan, although for different reasons. Trotsky was in favor of comprehensive planning and also supported a single plan for the development of transport. He objected to the *Electrification Plan* as "unrealistic," even a "dream."[83] Rykov hesitated to permit the centralization of the whole economy. He had already attacked Trotsky's suggestion for a single plan administered outside the Supreme Economic Council where Rykov and Miliutin held power. Rykov was concerned by the size of the capital investment assumed by the plan and spoke against hurrying too fast into it.[84] Lenin was angered by their comments.[85]

The suggestion that there might be another basis for economic planning made Lenin impatient. The *Electrification Plan* was "the one serious work on the question of the single economic plan," and any idea of a planning commission other than GOELRO was a mere "ignorant conceit." He argued vehemently in a *Pravda* article that this was not the time or place to write abstract theories or slogans; now was the time for actual work, corrections, and suggestions based on experience.[86] At a meeting of the Council of Commissars where Miliutin and Larin also spoke, Lenin argued in support of GOELRO, but in vain.[87] The council decided to terminate GOELRO and to replace it with a general state planning commission, Gosplan. At Lenin's insistence, Krzhizhanovskii, who had been head of GOELRO, became head of the new commission.[88] Despite the liquidation of GOELRO on May 28, 1921, its personnel was not widely dispersed. Most of the technical personnel associated with electrification continued to work in Glavelektro, the electrical trust, and in the Supreme Economic Council, or they moved into Gosplan.[89] The supporters of the electrification plan maintained an institutional base, albeit now in subcommittees of larger economic organizations.

The substitution of Gosplan for GOELRO constituted a compromise on the character of planning. In theory, planning by extrapolation and the coordination of goals set by individual enterprises through the agency of the Supreme Economic Council was to be replaced by long-range planning for the whole economy by an agency directly responsible to the Council of Labor and Defense, independent of the Supreme Economic Council and its industrial trusts. In practice, industrial planning, long- and short-term, remained the province of the Supreme Economic Council for numerous years. Competition between the two agencies festered until Gosplan won out and the Supreme Economic Council was dissolved in 1935.

The Importance of Electricity in NEP

In December 1921, the Ninth Congress of Soviets met. The country was experiencing widespread famine, and manufacturing had fallen to a new low. It was all too clear that the electrification plan would not be completed quickly. Lenin was aware of this circumstance, but he sensed the value of presenting a specific goal and enlisting participants in promoting it. Under his leadership, the Ninth Congress approved the section of the *Electrification Plan* dealing with electric power generation.[90]

In presenting electrification to the public during 1920 and 1921, Lenin had frequently spoken of the importance of electricity for the transformation of agriculture. He was concerned with the grain supply as well as with the social organization of the peasants and their political inclinations. His expectation was that only large-scale agriculture would wean the small peasant from his individualistic, capitalistic psychology, and only electrification and the most advanced technology would make possible large-scale agriculture. Lenin also sought increased productivity of agriculture through mechanization. The question of the grain supply became all too acute in 1920 and 1921. Peasant hostility and the lack of food for the cities had created an intolerable situation. In March 1921, at the Tenth Party Congress, Lenin introduced the New Economic Policy, NEP. A fixed tax replaced grain requisitioning. Peasants could market their produce after the tax was met. The free market was allowed except in heavy industry. At the same time, the conscription of labor was ended.[91]

The economy revived slowly. Capital, equipment, and technological knowledge were in very short supply. International boycott and the unwillingness of the Bolsheviks to conciliate investors sharply limited the role of foreign capital and foreign concessions. The destruction of existing capital plant caused by wars and their aftermath meant that the domestic economy had very little capacity for capital investment. In 1922 and 1923, with a good harvest and the NEP policies, agriculture and artisan industry revived, but the industrial sector lagged behind. Growing unemployment and serious price fluctuations revived the question of the relationship between peasant and worker—and between the agricultural sector and the industrial.

Lenin responded to the emerging critics of NEP with repeated assertions that the alliance between the peasant and the worker was essential to the survival of the Soviet Union. The workers' government, he wrote, had to retain the confidence of the peasants. The symbol of change from a "ruined peasant country" to a modern industrial one was large-scale machine industry, "electrification, the hydraulic extraction of peat [for fuel] . . . [completion of] the Volkhov Power Project, etc."[92] The view that economic development policies had to consider the needs of the peasantry was shared by numerous Bolsheviks and government officials and came to be associated primarily with the names of Nikolai Bukharin, A. Rykov, and the Right Opposition. Strong proponents of this view were in the agricultural, trade, and financial ministries.

Opponents to this view argued that the peasant was reestablishing his control over the economy. Development based on the petit bourgeois, unproductive small farmer would not sustain rapid industrialization. Cheap food and centralized, planned capital development alone would guarantee the construction of socialism, according to E. I. Preobrazhenskii, deputy chief of the Supreme Economic Council and then spokesman for what came to be the rapid industrialization group associated with the name of Trotsky and finally with Stalin.[93]

Argument over investment priorities, including the construction of large regional electric power plants, had a limited effect on policy in the years before Lenin's death. The economy had no reserves to support large investments of any kind. The party leaders also temporized during Lenin's frequent absences after his stroke in May 1922, in the hope that he would direct policy on his return. His death in 1924 threw them back on their own resources. The debate over economic planning began in earnest after Lenin's death and, in light of optimism engendered by the good harvest in 1924, expanded into a major party policy struggle.

Conclusion: "There Is Nothing That Is Not Possible for Electricity"[94]

The *Electrification Plan* had little impact on industrial construction while investment funds remained short. Soviet leaders did not welcome foreign investment, especially not in vital areas. The plan remained a draft plan, enhanced by the famous slogans coined by Lenin. But Lenin's legacy was more than slogans; he officially supported the view of science and technology as the servants of mankind and knowledge as a human tool. Essentially a politician and publicist, he strove to involve the party in the teaching of his views. He stressed the importance of technology in creating the material-technical base that would bring peasants and workers into the modern world of large-scale, scientific, and rational production.

The *Electrification Plan*—and, with it, Dneprostroi—embodied more than the sum of its parts, the individual projects culled from existing works on fuel, transportation, and resource development. The goal of the state's first official plan was to change the existing economic environment and transform the political and social legacy of the old Russian empire through a balanced, integrated plan. This was a plan to build the foundation not just for a powerful industrial state but for political and social transformation as well—a plan to build socialism. The plan was studied, it was approved in spirit, and specific parts were passed by the Congress of Soviets in 1921. Its execution became an official task and responsibility of the Soviet government. GOELRO left its legacy. The idea of central planning, the importance of electrification, and the immediacy and feasibility of building socialism were very much alive among the Bolshevik leaders. Work on the Dnepr project, described in the GOELRO plan, gathered momentum in 1924. Local town councils, the Ukrainian leaders, and I. G. Aleksandrov in the Supreme Economic Council apparatus cooperated to bring it to life.

2

The Decision

Dnepr:
>   Forgotten by all I fall into decay
>   My powerful current is weakening
>   But, with all, I have hope
>   That soon not one cataract
>   Will block my way.
>   Ships will beautify my breast.

Boatmen:
>   Eh, grandfather, don't have faith in that empty hope!
>   The cataracts will be as before.
>   You have been waiting for dozens of centuries,
>   Five hundred years, you will still be patient, grandfather,
>   They'll waste many projects,
>   But they won't save you, grandpop!

Verse on the front cover of the St. Petersburg
satirical journal *Budil'nik*, no. 21 (1887)

We have the technical knowledge to pour the Atlantic Ocean into the
Pacific—but we must know why it is necessary and how much it will
cost.

Ivan Gavrilovich Aleksandrov,
engineer, 1920

Economic revival in 1924 encouraged Soviet leaders to direct their attention once again to plans for industrial development. The translation of
the goals of "industrialization" and "building socialism" into specific
policies and concrete programs became a first-priority item. Members of
the state and planning organs discussed alternative strategies, especially
the tempo of growth, the ratio of industrial to agricultural investment,
and the degree of state intervention in the economy. Opposing programs
became linked to the political power struggle which came into the open

after Lenin's death. This competition shaped industrialization policy and affected the choice of specific projects, as can be seen in the debate over Dneprostroi.

Beyond the debate over grand strategy, what factors influenced the choice of projects? The Soviet Union covered a large territory, with rich resources widely scattered. The leaders had to choose where to invest; which area, which industry, had the best claim? How important was high technology and Lenin's legacy of a special interest in electrification? Should old plants be updated or new ones constructed? Some Bolsheviks argued that investment should spur social and political development in new areas, whereas others urged that it should capitalize on facilities and skills in established areas. The decision to build Dneprostroi reflected the interplay of varied interests. The changes incorporated in the project during the process of decision making and the redefinition of its purpose suggest that the goals of the Bolsheviks—industrialization and building socialism—were changing at the same time.

Economic Recovery

The revival of the Soviet economy in 1924 came after four years of slow recovery. After the revolution and during the years of War Communism, both industrial and agricultural production had declined steadily.[1] To stimulate recovery and avert political strife, the party introduced the new economic policy, NEP, in 1921.[2] With NEP, the party-state retained control of the "commanding heights," the finances, transportation, communication, and heavy industry. Peasants were required to supply grain to the state but were allowed to bring their surplus produce to a relatively free market. In 1924, their tax in kind was replaced by a money tax.

Agricultural production recovered rapidly, and more consumer goods were produced as well. The economy was not yet healthy, however. It was seized by a serious crisis in 1923. Low and falling prices for grain coexisted with rising prices for industrial goods. The shortage of affordable goods weakened the peasants' incentive to produce for the market. The crisis eased after October as seasonal adjustments helped farm prices and as the state took measures to force down the prices of manufactured goods. But the price reductions caused concern among some leaders who wanted industrial profits to accumulate to fund the faster recovery and reconstruction of industry.

Already in December 1923 and January 1924, the situation was becoming critical. Politburo optimism about the returning health of industry was challenged by members of the Left Opposition who attacked present policy and urged more planning and more investment in industry. The situation was also decried by labor, whose representatives pointed out that real wages in industry were not keeping up with the cost of living. Inflation was forcing the working class to pay for industrialization. The Thirteenth Party Congress agreed to wage supports for industrial workers but rejected the left's demand for extended control over planning and investment in favor of industry.

Incipient potential conflict between the predominantly private, agricultural sector and the state-owned and -run industrial sector stemmed from the general unavailability of investment funds for industrial development. Without growth, industry could not meet peasant demand, and the scissors were bound to reopen. The source of the necessary funds and also the size, timing, and type of investment needed were the issues of the "great industrial debate." It began in 1924 and was ended by the political ascendancy of Stalin in 1928.[3]

As available productive capacity in both light and heavy industry was reactivated, in early 1925, it became clear that further expansion depended on the reconditioning of old plants or the construction of new ones. One group recommended expansion of those light-industry enterprises that needed less investment than heavy industry and produced effects more quickly. An important exception was transportation. Almost all planners agreed that the transportation system, already overstrained before the war and still in a state of disrepair, needed improvement and expansion in order to promote the increase of trade and production for the market and, therefore, for the accumulation of reserves for investment.[4]

The moderate officials in financial and planning circles proposed to use light industry's profits to finance the development of heavy industry and hoped to attract foreign concessions. By returning to the gold standard and by increasing exports, they also hoped to increase foreign trade and to import machine goods, especially the farm machinery that the Soviet Union did not yet produce. Arguing that the transformation of the countryside could come only gradually and under conditions that maintained balanced growth in agriculture and industry, they recommended moderate taxation of the peasant and free-market profits.[5]

These views were criticized by the left wing of the party. The left argued that because productive capacity took a long time to develop, capital construction should be started immediately so that capacity would be ready when it was needed. It was not possible to wait for indirect accumulation of agricultural income through the medium of profits from light industry; rather, agricultural income had to be tapped directly. Analyzing the peasant economy and peasant behavior, Evgeni A. Preobrazhenskii, foremost theorist for the left wing, spoke out against concessions to the peasantry:

> In the period of primitive socialist accumulation the state cannot *do without the exploitation of small-scale production, without the expropriation of a part of the surplus* product of the countryside and of artisan labor.[6]

> *The more economically backward, petty bourgeois and peasant in character is the country making the transition to a socialist organization of production, the smaller is the legacy which the proletariat of the country in question receives at the moment of the social revolution to build up its own socialist accumulation, and the more in proportion this socialist accumulation will be obliged to rely on the expropriation of the surplus product of pre-socialist forms of the economy.*[7]

The Left Opposition argued that existing policies supported a capitalist element, the prosperous peasant, who they feared would dominate economic development and stifle both industrial growth and socialism. The left demanded long-term central planning, rapid industrialization, and the introduction of the most modern methods.[8]

Nikolai Bukharin answered Preobrazhenskii as spokesman for the right wing when party factions began to polarize in 1925. He supported agrarian reform which "extended NEP in the countryside by eliminating most of the remaining legal barriers to peasant farming."[9] Bukharin hypothesized that the peasant would buy industrial goods and also produce for the market. Opposed to squeezing the peasant for funds with high taxes and prices, Bukharin planned to obtain revenue by a progressive but not punitive tax and by encouraging the banking of rural savings. Not least important, he also expected to finance industry from its "growing profitability, based on increasing sales and decreasing costs."[10] Large agricultural and industrial enterprises, he wrote, would drive small and medium producers from the market, thus destroying the market and permitting evolution into a planned socialist economy.[11]

While grand strategy was being discussed in high party circles and among economists, industrializers at all levels regularly considered plans for increasing production and cutting costs. Individual trusts and enterprises built cases for their own industries and urged their causes in central planning offices. Such special pleading was particularly characteristic of certain favored industries such as the mining and metals trust and the electrical machine-building industry, certain departments such as transport and electrification, and the representatives of certain regions such as Leningrad, the Ukraine, and the Urals. Some of the most urgent pressure for funds came from the Ukraine—arguments of special need and high potential return. Some of the arguments found ready acceptance among the planners and fund allocators.

Special Interests—the Ukrainian Factor

The Ukrainian Bolsheviks represented the interests of long-established industrial cities and populations. Many of them had worked in the significant mining and manufacturing centers of the Ukraine before the war. They also represented the interests of the Ukrainian republic, a nation with a long history and its own particularistic goals. The republic had been independent until 1922, when it joined the Russian republic and others to form the USSR and accepted the Constitution of 1924.[12] It had its own political history and cultural heritage, in spite of many centuries of rule by the Russians. It also had rich natural resources. The majority of coal and iron produced in the Russian Empire came from the Ukraine, which produced seventy-five percent of the empire's industrial wealth. The Ukraine was also known as the bread basket of the empire.

During the revolution, parts of the Ukraine declared their independence. The Red Army, together with local Bolsheviks, had had to fight fiercely to establish Soviet power in 1920. The ravaged area suffered intensely from famine in 1921 and 1922. As peace returned to the area, memory of former riches and the potential of the area inspired Ukrainian leaders to rebuild the Ukrainian economy.

The Supreme Economic Council supervised the industrial efforts of the Ukraine through trusts, giving particular attention to coal mining and the metallurgical industry. Glavelektro was also active in the Ukraine, where former Red Army soldiers were mobilized into a labor army and sent to collect data for the electrification plan.[13] The Ukrainian Communist party and the Ukrainian Council of People's Commissars headed the state economic effort. In 1923, Ukrogosplan was formed to manage republican planning and to coordinate the various projects being investigated by local groups.[14]

The problems of the Ukraine were staggering. While agriculture began to recover when the harvests of 1922 and 1923 were good, industry stagnated. The coal mines were full of water and broken equipment. The formerly productive iron and manufacturing industries were plagued with out-of-repair, uncompetitive factories.[15] Although it was desirable to close uneconomic factories, a workers' government could ill afford to balance the budget by firing workers and adding to the ranks of the unemployed.[16] And unemployment was widespread and increasing. Lack of jobs had driven even qualified workers out of the cities. Unemployment, shortages, and inflation were rising.

During 1924, Ukrainian industry finally began to recover, helped by funds drawn from agriculture. The party-state councils directed funds, food, and goods to the Don Basin, for, as G. M. Krzhizhanovskii had said in 1920, it was "the most important economic region of the whole country, deciding the fate of our fuel supply and our metallurgy."[17] Coal production reached fifty percent of prewar levels by the end of the 1924 economic year. The large southen iron and steel trust, Iugostal', rebuilt with funds from the center and began to increase production, as did agricultural machine and tractor factories. Other important Ukrainian industries such as sugar found republican funds to enlarge and update their production.

Supporters of electrification were active. The Ukrainian electrification commission collected use data in the Don mines, in the factories administered by Iugostal', and in other industries. Mechanization through electrification seemed to promise higher productivity in the mines and metal factories of the Don Basin, Krivoi Rog, Nikopol', and Ekaterinoslav. The potential power production of Dneprostroi, in such close proximity to these areas, made it a particularly important project.

Dneprostroi had been kept prominent in the worst years of the economy by the chief engineer on the project for Glavelektro, Ivan Gavrilovich Aleksandrov. He was convinced of the feasibility of the project and of the grandeur of the economic plan of which Dneprostroi was the heart. He promoted its cause, seeking allies among metallurgical interests, regional planners, agricultural interests, and engineers. He spoke persuasively to the central Moscow committees of the Supreme Economic Council and Gosplan, to their Ukrainian committees, and to provincial and city, party, and state groups. As a result, he succeeded in securing funds to finance research and plan development. Some local support came from the provincial and regional organizations of the cities affected by the project. Ekaterinoslav, Zaporozh'e, and Poltava supported construction and requested central funds.[18] In addition, a joint meeting of representatives of southern (Ukrainian) mining and industry and Gosplan's energy section petitioned for and received research and planning funds.[19] In December 1923, Aleksandrov reported the work well along. Exemplifying the arguments of the left, he said the project needed funds for a 1924 start in order to meet demand for power in 1930.

The Ukrainian Planning Commission, Ukrogosplan, advocated starting Dneprostroi immediately. Elaborating on the resolution passed by the Ekaterinoslav provincial congress, Ukrogosplan argued that the project would give immediate employment to some ten thousand workers (nine thousand unskilled).[20] It would improve transportation with the seaway and electrified railways and would provide electricity for the Don Basin mines and backward metallurgical factories. Eventually, by making the production of metal more efficient and cheaper, Dneprostroi would promote the provision of agricultural machinery to farmers at reasonable prices. Finally, the very availability of power would act as a stimulus to growth. Dneprostroi would be more than a passive response to need; it would be a positive link between planning and the increased speed of development. Ukrainian planners argued that new industries would move in to profit from cheap energy and so provide the union economy with hitherto imported special steels, chemicals, and aluminum.[21]

The driving force in official support for Dneprostroi was provided by Vlas Iakolovich Chubar, chairman of the Ukrainian Council of People's Commissars from 1923. Chubar was also a member of the Supreme Economic Council and had long been associated with the central government's efforts to restore Ukrainian industrial production, especially coal. A member of the Communist party since 1905, he served in the Politburo of the Ukrainian Communist party and the party Central Committee and in 1926 joined the Politburo of the all-union party.[22] Chubar was in an excellent position to promote a project in which he had a special interest. His association with Dneprostroi had deep roots. According to his biographers, Chubar had been interested in the Dnepr rapids and in harnessing their power since his youth, for he had grown up in the area.[23] A metalworker and member of the Bolshevik party since the age of fourteen, he was well aware of the party's emphasis on industrialization and introduction of modern technology. Chief lobbyist for the Dneprostroi project, he carried its banner at national and union congresses. When the project finally received approval, workers from Chubar's home village had the privilege of being the first ones hired, underlining his close association with the project.[24]

Chubar was won over to official support for the project in early 1924. He received a briefing on it from V. E. Sproge, an engineer working in the Ukrainian economic planning office. Sproge was chief of the Commission for Water Development and an ardent supporter of Aleksandrov's design. Sproge had already gone to considerable lengths to clear the project's path through the bureaucracy. He had argued for it in the Engineers' Association and had written articles in the Ukrainian Gosplan bulletin and in Gosplan's *Ekonomicheskaia zhizn'*.[25] Chubar approved the project, and in March 1924, the Ukrainian Council of People's Commissars formed a special commission under the chairmanship of Chubar to support Dneprostroi.[26]

The immediate problem was financial. The Ukrainians had no independent funds for important industrial construction. Electric power construction was managed by Glavelektro for the Supreme Economic Council. A special bank, Elektrobank, was created in 1924 to help raise and coordinate funds for electrification. But in 1924, the sum of money sought for Dneprostroi was disproportionately great for a single project. The 10.6 million rubles needed for the first year of construction was 11.5 percent of all the union capital funds assigned to Ukrainian heavy industry and 10 percent of the union electrification budget for that year.[27] The completed project would cost an estimated 200 million rubles, or 30 percent more than was spent on all of industry in 1924–25.[28] Even greater funds would become necessary in order for industry to realize the full potential of Dneprostroi. Aleksandrov's plan had estimated that more than 75 percent of the electricity would be used by factories not yet built.[29] Construction of these factories presupposed a further investment of a possible 200 to 1500 million rubles.[30]

Chubar's commission sent Aleksandrov's materials on the development of the whole southern region and Dneprostroi to Moscow, seeking funding.[31] In July, the Ukrainian Council of Ministers reported to the Council of Labor and Security (USSR) concerning the consensus expressed by the Eighth All-Ukrainian Congress of Soviets. Work on Dneprostroi, it said, should start no later than January 1925. The council estimated the cost to be 144 million new or chervonets rubles, of which 15 million were to be spent abroad. Pointing out that "almost all large construction is finishing and therefore inclusion of Dneprostroi would not require the raising of the total funds assigned to electrical construction over 1923–1924 assignments," M. Vladimirskii (deputy president of the UkSSR) insisted that it was necessary to begin construction immediately.[32] He justified his case on the expected conclusion of Volkhovstroi, the hydroelectric project near Leningrad, already long overdue for completion. It was expected that trained workers and equipment would be available as well as a percentage of investment funds normally set aside for electrification. (Actually, Volkhovstroi was not finished until 1926.)

The Ukrainian Gosplan also argued that the Ukraine was not getting its quota of development funds. The "Ukrainian share, in accordance with her significant weight in the economic life of the Union, should be

25–26% and, taking into account that only 6% of funds appropriate to Ukrainian electrification have been spent," the sum to be spent should be 20.3 million.[33] In July, together with the Ukrainian party Central Committee and the Council of People's Commissars, Ukrogosplan told the Council of Labor and Defense (USSR) that it was necessary to begin Dneprostroi in 1925. Ukrogosplan requested the inclusion in the 1924–25 budget of 8 million rubles for the work on Dneprostroi and 2.6 million rubles for orders to be placed abroad.

The Gosplan (USSR) presidium turned down the request for funding a week later "on account of financial difficulties."[34] It also recommended to the Supreme Economic Council that it discuss power use with the commissariats of transport, agriculture, and others, and return to Gosplan with their plans.

When the new budget was being considered, in the fall of 1924, the Ukrainian leaders again made an active effort to draw more investment into their republic. E. I. Kviring, secretary of the Ukrainian party Central Committee, complained to the Moscow Politburo that "more goes faster to those who are closer and persistent."[35] In October, at the all-union party plenum, Ukrainian leaders spoke out again. They complained that the Ukraine had suffered more economic destruction than other regions.[36] This, in conjunction with the difficulty of obtaining investment capital, was hindering the achievement of normal economic development, not to mention prewar norms or parity with the tempo of restoration in other regions. These arguments fell on deaf ears. The poor harvest of 1924 caused a large increase in budgeted state expenditure to the agricultural sector, from 59 million to 88 million rubles. Large investments in industrial expansion and new construction were postponed.[37]

The debate on industrial development sharpened in 1925 as more funds became available. Recovery had continued and income remained stable in spite of the poor 1924 harvests. The party, in an optimistic mood at the January plenum and April conference, and the Council of Labor and Defense assigned top priority to metals production and manufacturing, including agricultural machinery, tractors, railway equipment, and military hardware.[38]

The Ukrainians were determined to obtain funds for their own development. They were competing with the Urals and Leningrad. At the party plenum in January 1925, they accused Dzerzhinskii, chairman of the Supreme Economic Council, of slighting the Ukraine. He flatly denied the charges, arguing that he thought only of the good of the union. He added that the southern Ukrainian metal industry had already profited from union funds, that pig iron production there had grown

233 percent in the past year, whereas in the Urals it had grown only 69 percent.[39]

The Ukrainians continued to press their case in republican and union forums. In May 1925, the Ninth All-Ukrainian Congress of Soviets met in Khar'kov and reviewed the state of industry. The resolutions passed there and those at the earlier Plenum of Trade Unions reflected the general concern of the party and planners with the shortages of goods and metal and the problem of prices. The expansion of production was identified as the basic task, and mechanization and electrification were identified as the chief means. The only funding available for this expansion was to be drawn from industry itself, through higher labor productivity, improved quality in production, and lower production costs.

The Ukrainian Congress again raised the question of the construction of the Dnepr hydroelectric station.[40] It repeated its claim that electrification was more important for the Ukraine than it was for the rest of the country because the Ukraine was the seat of the most important agriculture and industry.[41] Furthermore, reflecting current politics and the policy of conciliating the peasant, the Congress resolution emphasized the agricultural benefits to be derived from a series of Dnepr power dams which would promote the intensification and industrialization of agriculture.[42]

Shortly after the Congress in Khar'kov, the Third Congress of Soviets met in Moscow. Once again, the Ukrainians raised the issue of developmental funds. They added this time a complaint about centralization. Chubar began his comments with what might be interpreted as a veiled threat, referring to those in the Ukraine "who wish to help us get free of Moscow. . . . Building the union proceeds and will proceed on the basis of the independence of separate, national republics." He went on to criticize bureaucratism, a convenient and acceptable euphemism for centralism, which "not only causes technical problems but also ones of political significance, creating political loss." As an example, he referred to the All-Union Foreign Trade Ministry's cancellation of the republic's right to buy abroad and the annulment of orders creating "direct loss to the economic organs of our republic."[43]

Having established that the Ukraine was a nation—which some wanted to separate from Moscow and "Great Russia"—and having established that this same Moscow had acted to the economic and political detriment of the Ukraine, Chubar went on to offer Moscow a means of making retribution. "We must," he said, "develop our economy, as Lenin said, by electrification. I speak of the Dnepr electrical power station which will introduce and necessarily create an economic revolution in the Ukraine, that most important economic region of the Union of Soviet Socialist Republics, more important both in industry and agriculture." Without the improved transportation that the improved Dnepr waterway would provide, normal economic development could not proceed. Finally, he discussed cultural problems, asserting that for full development the union needed to give attention to two areas: those backward nationalities whose basic needs were unsatisfied and those regions which had had a more advanced economic development and therefore needed even more help than a previously undeveloped area because of the greater complexity of reconstruction. These areas in turn, he argued, would make productive resources available sooner.[44]

Chubar was not alone in his report of a deprived regional economy. Belorussians asked why their electrification was neglected, Leningraders asked for help with harnessing the power of the Svir River, the Volga representative wanted the Volga-Don Canal, and Turkestan wanted help for the cotton industry. The resolutions passed at the meeting made no direct reference to individual regional complaints; they stated only that industrial development should be useful to the whole economy and the interests of the national republics and provinces. They also recommended that an "effort be made to share financial authority with the republics."[45]

The Debate over Priorities

General concern over the rate of economic growth focused attention once more on means available for stimulating production, reducing costs, and raising productivity. Party members held different views on how to extract savings from the peasants, and planners were still divided between geneticists and teleologists. The discussion of Dneprostroi in 1925 reflects concern for growth and the sharpening debate over priorities and strategies.

The chief agency responsible for planning the economy was Gosplan. Gosplan had inherited the *Electrification Plan* as a first draft of a general plan, but continued development and change had made a new plan necessary. Most Gosplan economists belonged to the teleological school of thought; that is to say, they planned resources for economic sectors and derived yearly plans and strategies in accordance with an overall developmental plan. In this, they differed from the geneticists, many of whom tended to be in the Supreme Economic Council, who extrapolated growth from existing circumstances and shaped their goals accordingly.[46] In addition to differing about planning, these two bodies competed in authority. Gosplan was the official advisor to the government, but the Supreme Economic Council's president sat in the highest party and state councils and vied with Gosplan for policy direction.

While the Supreme Economic Council was intensifying the rehabilitation of heavy metals industry in the first months of 1925, Gosplan was endeavoring to force the Supreme Economic Council to work out a financial plan for the reconstruction of industrial development on the basis of the availability of an abundance of cheap power.[47] The Gosplan presidium had requested such a plan for the use of Dneprostroi power when it considered the project in July 1924. In January 1925, Professor A. A. Gorev, president of the electrification section and a longtime advocate of regional power stations, reported that the Dneprostroi project would soon be ready.[48] Gosplan asked once again for a review of the project and a plan for the utilization of the energy. The Supreme Economic Council answered with a general criticism of the GOELRO plan, which, though "objectively good," needed to be brought up to date.[49] But while the president and presidium of the Supreme Economic Council showed little interest in Dneprostroi or electrification, two subcommittees continued to support the project, giving it money and including it in the budget for 1925–26.[50] Thus, the enthusiasts for electrification continued to support the development of energy networks as the basis for large-scale regional planning and kept these plans alive in both competing planning organizations.

Electrification as the means of reconstructing industry on a new technical basis was a major topic of discussion during the next two months in both Glavelektro (VSNKh) and Gosplan. In Gosplan, the need for more funds and a broader financial base was discussed, as well as the need to review the original plan in the light of accumulated experience and in relation to the changing needs of the economy.[51] It was recognized that the creation of an integrated economy imagined in 1920 at the time of the writing of the *Electrification Plan* had proved to be more difficult than originally supposed. This point was illustrated by Professor Gorev. The Dneprostroi question, he said, was closely related to other economic problems—the reconstruction of the mining regions, transport, irrigation, and others—and should be studied from the point of view of the whole region; it also needed review by a technical commission. Gorev recommended that Gosplan create a commission to study the economy and transportation, inviting Ukrainian representatives and other interested parties. While most Gosplan members agreed to the need for a closer reconciliation of prospective plan, actual conditions, and future needs, P. S. Osadchii and A. Tsiurupa, president of Gosplan, refused the suggestion. Osadchii pointed out that this was the Supreme Economic Council's task, that it had been delinquent with its failure to interest itself in the rational reconstruction of the southern mining region. Tsiurupa agreed and requested the Supreme Economic Council to report on Dneprostroi in six weeks.[52]

In response to this request, the president, Dzerzhinskii, appointed a special interdepartmental commission to study the Dnepr project and make a report in mid-October, "perhaps in time for the annual budget."[53] He authorized the dispatch of specialists to consult with engineers in the United States and assigned the project thirty thousand rubles. But he sounded a note of caution: the government would feel justified in undertaking so large a project and so great an expense only if the lessons from previous experience (Volkhovstroi) had been learned and only if the project made sense in terms of world experience.[54]

The chairman of the new commission appointed by Dzerzhinskii was Lev Trotsky. Trotsky had come to the Supreme Economic Council when he was forced from his post as commissar of war by the triumvirate of Stalin, Bukharin, and Rykov in January 1925. His demotion was achieved by Stalin, who wanted no competition for political power, and by the propeasant majority among the leaders, who feared the left's repeated efforts to spend more on industrial development. Trotsky accepted appointment to the economic council, the electrotechnical council, and the commission on concessions, because, he wrote later, he was interested in applied technology and the modernization of industry.[55]

Shortly after his appointment, Trotsky called on Glavelektro for a report on its budget, accomplishments, and plans for the future. The proposed budget included an outlay of two hundred fifty million, an amount five times as large as that spent the previous year, justified by growth in industry and in the entire economy. Glavelektro aimed to aid local power-plant construction and to electrify transport, agriculture, and industry, in that order. Construction of regional stations was allotted 135.9 million rubles, including 8.3 million for the beginning of the Dnepr project. Electrification of transport was assigned 15 million, agriculture 18 million, mostly for the construction of transmission lines. The remainder, 81.1 million, was allotted to industry.[56]

Trotsky then called together the Dneprostroi investigative commission, including representatives of the Ukrainian government, transport, agriculture, metals, mining, the chemical and electrotechnical industries, and specialists associated with the project's plans. Addressing the commission, Trotsky explained its task. Choosing the correct moment to start was not less significant than choosing the correct design. Electrification depended on the level of industrial development and helped shape it in turn. It was better to spend an extra year making sure that financial resources, supplies, and the necessary equipment were at hand so that construction could take place without interruptions. Construction too early, before resources were available or before consumers were known to exist, would double necessary expenditure.[57] Trotsky made it clear that he felt Dneprostroi had to be considered not in isolation but as an integral part of an industrial combination; the Dneprostroi combine was to be a symbiotic conglomerate. Only research and planning could be done in 1925; a start would be made in 1926. He thought it possible that foreign firms would be interested in making resources available but that the subject had to be explored further.[58]

Aleksandrov challenged Trotsky's position. He agreed that special attention should be paid to finances and that foreign investment was possible. Regarding clients for Dneprostroi's electricity, his project description had identified the potential clients from the beginning. They included iron and steel production and factories producing metal manufactures and chemicals new to the Soviet Union. It was generally agreed that these industries were essential to the Soviet Union and that raw materials were available nearby. Aleksandrov claimed that considerable demand already existed and that the new factories would quickly be built. His answer was disputed by the representatives of the metals industries. They argued that demand did not yet exist, that almost ninety percent of the energy production was assigned to factories not yet built. Therefore, it was difficult to justify the grandiose costs of construction. The money could be better used, they argued, to build factories producing metal for existing demand.

Most Ukrainians wanted to proceed with Dneprostroi immediately. G. Grin'ko, president of the Ukrainian Gosplan, expressed the Ukrainians' wish to build according to their own plan.[59] He felt that the main evaluation of the project should be carried out in the Ukraine, and arrangements were made for the Dneprostroi commission to visit the proposed site. On the eve of its arrival, the presidium of the All-Ukrainian Central Executive Committee heard a report on Aleksandrov's plan. During the discussion, the Zaporozh'e town council recommended that the trade union and party organization mobilize to win approval for Dneprostroi. The presidium urged its members to complete identification of the lands to be flooded and locate funds for population relocation. It also urged that provision be made for an adjustment in the Ukrainian import-export plan; import requirements had already risen one hundred fifty percent over exports. Construction and plant equipment for Dneprostroi would worsen this disproportion.[60]

The Dneprostroi commission under Trotsky arrived in Khar'kov on August 29 and proceeded to Kichkas, the German Mennonite village at the dam site. There, in three days of discussion, the commission definitively redirected the project. Originally a chiefly navigational project for the transport of grain and coal, Dneprostroi was also to provide electricity for rural and industrial needs and improve irrigation. Now, Trotsky affirmed that the primary significance of the project was for industry, shifting away from the earlier emphasis on agriculture and transportation and disregarding Lenin's stress on cultural change. The construction of the dam was now explicitly linked with the combine, the specialized steel, ferro-magnesium, and aluminum factories, the clients for the new power. The combine, the commission estimated, would require an additional expense of 375 million rubles.[61]

Trotsky's commission resisted Aleksandrov's and the Ukrainians' arguments for an immediate start. Trotsky reported to the Ukrainian government that the commission was requesting nine hundred fifty thousand rubles to pay for a finished draft of the project and a review by American consultants. He wanted the Americans to check the project's technology and cost estimates, citing Soviet inexperience in calculating works of large size and the difficulties encountered in the financial planning for Volkhovstroi.[62]

On his return to Moscow, Trotsky wrote a summary of his trip for the press. While praising the work of the committee, he said more information was needed. When it was all gathered, the commission would submit its recommendation to the top government councils.[63] The commission sections were expected to report by the first of the year; work should be completed by April 1, 1926, well before the drawing up of the final 1926–27 budget. In answer to the question of whether construction would begin in 1926, Trotsky demurred. It might depend, he answered, on the availability of foreign capital, for the dam or for the combine. It would be important to get long-term credit for equipment. It was obvious, he said, that the use of foreign concessions could greatly facilitate starting in the new economic year. Trotsky then also pointed out that other major projects were being considered, especially the Volga-Don Canal, the Kuznetsk Basin combine, and the Baku-Batum oil line.[64]

The opponents of Dneprostroi mounted a broad attack. One objection was that the project cost too much money at a time when money was scarce. The estimated cost of one hundred forty million rubles, or about six percent of the national budget, was as much as was spent on all agriculture in the year 1924–25.[65] Building Dneprostroi meant not only mortgaging the future but limiting credit for other productive facilities under consideration.[66] These included projects that were important to both the agricultural and industrial sectors such as large tractor and agricultural combine factories and transport projects, including the Trans-Siberian Railroad and the Volga-Don Canal. The metallurgical interests contended that their development would do the most for the economy. They supported the large factories that would produce agricultural, transport, and defense goods and the capital industry on which such factories depended. Among these were projects supported by regional groups such as the hydroelectric power plant sought by Leningrad industry and the large industrial complex uniting the metal and coal of Magnitogorsk and Kuznetsk in the Urals.

The specific attack on Dneprostroi began with a vigorous offensive by R. E. Klasson. He published a critical article in *Torgovo-Promyshlennaia Gazeta*, the organ of the Supreme Economic Council. Klasson was a recognized expert in the field of electrical construction and transmission. He criticized the time-use base used by Aleksandrov. One could not count on six thousand hours of production or use a year; even American stations, which were generally the most efficient, could only count on three to four thousand hours annually. It was unrealistic to expect to transmit extra energy to Khar'kov and Kherson because it would be more lucrative to supply factories. Further, town needs were highest in the winter when water was low and less power available. Construction would take at least seven years, and southern industry was unlikely to want to wait so long. Dneprostroi would need a steam reserve plan because water was insufficient from December to February. A steam plant could be built in two and a half years and could use cheap coal. The example of the Americans who spent two thirds of their funds on steam and one third on hydroelectric power suggested that steam should be considered as a real alternative. Not all hydroelectric plants were cheaper than steam. Dneprostroi would be very expensive because of the size of the dam, and the slow movement of the water meant that the generators would have to be particularly large and expensive. Equipment would be very long in coming, four or five years. Finally, Klasson claimed that the project would cost more than estimated.[67]

Aleksandrov rejected Klasson's analysis on the crucial subject of annual hours of use. He cited *Electrical World* (USA) and claimed that seven stations worked more than six thousand hours, eight worked between fifty-five hundred and six thousand, and some worked as long as eighty-five hundred. Further, he claimed that 85.5 percent of Dneprostroi's energy would be sold to factories that worked all year without interruption. With respect to water levels, he reported that in forty-six years only four had had low water. Finally, it would take at least four separate steam plants to equal Dneprostroi, a significant cost difference.[68]

The opposition responded. A. Eisman, the commissar of transport, argued that Dneprostroi was too expensive for the present, claiming that the figures, if properly done, including all the supplementary projects of railroads, transmission lines, and factory construction, would reach seven hundred fifty million.[69] Two days later, Berstein-Kogan, another transportation expert, argued that Dneprostroi was too local. In the United States, for example, he wrote, deep-sea ships were rarely seen on rivers; for Dneprostroi to count on a large oceangoing traffic was unrealistic.[70] Other articles added that electricity for refining the Krivoi Rog ores was not worth obtaining because the ore was running out; the bauxite ores were too poor to bother with; the time necessary for construction—six to eight years—was too long, and it was impossible to leave factories "unreconstructed" for so long. Factories had their own steam plants which could be developed and used for mechanization. Further, modern factories used "waste gases," gas by-products of the production process, which gave them fuel independence.[71]

In late September, further facts negating the need for Dneprostroi were marshaled by the metallists. A group of engineers mailed a letter to Dzerzhinskii and Trotsky stating that the southern factories did not need Dneprostroi energy. Complaining that discussion of Dneprostroi had been progressing under heavy pressure from one side, the Iugostal' engineers stated that for rapid economic growth, in light of the capital shortage, the need was for cheap coal and iron which could be produced only with new mines and better factories, that is, not with hydroelectric plants. They challenged equally the cost estimate, saying it should be not one hundred thirty million but three hundred million. They pointed out that the estimates had been made in 1920 and 1921 and were out of date. It was claimed, they wrote, that technical advances would lower costs, but they pointed out that new technology was not in use and was unlikely to be available.[72]

In answer to this, Aleksandrov maintained that the gas-versus-hydro-energy figures were simply wrong, based on a technological possibility alone. Aleksandrov raised the question of how much technological novelty a capital-poor country could afford to use. He further argued that one of the signers of the letter, Lomov, had previously been anxious to reserve Dneprostroi energy for a metallurgical plant to be built by 1928: "In a year, Lomov can change his mind, but he shouldn't then write in such a tone as if a danger were threatening the fatherland." He countered the claim of out-of-date cost estimates, saying his numbers were based on 1925 prices, including prices given to him by Iugostal's own representatives.[73]

Aleksandrov's article stimulated a riposte from Engineer Gulia, one of the signers of the letter. Aleksandrov's numbers were incorrect. And, wrote A. A. Svitsin, director of Iugostal' and an appointee of Dzerzhinskii, metal production could not wait for Dneprostroi. Metal factories needed to be restored and new ones built. Among the plants listed as necessary was a ferro-magnesium plant.[74] It might be true that electrically poured magnesium was best, and used in the best steel, "but we do not have that sort of production, nor do we plan it in the near future."[75]

A Gosplan spokesman, N. N. Shaposhnikov, revived the teleological argument. It was incorrect to ask the question, he said, of whether there is being created, by itself, a sufficient regional demand for Dneprostroi's energy; rather, "can and should we use the Dnepr's energy, and what measures would be necessary to that end?" He answered his own question positively, concluding that "if a condition of the maximal development of our productive forces is the speediest industrialization of our country, we must give special attention to all which promises to speed that process."[76]

Klasson, whose article had set off the argument, returned to the fray. After chastizing Aleksandrov by asserting that "his long commitment" must be "the cause of his hot temper," he repeated that the operating-time figures were wrong; Aleksandrov was confusing capacity with maximum load. He raised questions about this available "head" and the amount of water available to pass through the turbines and recommended that one or even two steam plants be built first, since they would be needed in any case to carry the load when the water was low. Finally, he said, Dneprostroi was not necessary if the main reason for it was to supply energy to metallurgical factories.[77]

After this stormy exchange, the subject of Dneprostroi faded from view for a while. A few articles on irrigation and transport appeared, and Aleksandrov wrote another description of the project, defending it as a "factor of new economic formation."[78] Glavelektro approved funds for continuing research on Dneprostroi, but when the Supreme Economic Council discussed the budget for 1925–26, no allowance was made for construction.[79] The project had had significant support from the electrical committees of both Gosplan and Glavelektro, and the Ukraine had pressed strongly for it, but to no avail. The party leaders did not

approve so large an investment. This was because, in spite of agricultural recovery, the amount of grain marketed in 1925 had been a disap-
pointment and industrial revenues limited. The political climate was such
that conservative economic objections easily outweighed the visionary
claims of Aleksandrov. The Fourteenth Party Congress in December
embraced the goal of industrialization but promised no significant new
actions.

Dneprostroi in the Balance

Dneprostroi's supporters were not defeated or discouraged in their pursuit of funds and support for the great dam. At the close of 1925, the All-
Ukrainian Party Congress again affirmed its opinion that Dneprostroi
should be built as soon as possible. Lazar Kaganovich, the Ukrainian
party secretary who served as Stalin's appointee from April 1925 through
July 1928, repeated the official line that while Dneprostroi and electrification were important, there were insufficient resources available for
investment.[80] Chubar did not accept this as the final word. He claimed
that the fuel shortage and the lack of cheap fuel hindered metal production. He spoke vehemently about Moscow's interference in Ukrainian
budgetary and developmental plans, especially as it concerned Ukrainian
efforts to deal with the capital shortage: "The greatest difficulty was lack
of capital for the development of basic industry."[81] Reminding the Congress that Dneprostroi was of vital significance, he suggested that it could
be built if the Ukraine attracted capital from abroad. Yet he closed on the
same note of caution which had earlier been expressed by Trotsky: It was
not possible to proceed with construction until all research was complete;
his concern was not the waste of money but the loss to the Ukraine, for
"we cannot risk losing the funds which could be spent elsewhere."[82] The
Congress empowered the Central Committee to resolve the problem, but
nothing specific was achieved then or at the Fourteenth All-Union Party
Congress later in the month.

   Early in 1926, Grin'ko pursued the question of Dneprostroi at the First
All-Union Congress of Gosplan representatives. He argued again that the
Ukraine, which provided so much of the union's wealth, received too
little investment in return. He touched on the potential significance of the
Ukraine's border location, hinting perhaps at the danger of ignoring the
Ukraine's present loyalty. He observed that it was time for great collabo-
ration between the union and the republics. Turning to Dneprostroi, he
sought funds. Considering the arguments of the representatives of the

Iugostal' trust, he brushed aside their claims that they did not need Dneprostroi energy and emphasized the importance of cheap energy for the production of aluminum and ferro-magnesium. He stressed the importance of building new factories and concluded by calling on the whole Congress to direct its attention to the resolution of the problem of the Dnepr.[83]

At the same time, the Central Electrotechnical Council, a subcommittee of Glavelektro, reviewed the Dneprostroi project. It recalculated the costs, considered the possibility of attracting foreign capital, and prepared a list of questions for foreign experts. The council went on record in favor of Dneprostroi after hearing from all the commissions which reported to the Dnepr committee now headed by M. Rukhimovich, deputy chairman of the Supreme Economic Council.[84]

Under the auspices of Glavelektro, Aleksandrov led a delegation to the United States to study hydrotechnology and to "acquaint the Americans with the Dnepr project." This mission had a delicate task. While learning about the latest foreign technology, the delegation also had to negotiate for an experienced consultant to review the Dnepr plans. At the same time, it was to investigate the possibility of attracting foreign investment without making any commitments. The mission's work was complicated by the fact that there existed no diplomatic relations between the two countries, no overt friendliness, and no framework for business relations. Despite this lack of formal state relations, the mission was successful. The eminent engineer Colonel Hugh L. Cooper from the United States agreed to review the project.[85] Cooper visited the site in late August. He reported his very positive impressions to Rykov in the Crimea.[86] Then he and his assistants returned to Moscow, where they presented their conclusions to the technical council. Cooper spoke in the "Businessman's Club" (Delovoi Club) in approval of Dneprostroi. He recommended certain changes to reduce costs and shorten the time of construction by two and a half years.[87] His speech was well received, according to the Moscow daily press.

During 1926, new support for greater investment in industrialization was materializing. Although the advocates of rapid industrialization had suffered repeated political defeat and lacked the political power to press their preferences, they had won some attention to their concerns about the rate of development in industry. A party plenum in April discussed the poor growth of the economy. Party leaders there agreed that much more was now being produced, but, as the economy grew, more was needed. Industry now had to continue to develop without losing tempo in order to serve its own needs and those of the peasants. Machine building and electrification were essential for the development of the whole economy, for a high technological base, and for increased independence from foreign nations.[88] In spite of this favorable atmosphere, Dneprostroi was barely discussed at the plenum. According to Trotsky, all members of the Politburo were against the project at the time. Trotsky, as we have seen, had cautioned against it until a rigorous plan, including a financial plan, had been drawn up; he expected it to be included in the 1926 budget, but only if everything were ready. Stalin is reported (by Trotsky) as saying:

> Let us not fall into the position of the *muzhik* who had saved up a few kopecks and, instead of repairing his plow or renewing his stock, bought a gramophone and ruined himself. Can we ignore the decisions of the Congress that our industrial plans must correspond to our resources?[89]

Agreement that industry needed more investment characterized discussions during the summer, although there was little agreement on the amount of investment either necessary or possible. Specialists claimed that plant capacity was fully utilized and could no longer be counted on for productive expansion. Production of iron and steel lagged and was still far short of that in 1913. Industrial prices were rising, and goods were scarce.

The Supreme Economic Council continued to encourage the development of industry, especially metals production, but through the first half of the year, Dzerzhinskii's dominant theme was that industry had to finance its own expansion with lower costs, higher labor productivity, and improved production methods, especially in the application of high technology.[90]

However, planning took on a new urgency as both Gosplan and the Supreme Economic Council planned new construction, anticipating the full utilization of existing capacity by the end of the fiscal year. The size and rate of these investments were hotly debated in party and state councils. The Left Opposition attacked the slow pace of expansion once again. In mid-July, the party Central Committee met, and E. Piatakov recommended a budget based on raising the wholesale prices of industrial goods.[91] Dzerzhinskii called Piatakov's speech uninformed and attacked his suggestion for raising prices as a "senseless, antisoviet, antiworker program," based not on fact but on his and his colleagues' desires to mess up the programs of the Politburo and plenum.[92] Dzerzhinskii rejected the expanded budget and defended limited industrial investment during the meetings of the Central Committee and the Supreme Economic Council presidium.[93] He was taken ill during the second Central Committee meeting and suffered a fatal heart attack. His death left vacant an influential post in the economic hierarchy.

The Question Is Resolved

What direction would the economic leadership take? What size and form should the 1926 industrial budget take? What factors made Dneprostroi more attractive in 1926 than it had been in 1925? The discussion of the project reflects the party leaders' continuing difficulty in balancing economic and noneconomic factors in industrial planning.

The advent of Dzerzhinskii's successor, V. V. Kuibyshev, both marked and contributed to the strengthening of the advocates of more industrialization. Kuibyshev was a longtime member of the party. He had served as a military commander, in the management of the economy and in the Control Commission.[94] He was a proponent of radical reconstruction of the economy, technological change, and electrification.[95] The appointment of Kuibyshev as Dzerzhinskii's successor and other personnel shifts during the next few months reflected a shift in favor of industry within the Central Committee. The appointment coincided with the decision of the Council of People's Commissars that industry and transportation should receive increased allocations, a number of new power stations should be started, and exports should be encouraged.[96] Budgets were further increased on September 8.[97]

Kuibyshev reorganized the Supreme Economic Council, implementing a reform he had begun as commissar of the Worker-Peasant Inspection, at Dzerzhinskii's instigation. He reduced the central staff and reassigned some eight hundred persons from the center to enterprises.[98] At this time, significant changes were made in the organization of the armaments industry. A new war industry committee was established, and in September it began to report directly to the presidium of the Supreme Economic Council. Defense orders were given higher priority, and special personnel supervised their fulfillment.[99] Military requirements explained added chemical and metal investments the following year.[100] Discussion in the Communist Academy of the control figures of 1926–27 also demonstrated the shift within the party in favor of industry. A member of the Supreme Economic Council, I. Kraval, attacked Gosplan's "too conservative" investment figures, calling them "'a tremendous mistake' which had now been corrected by the party central committee."[101]

It was also in September that Dneprostroi again became the focus of attention. Impressive because of its size and scope, it suited the current policy of increased attention to industrialization together with continued attention to the worker-peasant alliance, or *smychka*. Rykov, chief of the Council of Labor and Defense, had expressed serious interest in the project when the American consultant Hugh L. Cooper discussed the project with him and Krzizhanovskii in September 1926.[102] Cooper also reported to Kuibyshev and, at a later date, to Stalin.[103] In these reports, Cooper approved the general engineering design but suggested changes that promised to save material and time.[104] He also made suggestions for mechanization. He encouraged the Soviet leaders to feel that the project was ready, that it could be successfully completed, and that it would serve as a showplace of Soviet progress.[105] Aleksandrov welcomed Cooper's approval and interest in the project; he admired American technology and supported its use at Dneprostroi. Aleksandrov said that Dneprostroi should be "an example of culture in building, an example proving the possibility of adapting American technology to our conditions."[106] Kuibyshev, too, was in favor of importing American technology and of making technological innovations a constituent part of economic reconstruction.[107]

In October, it was time to consider projects for inclusion in the new budget. The moment seemed particularly propitious for new construction; the harvest was good and the grain markets stable. Chubar, speaking to a joint meeting of the All-Ukrainian Central Executive Committee and the Council of People's Commissars on October 6, reported that it had been decided that one big construction project would be financed in the current year. He also reported that Rykov, Kuibyshev, and Krzhizhanovskii had said that it would be expedient to start Dneprostroi in the coming year; the main difficulty was financial. Now, he continued, it was necessary to demonstrate the outstanding significance of Dneprostroi in the union so that it would win the special funds.[108]

Kviring, deputy president of the Supreme Economic Council, also announced the special fund. "According to a resolution of the government, in the current year, it is necessary to begin one great [*krupnyi*] construction project of all-union significance. . . . We must decide which project is economically worthwhile."[109] Kviring, who had once been president of the Ekaterinoslav council, chief of the Ukrainian economic commission, and secretary of the Ukrainian party committee, was well acquainted with the Dnepr project and felt it was the best of the contenders. "What could be done to prepare the Dnepr project, could everything be made ready for construction to begin?" Despite some opposition, the presidium agreed that it should recommend Dneprostroi.[110]

A forceful speech by Chubar was published on the same day as Kviring's remarks. Chubar brought out some new themes, raised often thereafter. He argued that the economy was stronger than it had been when the Soviet Union had begun the construction of Volkhovstroi. Workers were interested in the project, he said: "A big step forward was needed. Construction of Dneprostroi would show those of little faith within the republic and the skeptics outside the USSR that socialist construction was moving forward."[111] Two days later, in an interview, Chubar said that the Dnepr construction would promote the reconstruction of industry and agriculture significantly.[112] In other interviews, the president of the construction workers' trade union, the president of the Ukrainian Central Executive Committee, and the deputy president of the Ukrainian Gosplan agreed that it was time to begin construction.[113]

However, at the First All-Ukrainian Party Conference a week later, the enthusiastic supporters of Dneprostroi encountered some opposition. Dashkovskii and Efremov, later expelled from the party as Trotskyites, complained that the expense was too great, too large for the present level of the economy. The project would put an unbearable yoke on the peasant.[114] Another party member, Shumskii, later expelled as a renegade nationalist, expressed his concern that the influx of Great Russian money would be accompanied by more control and interference in the Ukraine.[115] The majority of the party supported the project and passed a resolution incorporating it into the republican budget for the year. It also empowered the Central Committee to press for union funds.[116]

A joint meeting of the Ukrainian Trade Union Council and the Council of People's Commissars followed the party conference. The Ukrainian members of the Dneprostroi commission, the Moscow committee for the Dnepr, and the American specialists all reported. V. K. Viktorov, deputy president of Ukrogosplan, reported on the estimated costs and benefits.[117] According to the Americans, the project, not including the railroad, would cost 120 million rubles; the Gosplan estimate was 109.5 million. There would be annual savings of 31 million rubles on fuel and transportation costs and quantities of cheap fuel for aluminum, mechanization of factory and farm work, and related savings in imports. Viktorov said that all new construction in the Ukraine was dependent on the starting of Dneprostroi and implied that economic catastrophe would occur if the country waited any longer.[118]

Aleksandrov argued that it was important to decide immediately, because technical drawings had to be given to factories and materials ordered so that all would be ready when the spring high waters subsided and the construction season began. He reviewed the latest competing projects and eliminated them: Kuznetsk was not ready; Svirstroi was not Dneprostroi's equal for all-union economic significance; the Volga-Don

Canal was unnecessary; and the Moscow-Don railroad and Rostov port not immediately essential.[119]

The teleological point of view was expressed by Dudnik, from the Commissariat of Agriculture. Dneprostroi, he felt, should be viewed as exceptional because of the special technology involved, the new beginnings, the new tempo. Further, it was not necessary to expect profit. Gosplan had neglected to say that the Dneprostroi would have an enormous influence and effect on the economy as a whole. Dudnik was against a foreign concession: "We must have only our own [capital] in all that relates to the production of energy." He wanted to encourage public support and recommended the formation of a committee that would "let people know" and attract local organizations to the work of financing.[120] A representative from Zaporozh'e testified to local interest and suggested that since Dneprostroi had such colossal signficance, a loan for it would be immediately subscribed. The other speakers all supported the project, citing not only the cheap energy and new factories but also the contribution to be made to the intensification of agriculture. One quoted Rykov, who called Dneprostroi the "*muzhik*'s project," demonstrating the turnabout since the days of April 1926 plenum.[121]

The Ukrainian party members went on to Moscow to the Fifteenth All-Union Party Conference. There Chubar, supported by Rukhimovich, argued strongly for Dneprostroi. Creatively shaping his arguments to the new mood in the leadership, Chubar argued: "We must find those economies, those improvements which will give us new resources. . . . [We need] a plan, a framework, big industry—electrification and Dneprostroi. . . . If we do not build it, we will build small ones which will produce twelve times more expensively."[122] The representatives from the various geographic regions all argued for their own projects—Svirstroi, Volga-Don Canal, and the Turk-Sib, the railroad which linked the Soviet heartland with Turkestan, Siberia, and finally the Pacific Ocean. Industrial trusts cried out for investment in cotton, gold, and an oil pipeline. In his summary of the economic situation, Rykov warned each area against thinking of itself as standing alone. He indicated that his choice, if there were means only for one project, would be the Turk-Sib, Dneprostroi, or the Volga-Don, in that order.[123]

With nothing specific said about Dneprostroi or any of the other individual projects, the conference resolved to spend not less than nine hundred million rubles on industry and, with electricity, not less than one billion. Even more than the previous year, *capital* construction was to be directed to reequipping and reconstruction of heavy industry (metal, fuel, power station construction): "In particular, sufficient attention must be directed to the development of the light metals (copper, tin, lead, and aluminum)." The resolution went on to stress the importance of developing the production of the implements of production and machine building with the aim of eliminating dependence on the capitalist countries.[124]

On November 6, after the party conference, the Gosplan presidium met in Moscow. The meetings were attended by the representatives of the various republics and by the leaders of economic councils, including Chubar.[125] The possibility of a large construction of general union significance able to force the development of the economy as a whole was discussed, as were seven candidates. The next day, Gosplan announced support for both Dneprostroi and the Turk-Sib, a combination designed to strengthen the "leading role of heavy industry" and the "socialist transformation of the peasant."[126]

On November 9, Kuibyshev addressed the "unofficial" meeting of the presidium of the Supreme Economic Council. He pointed out that their chief concern was "Why Dneprostroi and not something else?"[127] In order to get the fullest discussion, he had invited Dneprostroi's opponents and warned Aleksandrov that he would have to answer them. At the end of the session, Kuibyshev announced that another meeting would be held after all members had a chance to study the materials, but in the meantime, he concluded that Dneprostroi would, alone of all the projects discussed, make a qualitative difference in the development of future capacity.[128]

The executive committee of the Russian Republic challenged the decision favoring Dneprostroi, arguing that the Volga-Don Canal would cost less, was less dependent on imported technology, and would contribute more to agriculture and to more regions than Dneprostroi.[129] This effort did not sway support away from Dneprostroi.

On November 25, the Central Committee resolved that Dneprostroi and the Turk-Sib were projects of primary importance. The next day, the Ukrainian party Central Committee passed the same resolution. This ranking meant that these two projects had a prior call on all resources of labor, materials, and finance. [130] On December 3, Krzhizhanovskii presented his arguments to the Council of Labor and Defense, which resolved that the two projects should be built.[131] Finally, on December 4, in Khar'kov, there was the first meeting of the Dnepr Construction Commission, Dneprostroi, under Chubar. Chubar assigned tasks to the various committees, and the project moved into a new stage.[132]

Conclusion

The rewriting and redirection of the Dneprostroi project and the arguments over its approval reflect the evolution of the party's goals and
policies. Presented at first as an integral part of the first unified plan for
the development of the whole economy, Dneprostroi was viewed primarily as a transportation project which would benefit first agriculture and
then industry. It was conceived of as part of a unionwide effort to
improve transportation of goods, much as it had been during the end of
the imperial period. Later, it became a specifically industrial project,
important to specialized interest groups. Finally, it became part of the
effort to transform the economy and society and a symbol of socialist
construction. The project reflected the evolution of the leaders' thinking
and practical work. Firmly rooted in Lenin's utopian vision of a transformed society, reworked to satisfy the aims of the decision makers, it
was the bridge between Lenin's electrification plan and the first Five-Year
Plan which was approved by the party in 1928 and which gave priority to
Dneprostroi.

The choice of Dneprostroi for the first large commitment of funds
could not be justified on simple cost-benefit grounds. Its economic rationality was never proven. Although Aleksandrov was adamant about
the validity of his analysis, major elements were regularly omitted from
his calculations. He allowed a flat six percent interest rate on investment,
a pseudo-official figure and one with no real basis; there was no comparative measure for competitors for funds. His estimate did not count the
costs of the necessary services for the working population—housing,
schools, shops, and medical care. He allowed nothing for the very low
level of labor skills. Most serious of all, calculations were made on the
assumption of a certain demand for power, but the new factories did not
exist, and, if built in time to consume the newly generated power, they
would compete during construction with Dneprostroi for funds, materials, and labor. In addition, the attacks of Klasson and others were never
satisfactorily answered. Even if Aleksandrov had rebutted them, there
was still no practical way to compare quickly built thermal stations using
finite organic fuel with those taking measurably longer to build but using
water power; neither were there models for comparing alternative investments even within the heavy-industry sector. Clearly, the decision to
build Dneprostroi was made on other grounds.

In the plan, the project was expected to put twenty million rubles into
the Ukrainian economy and provide jobs for two thousand workers in

1927 and, by 1932, an investment of more than five hundred million and thousands of jobs in a modern industrial combine. The Ukrainian lobby had won over the central political and economic agencies to their cause. At the same time, the promoters of electrification also could claim success. They included the engineers and other promoters of high technology who argued that electricity would play a vital role in the modernization of production. They also included economists who felt that energy was a basic resource around which manufacturing should be planned. These two groups kept the Dneprostroi project before the eyes of the political leaders who had the power to set priorities and allocate funds.

Their advocacy was successful in part because in 1926 the harvest was good. The stronger economy encouraged party leaders to commit themselves to greater capital investment. At the same time, the protagonists in the great industrial debate had moved closer together and agreed that increased capital investment was necessary. The majority which had been concerned about agriculture looked forward to improved transportation, rural electrification, irrigation, and, in the future, improved industrial production and therefore cheaper fertilizers, tractors, and combines. Industrialists liked Dneprostroi's energy capacity and the new factories planned in combination with it.

The Dneprostroi project was supported, moreover, by members of the party who saw in it an opportunity to direct the economy, to stimulate development in a chosen fashion, and to expand the socialist sector. By concentrating investment in one large, multifaceted project, they expanded centralized control over the economy. They also expanded the potential for party influence in society by drawing more workers into the state-owned and -run sector.

It is difficult to evaluate the direct influence of individual leaders in the final decision to build Dneprostroi. The death of Dzerzhinskii permitted the rise of Kuibyshev, experienced in industrial planning, electrification, and organizational matters. He took the lead in suggesting that one project should be built to stimulate the economy to transform itself, not to just produce more of any given product. Kuibyshev's interest in Dneprostroi was probably supported by the military; its construction would hasten the production of strategically important chemicals, aluminum, and other metals.

Trotsky clearly played a role in the postponement of the project in 1925, a fact that casts some doubt on the common characterization of him as a consistent super-industrializer. The other political leaders rarely mentioned Dneprostroi in published discussion, except for Rykov, who supported the project in the context of the accepted party line in 1926.

Stalin had not been one of the electrification plan's first supporters in 1920, and he had not come out in favor of it until Trotsky had ranged himself among its critics. Only then, three months after it had been published, did Stalin read the plan and write to Lenin praising it. "The last three days," he wrote, "I have been able to read through the collection, the *Electrification Plan*. Being sick helped (there is no cloud without a silver lining)," indicating that he had not read it before.[133] Even then, Stalin's support was couched in Lenin's own words and offered no evidence that he had thought about the economics of the GOELRO plan or its broad political and social implications. It suggested only that he chose to support Lenin against Trotsky. In April 1926, Stalin voted against Dneprostroi at the party plenum. It is likely that he changed his mind before the year was out, as it is unlikely that the party and state officials would have endorsed it in the fall without Stalin's agreement. A number of factors could have contributed to this change. The most important may have been a desire to satisfy the demands of the Ukrainian interests, particularly to reward Chubar for keeping the Ukrainian party unified, disciplined, and obedient to the leadership. Perhaps he thought he could guarantee Chubar's support in the continuing leadership struggle. For Stalin and those advocating self-sufficiency, the Dneprostroi combine was vital for the production of aluminum and special steel alloys. Moreover, Dneprostroi may have had a special appeal to Stalin and others who felt it was time the Soviet Union proved it had come of age. Dneprostroi was the first of several giant projects designed to control nature and exploit its riches in the socialist cause.

3

Management Policy

Our forces . . . must create a cadre of workers who will relate with love to this great construction and who will themselves carefully watch the spending of each Soviet kopeck. This can only be done when the administration relates sensitively and attentively to the needs of the worker-constructor. . . . It is very important under the circumstances to start well, we need to have a friendly family of all builders, from the chief engineer to the unskilled worker.

N. P. Bogdanov, president of the construction workers'
union and member of the Dneprostroi Board of Directors,
Postroika, February 16, 1927

The Muscovite and Ukrainian press hailed the decision to build Dneprostroi as an important step in building socialism, in planned development, in technological modernization. The evolution of the discussion on who was to build the Dnepr project reflects important issues of the mid-1920s. Soviet leaders wanted to industrialize quickly, using the most modern technology. Hiring an experienced European or American firm was potentially promising. The Soviet leaders, however, like their predecessors in the imperial bureaucracy and business world, were suspicious of foreign investors and extremely sensitive to any intimation that their science and technology were inferior to those of the West. An alternative to a foreign firm was a Soviet specialist, but who was available for a task of this magnitude?

As they began to explore these questions, Soviet leaders uncovered scores of others relating to the allocation of authority and responsibility. The central planning organs in Moscow—Gosplan and the Supreme Economic Council—tried to control decisions affecting planning, project design, and resource use. Individual enterprise chiefs wanted to make the decisions affecting their individual enterprises and to control the resources under their direction. And the technically trained supervisors had differences with the party and trade union organization. What powers and rights did each one have, and what roles were the different levels of the community organizations to play? The task was challenging; there were no precedents for resolving these issues while creating a socialist environment, yet part of Dneprostroi's purpose was to serve as a model of socialist construction.

The Issue of Foreign Aid

After Soviet leaders chose Dneprostroi to help transform the economy, they wished to proceed as rapidly as possible. Soviet engineers, however, had little experience with complex, large-scale projects or mechanized construction work. Since rapid completion of the project was predicated on intensive use of modern mechanical equipment, two foreign firms were invited to submit construction proposals and bids, and their bids were considered along with other options.[1] Using foreigners to help Soviet development was not a radical departure from Bolshevik procedure. Lenin had argued, as did many of his successors in 1927, that one had to build socialism on a high technical level.[2] In order to share in the progress already achieved by various nations, the Soviet government, under Lenin, resolved to avail itself of foreign experience. Since it had limited foreign exchange, this was accomplished to some extent through the lease of concessions, a system that had the positive attribute of supplying investment capital necessary for plant and other construction. In a concession, a foreign company manufactured a product or developed a natural resource in return for a percentage of the profits and an option to buy the product. After an agreed period of time, the manufacturing or processing plants and technology reverted to the Soviet Union at a price. But concessions were unpopular with many of the Soviet leaders to whom they represented collaboration with capitalist "exploiters" and "foreign imperialists." They so ringed the concessions with rules and regulations that foreign firms had difficulty in making any profit whatsoever, and potential investors became fewer, were less qualified, and demanded more guarantees than the Soviet government was willing to concede.

The Soviet government also bought advanced technology through technical assistance contracts. Although these did not make capital available, they generally involved some special access to long-term credits supplied by the manufacturer of the high-technology product in question. These agreements were more palatable to the Soviet leaders, involving fewer foreigners on the Soviet soil, short-term agreements, and more direct control over the actual project. In addition, the Soviet government felt it had more control over which technology was imported; contractors were sought out and hired for projects proposed to foreigners according to national priorities. In practice, technical assistance agreements were limited to those areas in which long-term credits could be negotiated, especially in the 1930s when the Soviet Union had diminishing foreign exchange reserves.[3]

The merits of hiring foreigners to build Dneprostroi were reviewed by a special committee of the Council of Commissars under A. Rykov, chairman.[4] In the discussion of whether or not to invite foreigners to participate in the construction of Dneprostroi, Aleksandrov, chief designer of the project, and others argued the the Soviet Union was far behind the West in the development of technology, especially in the sphere of mechanization.[5] Soviet engineers lacked practical experience. Their training, based on a German model, emphasized theory over practice. Many chose careers in universities and government offices over careers in industry.[6] Further, war and revolution had thinned the ranks of the technical intelligentsia. It was important to use foreigners to fill this gap while Soviet practitioners were being trained.

Weighing the advantages and disadvantages of putting Dneprostroi out as a concession or, alternatively, arranging some kind of technical assistance contract, the Council of Commissars invited two firms to present estimates. One was the small New York City firm of Hugh Lincoln Cooper, Inc. Colonel Cooper had supervised the construction of three major dams—Niagara, Keokuk, and Muscle Shoals—and had vetted Aleksandrov's plan for Dneprostroi in 1926. He was known for his skill and ingenuity in mastering difficult engineering problems. He was a maverick in the United States, where professional training was already developing and a degree was becoming more important than experience. He had no formal education; his diplomas were his dams.[7] For Soviet discussants, this was both an asset and a liability. On the one hand, they were accustomed to placing great value on formal academic training and theoretical knowledge. On the other hand, Cooper had risen through the ranks on the basis of practical experience and was remarkably successful and highly respected. Although he was a capitalist millionaire, Cooper had humble origins, and his lack of professional snobbery added to his already formidable standing as the foremost builder of big dams. Cooper's attitude toward the Soviet Union was another important positive factor. He was very much in favor of trade with the Soviet Union, and business contact with him was liable to bring in its train favorable publicity, perhaps additional credits, and even diplomatic recognition.

The Council of Commissars also contacted Siemens Bau Union, an outstanding German construction firm with a long tradition of cooperation with imperial Russia. Many Russian engineers had completed their education in German universities or worked in one of the numerous Siemens concerns. They were accustomed to looking to Germany for ideas and equipment. Siemens Bau Union prepared extensive plans and estimates for Dneprostroi and even a model of the dam and installations; their work was characteristically careful and detailed. The German government announced its positive support of the policy of granting credits to the Soviet Union, a policy that promised to facilitate credit negotiations for the project's needs.[8]

The issue of the involvement of foreigners was resolved on January 31, 1927. The Council of Commissars announced that a Soviet hydrospecialist or a collegium of several specialists would manage Dneprostroi.[9] Consultation with foreigners was not ruled out, but the council emphasized the fact that there were good Soviet engineers available. They, said Kuibyshev, would know better than foreigners how best to introduce new methods and how to create friendly teamwork with the workers.[10] The use of Soviet personnel would entail reduced expenditure of foreign exchange and avoid damage to prestige. Finally, although both Cooper and the Siemens Bau Union firm estimated that they could do the job in four and a half years for one hundred million rubles, neither one would offer significant guarantees or accept any substantial penalty clause for delays or cost overruns.[11]

This decision reflected the general mood of antagonism toward concessions which had also existed in the years just preceding the revolution. National pride played a part in this antagonism, as did the argument that Soviet personnel and technology were available and that their use would keep the profits of industrialization at home where it belonged. Opposition to foreign investment had been refueled by Western intervention in the civil war. In addition, many Bolsheviks regarded the granting of concessions to foreigners as an invitation to capitalists to exploit Soviet citizens and Soviet resources—a real contradiction, they argued, after they had just fought to throw capitalists out![12] The argument over concessions grew more complicated when it became embroiled in the political debates between Trotsky and Stalin. Trotsky looked to foreign revolution and technical help from friendly, victorious, proletarian states to help Russia overcome its economic backwardness, but the revolutions failed to materialize. Trotsky argued in 1925 that industrial development and, therefore, military power depended on foreign machinery. Even when hopes for help from a friendly advanced socialist country faded,

Trotsky argued that industry could not develop on internal resources alone, that the Soviet Union had to import foreign machines despite "cruel dependence."[13] Stalin accused Trotsky of kowtowing to the West and having insufficient faith in the power of the Bolsheviks to succeed independently of foreigners. He reaffirmed this emphatically in 1924, when he repeatedly asserted that the Soviet Union could and would build "socialism in one country."[14] This appeal to national pride later became an indispensable part of his political program. It struck a receptive chord among prominent Russian technologists, such as A. V. Vinter, who said in 1926 that it was time the Russians "showed the world they could stand on their own two feet."[15] The decision to build with Soviet specialists reflected the shortage of foreign currency. More importantly, however, it was an expression of national pride and determination to surmount obstacles independently. Finally, it was an assertion by the Bolsheviks of their intention to control the reconstruction of the economy and the laying of the foundations for socialism.

Foreign Consultants

Having decided that Dneprostroi should be directed by a Soviet engineer, the Politburo turned to the question of access to the most up-to-date technology. Should the Supreme Economic Council retain foreigners as consultants on the project, and, if so, which firm? The consensus in the Supreme Economic Council and in the Council of Commissars was that the foreign technology essential for the mechanization of the project and its rapid completion could be fully utilized only with the aid of foreign consultants. Vinter, whose choice as chief engineer is discussed below, argued that he could do without foreigners. The highest political and economic authorities discussed the matter for a week.[16] Cooper's experience was a very strong factor in favor of his employment, but some members of the Dneprostroi committee feared American tempo. Cooper's plan, which had cut two years off Aleksandrov's estimate, was predicated on the extensive and efficient use of machinery. Soviet workers were unaccustomed to machinery and, it was feared, would have difficulty mastering its use and maintenance. The Germans, it was suggested, would not work so fast, and their machinery was less expensive.[17] There is no evidence that the different management styles and the context of their past successes were discussed in the comparisons of the two firms at this time.

The Supreme Economic Council appointed Cooper chief consultant for Dneprostroi on February 27, 1927. His record and his creative adaptations of the project apparently more than balanced Siemens Bau Union's elaborate sketches and available credits and Vinter's preference for the German firm. It may well be that Cooper's enthusiastic commitment was a significant factor, in addition to his specific "large dam" expertise. As he had won Rykov and Stalin over in 1926, he now spoke convincingly in the Businessman's Club in Moscow. He was willing to be interviewed for New York, European, and Soviet newspapers, and he always pointed out the importance of Dneprostroi, its significance for regional development, and, not least, its record-breaking size and capacity.[18]

As chief consultant for the whole project, Cooper was required to keep four of his own (U.S.) engineers in different specialties on the site and to come himself yearly for a minimum of four weeks. His duties included investigation of project questions as they arose and suggestion of appropriate responses. He was to specify and locate the machines and equipment. All plans and orders were subject to final review by the Dneprostroi administration and its board of directors. In payment, Cooper received six percent of Dneprostroi costs. Siemens Bau Union was also retained to advise on the selection and use of construction equipment.[19]

The retention of Cooper and Siemens Bau Union as consultants affirmed the desire of the Soviet leaders to get the best and most recent technology and their willingness to pay for it. The selection of Cooper as chief consultant was propitious. Cooper was dedicated to his work, thorough, and responsible, and he maintained good communications with the Dneprostroi staff as well as with the home office. Because of their technical knowledge and the appropriateness of the equipment they recommended, and because of their agreeable personal characteristics, Cooper and his staff made it possible for the Dneprostroi administrators to learn a great deal during the period of their collaboration.[20]

Organization

Having decided to keep the direction of Dneprostroi at home, the Soviet leaders moved to create an administration with an appropriate managerial structure, technical expertise, and financing. In order to be in close control, the Supreme Economic Council created a board of directors, directly responsible to the council and therefore an agent of both the central economic authority and party authority.[21] Its president, Emmanuel Ionovich Kviring, was deputy chief of the Supreme Economic Council and member of the party's Central Committee. He had been intimately involved in the discussions which immediately preceded the decision to build Dne-prostroi and had supported the project as a suitable prototype of the big, regional reconstruction projects the government was contemplating.[22] Kvir-ing had long worked in the Ukraine. He was one of the founding members of the Ukrainian party in 1912 and had regularly been involved in Ukrain-ian economic matters. He was well acquainted with the area and with Ukrainian personnel.[23] The other board members were deputy chief V. K. Viktorov, member of the Central Committee of the Ukrainian party and of the Ukrainian Gosplan, and N. P. Bogdanov, party member, formerly chief of the military economic planning, then president of the all-union union of construction workers. The nonparty members were both technical special-ists, Aleksandrov and A. V. Vinter, chief engineer.[24]

The board's task was to provide leadership and supervision over con-struction, a general plan, and annual work and finance plans. It was also responsible for planning and buying material supplies. It had the right to give final approval to expenditures of assigned funds without reference to state organs.[25]

Operational management was concentrated in the hands of the chief engineer, not a collegium as had once been discussed. There were three major contenders for the position. Aleksandrov, designer of the project, seemed the most likely candidate because of his close connection with the project and his past experience in construction. There is, however, no evidence that he was offered the job. Though an outspoken supporter of large-scale regional planning and as such a target for economic conserva-tives, he was not a political revolutionary and had no ties to the Bolshe-viks. His ardent advocacy of the expensive, complete mechanization of the project may have worked against him. In addition, the bulk of his recent experience, and perhaps his preference, too, was in the design of projects and in regional planning. The rest of his career suggests that he enjoyed living in Moscow and working in the central planning councils and that he may have preferred such a career to the practical construction work of Dneprostroi.[26]

The second candidate, Hugo Graftio, had designed the 1905 Dnepr project and was chief of Volkhovstroi, the hydroelectric project currently being built near Leningrad. Volkhovstroi was far behind schedule, how-ever, and had become very expensive, costing one hundred million rubles for eighty thousand horsepower.[27] Graftio's past was against him; he had been a tsarist official and had been arrested after the revolution. Only Lenin's intervention had restored him to work at Volkhovstroi.[28]

Aleksander Vasil'evich Vinter, a construction engineer, was selected. Vinter had recently completed the construction of Shatura, a central thermal power station. He was also serving on a number of committees concerned with power station construction. Though not a hydroengineer, Vinter had an appropriate social and professional background. Son of a tradesman, he had been expelled from Kiev University in 1901 for student revolutionary activity. He found work in the construction of a power station in Baku. There he worked under R. E. Klasson and L. Krasin, who later helped him find a place in Petrograd University. After defending his thesis, Vinter worked at Elektroperedacha, the first peat-burning station in Russia. He also married Krasin's sister, strengthening his connection to this eminent Bolshevik.[29] Vinter was not a member of the party, although he had been a Social Democrat before the war. One memoir suggests that Vinter compared favorably to Graftio in his capabilities in financial matters. Vinter was willing to make a firm estimate of cost, including costs abroad. This may have acted decisively in his favor.[30] V. Sproge, the engineer who presented the project to Chubar and who had translated for Cooper to Rykov and Kuibyshev, claimed that Vinter was appointed because he was a friend of Rykov's.[31] This friendship may have been important, but it is also true that Vinter had broad experience and a good record.

Vinter's two chief deputies were also appointed—Boris Evgenevich Vedeneev and Pavel P. Rottert. Vedeneev had graduated from the Petersburg Institute of the Ministry of Communication in 1909. His career included lecturing on hydroengineering as well as construction and irrigation work in Vladivostok and Turkestan. He had worked in GOELRO and Volkhovstroi, where he headed the hydrotechnical department.[32] Rottert had graduated from the same institute in 1911. He was active in construction work in Ekaterinoslav and for the Southern Railway. He came to Dneprostroi from Khar'kov, where he was chief engineer in charge of building the fourteen-floor Dom Promyshlennosti, then the city's largest multistory building.[33]

A vital issue at this time was the division of authority between the central councils in Moscow and the enterprise. As Kuibyshev pointed out in a speech in February 1927, the existing system did not encourage responsibility or initiative, and it was proving difficult to reconcile responsibility and control.[34] Individual directors complained about their limited rights and objected to the review of their work by control commissions. Moreover, regional and national groups sought to assert their own local controls. K. V. Sukhomlin, president of the Supreme Council of the Ukraine, commented on Kuibyshev's speech concerning correct administrative procedure, saying that builders in direct contact with responsible workers could solve organizational questions; not everything had to be decided at the center.[35] And the All-Russian Congress of Engineers and Technologists argued for decentralized operations.[36] Some argued that engineers would be more likely to concern themselves with economic effectiveness if they were personally responsible for the enterprise operations and more likely to introduce the latest technology promoting such effectiveness. The Dneprostroi principals met together twice to define their functions, powers, and responsibilities. There were to be no duplicate structures. The board would provide general leadership and financial plans, give orders for materials, and make collective agreements. The chief engineer in Kichkas was still responsible for all work on the site. Kviring affirmed that the chief engineer would have all the power (*vlast'*) he needed for the construction, that the board's basic principle was faith in the chief engineer.[37]

The individual members of the administration were hard at work in February. As board officer, Kviring arranged for financing to supplement that provided by the state budget. He went to Gosbank, Elektrobank, and Prombank.[38] He negotiated for material supplies, including timber, brick, and cement. He also negotiated for funds from the agricultural bank (Sel'khozbank) to finance the relocation of more than twenty-five hundred peasant households from Dneprostroi's flood plain.[39] Kviring represented the board at meetings in Moscow, Khar'kov, and Kichkas, where policy issues were discussed or explained to the public at large.

N. P. Bogdanov, president of the construction workers' union and a board member, negotiated concerning the labor force with Chaiko, president of the Ukrainian construction workers' union, the Zaporozh'e district council of trade unions, and the labor exchange board. Local agencies wished to ensure employment for their unemployed, while Dneprostroi wanted access to the most skilled labor force. Dneprostroi's managers contracted to hire local applicants and to recruit only if the needed skilled workers were not available locally. This soon happened. Representatives of the board and the chief engineer's staff applied to the Ukrainian Labor Commissariat for help. Dneprostroi tried to recruit specialists from other enterprises but stopped when the trusts complained against raiding.[40] The Zaporozh'e Labor Exchange also complained that Dneprostroi bypassed its offices and hired all sorts of workers directly at the site, not only those with special skills. Bogdanov and the board of directors did not become involved in this quarrel, which became one of a number of long-standing arguments between the chief engineer and the local organizations.

Bogdanov, Chaiko, and the District Trade Union Council also set wages. When the administration tried to set the pay very low and refused to raise it, Chaiko journeyed to Moscow to the board members there.[41]

His complaints included the low level of pay, the bypassing of the labor exchange, and the absence from the site of Vinter's staff, away buying supplies and equipment in Khar'kov, Moscow, and abroad. Kviring and Bogdanov came to Kichkas to smooth matters over and signed a temporary collective agreement with Chaiko.[42] Rottert resisted the pay raise. The board went on to Khar'kov, then capital of the Ukraine, to settle the matter. An agreement in June covered pay and labor recruitment.[43] Vinter, when he returned from Europe, became very angry that pay had been raised, but he had to accept it.[44] Such disagreements over pay and labor recruitment continued to exacerbate relations among the local union, Vinter, and central party authorities throughout the next three years.

Work on the site began in March 1927. Before any work on the dam, locks, and power station could begin, rail transportation was needed for equipment and materials and facilities for the workers. Aleksandrov, in his capacity as former chief of the project as well as a member of the board of directors and president of the Technical Council, saw to it that work was begun on the railroad spurs that would allow the movement of materials to the site. Viktorov, the ranking Ukrainian party official, supervised the sensitive negotiations with the peasants whose houses were requisitioned for workers and whose farms were in the future flood plain. Vinter and Rottert planned and supervised the transformation of old factories into housing; the construction of barracks, dining halls, warehouses, workshops, and bathhouses; the organization of food, goods, medical supplies, and services. The great concern of all the officials was that work should get started so that the construction season should not be lost.

The overall plan of the work involved diverting the water from its normal channel so that the separate parts of the project could be built. These included the dam foundations, the piers, and the gates used to control the water flow; the powerhouse, which consisted of an underwater channel and turbine section and the housing for the generators above it; and the lock chambers. The procedure called for workers to build and sink rock-filled timber cribs until they enclosed a section of the riverbed. They then pumped out the water behind the temporary coffer dam, exposing the riverbed, which they leveled, cleaned, and strengthened, preparing it for bonding to the dam foundations. On top of the foundation, they built concrete piers between which steel gates were hung, holding back the water.

While the workers prepared the site, the engineers were embroiled in conflict. The Supreme Economic Council had allocated responsibility for design to the Technical Council on which both Vinter and Aleksandrov served. It had to prepare plans, produce design specifications, and respond to technical difficulties and opportunities as they arose during the process of construction. It was staffed by fifteen experts in the fields of hydroelectric construction, electric power, waterway transportation, and irrigation. The Technical Council's members, nominated by the Supreme Economic Council and confirmed by the Council of Labor and Defense, were nonparty specialists. Most of them, including the president, Aleksandrov, had served on the original Dneprostroi commission. The council had three divisions, one each in Kichkas, Moscow, and Leningrad.[45]

As the council began its work, the very life of the project was challenged by the Commissariat of Communication. The commissariat wanted two dams and was not satisfied with the location of the proposed dam. Further, this commissariat wanted the locks bypassing the dam to handle seagoing ships and therefore wanted them deeper, larger, and farther apart.[46] The official representative, Mogilko, presented his own plan and argued that it would cost less. Kviring countered, saying that Mogilko's was not a finished project but just a plan—that the way to save money was to stick to the plan and schedule.[47] River traffic was losing its importance relative to railroads, Aleksandrov argued. Part of the Dnepr project was its bridges over the river, and the newly electrified railroad transport would play an essential role in linking the developing industrial areas. It was at this time that a new railway bridge became an integral part of the project.[48]

The latent disagreement between Vinter and the Technical Council under Aleksandrov flared at this time. Major concerns of the chief engineer and his deputies as well as the Technical Council included the final choice of construction method, the purchase of equipment, and the preparation of the site. Vinter went to Europe twice during this period to compare construction methods and to purchase necessary equipment. Aleksandrov went to the United States.[49] Up-to-date equipment for earth moving, concrete preparation and pouring, and machine workshop did not exist in the Soviet Union and had to be bought abroad, along with special equipment for dam construction. Cooper's and Siemen Bau Union's construction methods differed radically and involved the purchase of different types of equipment. Choosing between them required study and time.

Finally, in June, the Technical Council recommended the adoption of Cooper's method of construction. The council pointed out, however, that the delays that had occurred in ordering materials from abroad meant that Dneprostroi could not meet the original schedule for completion.

Current from the first three generators, one hundred fifty thousand horsepower, would begin in five and a half years, rather than four and a half, from June 1927.[50] Some current might be available in December 1931, the engineers conceded, if equipment arrived quickly.

Vinter overruled the Technical Council's recommendation. He wanted to speed the work by using both Cooper's and Siemen Bau Union's methods and types of equipment and by building from both sides of the river at the same time.[51] Ignoring Aleksandrov's warning that the German method was dangerous and unsuitable, the board of directors and the Council of Labor and Defense accepted Vinter's new plan. Kuibyshev announced for the Supreme Economic Council that Dneprostroi had to be finished on time (December 1931).[52]

Vinter also forced the pace by hiring extra hands, adding substantially to costs. He ordered work that was to have been done by machine started by hand, especially drilling, digging, loading, and hauling. Many hands, many more than originally planned, became necessary. By October, the work force was four times as large as that originally planned—ten thousand instead of two or three thousand.[53] The substitution of men for machines entailed many other changes. Certain parts of the project scheduled for completion had to be delayed, while others, more easily translated into hand work, were done ahead of schedule. Extra buildings were constructed to house and serve the additional workers. These changes required more materials and especially more funds. Some came from reserve funds and special long-term loans, but much of the work was financed by expensive, short-term credit, raising the cost of financing.[54]

Vinter's expenses came increasingly under scrutiny as he exceeded the budget and asked for more money.[55] Kuibyshev proposed a special commission under A. P. Serebrovskii to keep an eye on Dneprostroi's expenses. This commission conducted an examination and reported a few days later that although there were some unnecessary expenses and mistakes, there was "no need to correct Vinter."[56]

Most expensive and wasteful was Vinter's decision to use the different methods, working from both sides of the river. His decision was contrary to the advice of the consultants, who said that their designs fit together "like oil and water."[57] He persisted in spite of the Technical Council's disapproval. His attempt to build the complicated German coffer dam was a complete failure. Materials and equipment were wasted. Time was lost. In November, orders were hurriedly given to construct coffer dams of Cooper's design in place of the German ones, and more American equipment had to be ordered.[58] Vinter survived this serious miscalculation with his authority intact. It is likely that he was protected by his acquaintances among Bolshevik technical specialists. The engineer, Sproge, claims it was his friendship with Rykov that saved him.[59] It may also have been that Dneprostroi was so new and important a project, and so expensive, that those close enough to it to know about its difficulties were perhaps also close enough to it to want to hide them and so protect its future. In spite of the delay and cost overruns, Vinter consolidated his position. During 1928, he succeeded in enlarging the project and his role in its management.

Vinter's changed plan of construction for the left-bank coffer dam required more men and more equipment if the schedule was to be kept, and therefore more money.[60] If the schedule slipped, the energy requirements of the new factories planned as Dneprostroi clients—the aluminum, coke, steel, and chemical factories—would not be met.[61] Vinter reported this to the Committee of Support for Dneprostroi, a committee of interested Ukrainian officials, headed by Chubar, in Khar'kov, and then went to Moscow in January to defend his accomplishments and urge increased financial support.[62]

Gosplan's *Ekonomicheskaia zhizn'* publicized many of Vinter's mistakes at this time.[63] Some buildings on the site had been built too substantially with inappropriately expensive materials, others so hurriedly and with such poor workmanship that they needed extensive repair within a year. The many housing designs (nineteen) and lack of standardization caused further expense.[64] The woodworking shop, which was built in late 1927 and equipped with expensive German tools, was readied too late to be of use for the extensive building carried on in the first year. Fear of running out of certain materials and dissatisfaction with the quality available caused the Dneprostroi administration to invest in manufacturing, to produce items also made elsewhere, and to hoard supplies.[65] The carelessness and inexperience of the workers, compounded by poor supervision by technical personnel, caused further delay and expense. Vinter overspent the budget in the first year by thirty-three percent.

Moreover, the Moscow-based board of directors and the Kichkas-based chief engineer "got in each other's way" and communicated badly.[66] This was an issue that Vinter turned to his own advantage. In the interest of better management and economy, he argued that he alone should direct the project. Elimination of the board would end the duplication of staff and effort, would save time and personnel, and would clarify responsibility.[67] Within the month, he had won a vote of confidence from the Supreme Economic Council in the form of the dissolution of the board and an extra assignment of funds from Gosplan.[68] With the board gone, Vinter controlled the Technical Council which reported to him. Vinter cut staff in Leningrad and Moscow and brought the design and comptroller staffs to Kichkas. Within the year, Vinter had also made a number of changes in the administrative organization, consolidating his local authority as well.[69]

Vinter's disagreements with the board and the central planning authorities had two aspects. One was simply a matter of power. The board saw itself as the director and final authority for Dneprostroi with the chief engineer as its agent. As such, it intended to make Dneprostroi a model of mechanization and organization, thereby keeping costs down while achieving high productivity. Vinter saw himself as a project director, with a deadline to meet, needing the power to command and direct resources without having to justify them within the context of the plan or the "ideal" set for Dneprostroi. But this was not a conflict over power alone; the second aspect of their argument involved their different approaches to industrialization and the balance between central control and planning and decentralization. At Dneprostroi, Vinter, supported by Chubar and the Ukrainian Council of People's Commissars, and with allies in Moscow, succeeded in strengthening his authority and freeing himself from direct control. The general agreements for the liquidation of the dual authority were made in January and confirmed by a Supreme Economic Council protocol dated May 14, 1928.[70]

Expansion of the Project

Turning to the linked problems of the tempo of construction and the schedule for completion, Vinter urged that the project be expanded to its original size. He argued that it was being built to accommodate five generators and could, with only a little additional cost, be built for seven, guaranteeing energy for the new factories. Moreover, the expanded project would have the right to twenty million additional rubles, approved earlier for such work by the Council of Labor and Defense and currently needed.

A. N. Dolgov, representing the commission planning for the use of Dneprostroi energy, defended expansion at a Gosplan meeting.[71] Others supporting the expansion included Chubar, who saw in it the beginning of an integrated industrial center at Zaporozh'e.[72] The power plant would serve ore-processing plants, which were linked to manufacturing plants. The factories would use each other's products and by-products, forming an interrelated unit or combine. Vinter argued that the project was going well. Men were being trained to assemble, use, and maintain the machines that had finally come. The coffer dams for closing the river were growing at a rapid rate, particularly as carpenters learned to use the foreign pneumatic drills and foremen learned how to assign efficiently the limited number of skilled workers. Now, in 1928, he could compensate for time lost if he were allowed to build the full capacity planned by Aleksandrov but cut down in the approved plan; he proposed to build three hundred fifty thousand horsepower instead of one hundred fifty thousand horsepower. The client factories could be built for about sixty million rubles and could be ready quickly to utilize the extra energy thus produced, he said.[73] The Supreme Economic Council agreed with Vinter and in March 1928 decided to proceed with installation of seven generators.[74] The completion date was moved forward one year, to December 1932. Supporters recalled that Dneprostroi was important not only as a source of electric power but as a stimulus for total change in the economy.[75] It was wrong, argued S. A. Kukel-Kraevski, to say that there was not enough money for Dneprostroi;[76] and, argued another, criticism of Dneprostroi was only illustrative of enmity to the party policy of industrialization and demonstrated a lack of faith in the party and country.[77]

Those who opposed Dneprostroi's expansion spoke up in party meetings and in the public press. Their opposition extended beyond Dneprostroi and challenged the rising pace of industrial development. At the July meeting of the Central Committee, N. Osinskii argued that funds spent on Dneprostroi and similar grandiose projects might better be invested in the countryside to restore lagging agricultural production.[78] Nikolai Uglanov, in Moscow, argued against the aggrandizement of Dneprostroi and further unbalanced excessive investment in industry. The escalating costs of the project, which exceeded estimates by 161 percent, drew stringent criticism.[79] One critic concentrated on the mistaken assumptions on which Dneprostroi's production costs had been based and argued that hydroelectric power, at present costs of capital and amortization, was undeniably more expensive than thermal plants using coal or peat.[80] Other critics noted that there were as yet few clients for the energy that Dneprostroi was to have produced in the smallest variant.[81] Finally, a wing of the Ukrainian party, categorizing Russian involvement in the Ukraine as colonialism, advised the Ukrainian republic to confine itself to projects that it alone could build and use.[82]

But Vinter was not deterred by such criticism. In mid-November, he again proposed expansion in a formal report to Glavelektro, asking to install larger generators, raising Dneprostroi's capacity to eight hundred thousand horsepower.[83] In spite of antagonists, Vinter and the planners in favor of this largest variant succeeded in December in gaining approval from the Supreme Economic Council. The council also approved the draft plans for the complex of factories which were to consume Dneprostroi's expanded production.[84]

The council's approval capped the process of expansion that Vinter had embarked on in early 1928. He was not alone in this kind of action; his contemporaries among field engineers and project directors provided strong impetus for expansion of the industrial plan. Ambitious men, they believed that they would master existing shortages and meet schedules with just more men, money, and more machinery.[85]

Their ambitions corresponded with those of Stalin and his faction who had come to dominate the Supreme Economic Council and, to a lesser extent, Gosplan.[86] The original planning for industrial development, including the early drafts of the Five-Year Plan, had set moderately high goals.[87] The Bukharin-led right and the Stalinist center had agreed in 1926 that industry needed additional long-term capital.[88] This had not implied a departure from NEP but had been within its framework. The right urged moderation in the taxation of successful peasants. The government bought grain from the farmers at low prices but abstained from forceful requisitioning. Rather than financing industrial development from agriculture alone, Bukharin advocated internal economies in industry and the careful reinvestment of profits in further development.[89]

Then, in 1928, Stalin pressed for greater tempo in industrialization and greater pressure on the peasants to make them contribute to national capital accumulation through low grain prices and high taxation. Stalin renewed grain requisitioning in the Urals and Siberia in early spring 1928. This marked the demise of NEP. The relations between the right and Stalin became very strained. Bukharin argued that violent measures against the richer peasants would lead to civil war and an end to the policy of union, or *smychka*, which had made the revolution successful.[90] Nevertheless, with Kuibyshev at the head, the Supreme Economic Council was Stalinist in its views and pressed for the acceleration of industrialization. Vinter took advantage of the expansionist spirit according to which what had been extravagant before now became permissible.

The council and the Soviet leaders were responsive to Vinter's confidence that he could do more, faster than planned. They approved the expanded project just as they had accepted his demand for freedom from direct council supervision and expanded administrative power. But there were other organizations on the site that competed with Vinter for authority and power—local organizations that, like the site administration, were working out their own goals and strategies and their relationships with the leaders at the center. They included the Communist party, the Leninist Communist Youth League, the Komsomol, and the trade unions.

The Communist Party at Dneprostroi

How did the party-led organizations define their areas of responsibility and competency? Did their different claims compete, and did the administration and party organizations conflict with one another? Responsibility for communist leadership on the site belonged to local organizations—the site cells, district councils, Ukrainian party leaders—and to the Central Committee and Politburo in Moscow. Exactly what sort of leadership was to be exercised, how, and to what ends were matters not fully defined. The pressure of events both on and off the site shaped the issues of power.

Party leaders charged with economic decision making at Dneprostroi were those on the board of directors, particularly Kviring, who represented the Central Committee. The special Ukrainian party interests were represented in the project leadership by Viktorov and through the special Commission of Assistance for Dneprostroi under the presidency of Chubar.[91] Such direct participation by party members was interrupted in early 1928, when Vinter asserted his independence and won the dissolution of the board. The party leaders retained indirect authority through their control of the Supreme Economic Council and the Council of Labor and Defense, where Vinter's major decisions were reviewed, and through the party Central Committee and Politburo, where major policy questions received definitive resolution. Vinter could be called to account by these councils, but he had aggregated technical and managerial initiatives and authority to himself.

The party exercised leadership on the site through its local organizations and, periodically, through the emissaries of the party Central Committee and the Commissariat of Workers' and Peasants' Inspection (RKI). The duties of the party organization included broadening and strengthening party leadership in the enterprise; carrying out assigned economic, party, and trade union tasks; improving the material-cultural position of the workers; and strengthening the ideological education of the party members and their internal organization.[92] Strengthening party leadership included recruiting new party workers and mobilizing them to follow party leadership.

The basic membership unit was the cell. It formed in the work place, at Dneprostroi—in the mechanical workshop, the earth-moving sector, the depot, or administrative office. When there were too few for a cell, members from different workshops formed a link, *zveno*, but did not elect their own secretary.

The lowest-level party cell had two major functions: training the individual and expanding party influence over the masses in all political, economic, and cultural activity. The individual member's duties were to persuade those outside the party to execute party decisions and to prepare nonmembers to join the party.[93] The individual therefore had to educate himself through regular attendance at meetings and the study of materials presented there, the study of party resolutions and protocols published in the press, and participation in party schools. Then he had to execute party commands and lead others, even command others, through the party hierarchy to do the same.[94]

The founding meeting of the Dneprostroi call took place on May 7, 1927.[95] Forty-five party members and fifteen candidates elected a bureau of seven (two of them candidate members). They held their second meeting two weeks later when their numbers had increased to 80—out of a work force of 2211.[96] Ten workshop cells formed in the summer of the first year. Each elected a secretary who was usually assisted by one or more activists. These party activists, as their title suggests, were those who accepted special responsibility and therefore had specific tasks and usually received extra training. Those serving as party bureau members were often released from production duties and served as paid staff.[97] The members also elected a party bureau, headed by a secretary. The Dneprostroi bureau included the head of the trade union committee, a member responsible for agitation and propaganda (*agitprop*), and three other members.

The Dneprostroi bureau told the workshop cells to battle against bureaucratism, promote the development of the economy, improve knowledge of technology, and raise productivity through its application, to rationalize production and to battle with absenteeism.[98] Cells were expected to meet at least once monthly, to review the activities of individual members, and to promote ideological education.[99]

Difficulties in internal organization hampered the party development from the outset. The ten cells tried to attract candidate members and interest workers in party teachings. However, conditions were unfavorable for cell development.[100] Instead of a stable factory force, reporting daily to a known location, the Dneprostroi labor force was spread over an area of twenty-five kilometers and lacked cohesiveness. The makeup of work groups, even of *arteli*, frequently changed, particularly as the work force grew and cell members were scattered all over the site. In addition, most party members had to do a full day's work in production before turning to party work. Good workers with such energy were scarce.

In spite of difficulties, the party had grown along with the work force. By early September, the party reported 358 members and candidates, three percent of the site population.[101] They were predominately Russian, white-collar males (335 men, 23 women) who had joined the party during the Leninist draft of 1924 or later. Their characteristics are listed in Table 1.

The collective continued to grow together with the work force (see Table 2). New members came largely from outside the site. Thirty-five new candidates were finally recruited in December.[102] This number was considered insufficient by the Ukrainian Central Committee Orgburo, which reprimanded the Dneprostroi cell in January 1928 for its inactivity in recruitment of workers.[103] The slow growth that did occur was caused by the import of cadres from off the site. The cell also had difficulty in finding trained party members to promote into positions of responsibility in either community organizations or the administration. A major complaint of the cell throughout the year, one seconded by the regional bureau, was that there was no local party member with enough authority to control the chief engineer.[104]

In order to inform members of party policy and to mobilize them behind it, Dneprostroi activists discussed in the cells the site's production plan, the progress in party tasks, workshop production matters, and the work of the youth group, the Komsomol. Some organized Marxist-Leninist study groups and a school of political literacy. The number of activists in a workshop cell grew from between three and five to between seven and ten during the year, and two activists were assigned places in the regional school of political activism.[105]

The party worked directly with the labor force, assigning activists to present lectures and lead discussion groups in the barracks, on the train and boat between the site and Zaporozh'e, and in the cafeterias.[106] In their summer work among the workers, the activists conducted information campaigns and discussions on many topics, including the international position of the Soviet republic in connection with the murder of the Soviet consuls in China and Poland, the rupture of trade relations with England, the tasks of the Dneprostroi construction, "our internal position," and a protest against the Sacco-Vanzetti trial.[107] There were campaigns to publicize the danger of war and the importance of defense

Table 1. Dneprostroi VKP (b) Membership, 1927

Nationality

Russian	Ukrainian	Jew	White Russian	German	Latvian	Other
180	126	27	6	3	9	7

Year of entry into VKP(b)

pre-1917	1917	1918	1919	1920	1921	1922	1923	1924	1925	1926	1927
4	12	9	34	32	14	9	6	40	58	39	17

Occupation

Administrative personnel and employees	Bench workers
209	149

Social origins

Workers	Peasants	Employees	Other
261	41	52	4

Source: "Iz doklada sekretaria partbiuro o rabote partiinoi organizatisii Dneprostroia," 3 September 1927, Document 30, *Pervenets industrializatsii strany—Dneproges: Sbornik dokumentov.* Zaporozh'e, 1960, p. 41.

Table 2. Dneprostroi VKP (b) Membership, May 1927–January 1928

	May	June	July	Aug.	Sept.	Oct.	Nov.	Dec.	Jan.
Work force	2184	3210	6140	8937	11449	13117	12765	8785	8622
Members	16	38	68	144	237	312	383	439	459

Source: "Iz otcheta o rabote partiinoi iacheiki Dneprostroia s maia 1927g. po le ianvaria 1928 g.," 27 January, Document 40, *Pervenets*, pp. 56–65.

preparations. The activists urged participation in voluntary organizations offering Red Cross medical courses and military training. They also urged workers to invest in savings banks and special loans that would help finance the development of the country and to join the food cooperative.[108] Although workers were generally more interested in wages and their own living and working conditions than in these topics, the campaigns had some impact. Workers joined the Red Cross medical course (though it collapsed when the instructor left) and Osoviakhim, the military preparedness society which held training courses and outings. Participation in the loan campaign was poor until it was made nearly obligatory. The class war and antiforeign slogans appealed to those who hated land and factory owners, especially foreign owners, and reminded others of recent foreign invasions. On the other hand, many admired foreign goods and foreign technology. Party campaigns introduced workers to a variety of slogans, but they were shallow in content and limited in effect.

The party secretary had ample opportunity for informal influence. He had an office in the main office building and a telephone and could contact the department officials. He had a strong potential bargaining position because party members staffed the trade union committee with which the administration had to negotiate labor contracts. Perhaps the party's strongest potential tool was its local newspaper, *Dneprostroi.* The paper publicized state and party resolutions and carried international, national, and local news. Experienced editors were scarce, however, and the paper underwent frequent reorganization. It only began to appear regularly in 1928. It tried without success in the first year to develop a network of local workers' correspondents to report public and private job mistakes and misadventures. Such *rabkory* were unpopular. Fearing public censure, administrators fired them, coworkers shied away from them, and recruits were hard to find.[109]

In addition to creating an organization and extending its influence over the work force, the Dneprostroi party was expected by the Central Committee to be able to influence the administration. One of its major tasks was to control costs, particularly personnel costs. It had, however, little direct authority in management decisions. None of the chief managers was a party member. Even after two years, only six percent of the staff belonged to the party.[110] The party secretary on the site complained to the administration of inefficient use of material and workers with no effect, because, he reported, there was no Communist in the administration.[111] The administration kept inefficient workers, paid unequal wages for equal work, and ignored infractions of labor safety procedures, and the party organization was unable to change the situation.[112]

In addition to work with its own members, the administration, and the public at large, the party cell supplied the leadership core for community organizations formed at Dneprostroi. In 1927, of the five most important community organizations, two were just getting started: the International Organization of Aid to Revolutionaries (MOPR) and the Society of Assistance to Security, Aviation, and Chemical Construction in the USSR (Osoviakhim). The other three, already established by the end of 1927, were the trade unions, the youth organization, and the women's organization. The nucleus of party members belonging to these organizations planned their activities in private caucus and guided the decisions of the executive committees to support party goals. It was in cooperation with these organizations, and especially with the trade unions, that the party pursued its goal of broadening party leadership in the enterprise, especially by involving the workers in volunteer activities related to improving production and living standards.

The Leninist League of Communist Youth

One branch of party activity that grew to be particularly important on construction sites was the recruitment and training of young people. The party-led youth organization, the Komsomol, served as a training ground for future Communist party members. It provided special instruction and practical leadership opportunities for young people aged fourteen to twenty-five.[113]

The Dneprostroi Komsomol organization was founded in May 1927. It grew out of the rural Kichkas cell.[114] In February 1927, fourteen of the thirty young people on the site were members of the Komsomol; in September, their number had grown to 505, one quarter of the young, and four and a half percent of all workers. The numbers of Komsomol members fluctuated widely, indicating that they came during the slack farm seasons.[115] In the fall of 1928, there were 750 members, seven percent of all workers.

The chief emphasis in the Komsomol was on self-education. Komsomol members were urged to form circles for the study of Marxism-Leninism and party directives. In early 1928, they were also urged to recruit new members and to establish their influence over incoming young people and peasants. But the Komsomol did not become very active in the first two years, in spite of prodding from the party bureau and the assignment of party instructors. Many members found excuses not to attend meetings. The party collective assigned one member full-time to supervise and develop youth activities. It organized five schools of communist studies, and encouraged all to enroll in courses. The one member with spasmodic bureau support achieved little success. At the end of the year, the Komsomol tried to reach out to the nearby peasant villages over which it established patronage, or *sheftsvo*. It promised to raise their cultural level and strengthen the bonds between the village and site youth but accomplished little.[116] The local press and party reports expressed concern that there were few activities planned for young people after dark, that get-togethers for talk and singing turned into noisy drinking bouts and even fights. Young and old workers annoyed one another in the club areas, while their trade union sponsors fretted over the rudeness of the young and the conservatism of the old.

In early 1928, party interest in young people grew. Party leaders recognized their work energy, their potential for mastering new knowledge and technology, and their capacity for loyalty to the regime that gave them opportunities. The party wooed them and directed both party and trade union officials to involve the young more fully in their organizations.[117]

Organization of the Trade Unions

The trade unions at Dneprostroi faced formidable obstacles. The two purposes of the unions carried potential conflict—they sought to represent the interests of the workers vis-à-vis the party-state and, at the same time, to mobilize the workers to carry out the party line.[118] Trade union history at Dneprostroi is illustrative of the problems trade unions were encountering elsewhere at the same time. In addition, special problems developed at Dneprostroi because of the size and diversity of the working population. Solutions found there were applied in succeeding projects.

The unions had a difficult time getting established at Dneprostroi in 1927. The predecessor to all unions was a workers' committee, Rabochkom, elected in October 1926 by three hundred workers and research personnel then on the site.[119] The following April, the membership attacked the committee for its failures—committee members were unavailable to the membership, they published no accounts, and they had failed to assist workers in getting medical care, drinking water, or announcements of the end of a shift by means of whistles.[120] A new committee of thirteen was elected, with seven party members and one Komsomol, including party members P. Timoshkin, president, formerly president of the Dnepropetrovsk construction workers' union, and Nekrasov, chief of the wage-setting department at Volkhovstroi.[121] A week later, the new Rabochkom presided over "a stormy meeting," where it was again attacked.[122] "[The Rabochkom] sat in a little shed and played with trifles," the members said. It offered no protection for labor, did no cultural work, ran no labor conferences, and did not know what was going on.[123]

One of the causes of these shortcomings was the influx of new workers. In June, for example, two hundred to three hundred new workers were hired a day. By the end of the month, there were already 3110 workers. Only 1250 were members of the union (forty percent), in spite of the fact that workers with six months of consecutive work experience were allowed, even expected, to join the union.[124] Concerned over their lack of drawing power, the Rabochkom held a union conference in July at which the committee was enlarged to twenty-three members and candidates so that there would be more staff members available for organizational and recruitment work. Six of them were relieved of production duties so that they could work full-time for the union. There were fourteen party members and two Komsomol; two women were on the committee.[125]

The Dneprostroi Rabochkom was the elected representative of the construction workers' union. Members elected representatives to a delegates' institute on the basis of a ratio of one to ten.[126] These delegates elected the Rabochkom. There were other unions, including food service, store clerks, medical staff, and seasonal workers.[127] The construction workers, however, had by far the largest union on the site. Their Rabochkom, while nominally the elected representative of the construction workers alone, represented all the workers on the site. This was because Vinter, chief engineer, preferred to deal with just one union and refused to deal with more.[128]

The basic unit in the organization was the cell. The cell usually formed within a single workshop and elected a secretary and a *profburo* of four or five members. The *profburo* members were responsible for the regular meetings and for the work of the committees for the regulation of conflicts between workers and management, the *rastsenochno-konfliktnye komissi* (RKK). They were also responsible for the recruitment and processing of new members and for elections.

It was difficult, however, to organize the pieces of this structure. During 1927, the Rabochkom established *profburo* in only four of the seven sectors of the site. They held elections, but only two *profburo* had begun to meet by September.[129] Applications for membership were handled through meetings of elected representatives and then through large meetings for the whole membership. In September, an effort was made to return applications to the smaller, more controllable meetings where prompt attention could be given to them.[130] Members' duties were to pay dues, obey union rules, and participate actively in union activities. Union members were supposed to attend meetings, contribute to loan and special project campaigns, and participate in extra production work when necessary.[131]

The Rabochkom kept in touch with its individual members through activists, those who accepted extra duty and responsibility.[132] Some served as elected representatives of union members and met irregularly in delegates' institutes. Others served on various commissions organized by the Rabochkom: production, labor, "red corners," and one that collected dues. The Rabochkom supervised the election of these activists and urged them, in turn, to go to trade union schools to learn their practical tasks and something of the history of the working-class movements and the Communist party.[133]

One of the primary responsibilities of the trade unions, and the Rabochkom in particular, was the daily defense of the rights and interests of workers. At this time, a major problem for workers in Zaporozh'e was growing unemployment, directly related to the news of Dneprostroi. Workers were applying to the local construction union from across the union. They were told to apply only, not to come, but they continued to arrive. The local union secretary, Abazin, went to Moscow to discuss how to create jobs. The Zaporozh'e Trade Union Council (OSPS) noted that even among those lucky enough to get jobs at Dneprostroi there was dissatisfaction. All ranks had very low pay; they complained that they did not know the rates for which they were working; and their pay did not come on time. The OSPS further complained that food at the cafeteria was expensive and of low quality; workers had to bear the cost of transportation and needed a monthly commutation ticket; and that as the chief engineer was regularly absent there were no responsible authorities on the site. The argument went to the Workers' and Peasants' Inspectorate who asked for higher pay scales but the administration refused. The OSPS sent another representative to carry their complaints to Moscow.[134] The chief of the Ukrainian construction union, Chaiko, also journeyed to Moscow where he succeeded in winning a slight improvement in wages.[135] Worker-administration conflicts over living and working conditions multiplied, however.[136] During the summer, the enlarged Rabochkom helped negotiate new collective agreements, *koldogovor*, with improved pay and allowance for housing and travel; fuller enumeration of the administration's obligations to provide baths, medical services, and schools; and a reiteration of the administration's obligation to hire through the labor exchanges where union members had priority.[137]

The Rabochkom played a limited role in defending the interests of the workers. It collected information on wages and labor safety which it reported to the Zaporozh'e OSPS, inspectors for labor safety, the Workers' and Peasants' Inspection (RKI), and the newspapers.[138] It identified inequalities in the wages of men and women and investigated accusations of protectionism and nepotism, frequently publishing news of wrongdoings in hiring and firing. It handled and published complaints about living conditions and sought to pressure the administration into observing its obligations under the collective agreements. When individual complaints could not be resolved, the Rabochkom referred them to the RKI for third-party arbitration. The trade union negotiated nonunion grievances as well as those of their members and claimed responsibility for defusing most conflicts. In spite of their efforts, however, there were occasional strikes; for example, the wagoneers refused to work in the fall of 1927 at existing rates and only went back to work when their pay was raised.[139]

The Rabochkom sought to stimulate worker interest in and commitment to the project and their work. It organized ten bureaus for production and one for economics and held a number of production meetings in the workshops and construction departments. Production and economic information meetings and all-site production conferences were planned as means for attracting workers into the work of administration. Through their suggestions at the workshop level and their critique of management reports, workers ideally would recognize both the importance of their personal contributions and their ability to comment usefully on the work of administrators. The party defined the production information meeting as the vehicle through which the trade union would introduce the masses to the problems and progress of the project.[140] When they became knowledgeable about the overall project, the party hoped that the Dneprostroi workers, Dneprostroevtsi, would better understand and value their own contribution to the project and to the goal of Soviet industrialization, therefore maintaining good labor discipline, improving productivity, and studying to improve their skills. Activists gave lectures on these topics to specially convoked groups of workers. During the first year, 230 such meetings were held, 24 large meetings with a total attendance of 4505 (average attendance 187); 58 at the workshops with 4814 in attendance (average attendance 83); and 148 among groups with 3552 in attendance (average attendance 24).[141]

The trade unions pursued their goals of informing and educating the workers, urging them to participate more through meetings in which the activists discussed the significance of the Dneprostroi project, the particulars of the collective agreement, and the importance of elections. They organized six campaigns for the mass of the workers: popularization of the collective agreement, the week of defense, the Sacco-Vanzetti trial, the industrial loan, October creativity (in honor of the tenth anniversary of the revolution), and unemployment week. Meetings took place on fifteen evenings, drawing an audience of 4560.[142]

The Rabochkom also organized schools. Illiteracy was common on the site, and the five "Liquidate Illiteracy" centers were very important. A start was made on organizing general education on the site—evening schools and a school for children—a responsibility of Zaporozh'e but one for which the district lacked funds. With respect to industrial education, the Rabochkom, with the chief engineer's assistance as required by the October collective agreement, organized two construction schools.[143] It also set up "red circles" for the study of technology and two circles where workers could improve existing skills.[144] American instructors, who came with the new cranes and excavators, taught Soviet engineers and technologists how to use them, and they in turn taught the workers.[145] In all the schools, however, there were problems with absenteeism and high drop-out rates as workers and their teachers transferred from one job to another.

The trade unions supplemented educational work with cultural activities. The Rabochkom organized four large red corners and a club whose presidium organized groups in drama, chorus, sports, and orchestra. The unions supported a library with mobile divisions, a radio station, and *Dneprostroi*, the enterprise newspaper. They also provided entertainments, lectures, and movies. Between mid-June and mid-August, there were twelve spectacles (for 10,150), sixteen movies (for 4800), and twenty-one lectures (for 5560).[146] The workers were not deeply involved in many of these activities, saying, "The club exists in name only" or "club work is work of the council only, workers don't come." Red corners were often dark, empty of chairs and tables, bare of reading materials. Only subscribers could take out books, and desirable technical books, complained one report, were still "packed" and unavailable. Movie projectors failed to work regularly, and available seats were oversold. In November, a permanent meeting place was found for "cultural work," and a special cultural committee of fifty-nine members was formed to provide more direction and greater quality and consistency in cultural activities. In December, the Rabochkom reported more reading of newspapers, new evenings of questions and answers, more books and readers, and the opening of the seven-year school for workers' children.[147]

The unions had a particularly delicate role to play in mediating the relationships of the bourgeois specialists, the newly trained specialists, and the workers. Until new specialists were trained, the party and state had to rely on the bourgeois specialists for technical guidance.[148] The trade unions were responsible for mobilizing these specialists to reach beyond their professional tasks into educational and community work. The unions were also responsible for checking specialists' work to make sure that it was in accord with party and state directives. The workers' Rabochkom frequently reminded the engineering-technical personnel's union, the ITS, of its obligations for the rationalization and mechanization of construction, cost containment, and helping to train workers in administration and new technology. Examples of poor management, extravagance, and poor-quality work were reported in the press and in party and union reports along with infractions of safety rules, nepotism, and abuse of position. Such public attack initiated by the unions and by workers themselves undermined the already weak authority of the specialists. Engineers and other persons professionally trained before the revolution were automatically suspect as actual or potential members of the bourgeois class. When old forms of authority of all kinds were being tested, the authority of the engineers and technical supervisors was no exception.

The engineers at Dneprostroi and other prominent work sites were particularly vulnerable in 1928 and thereafter. Engineers and specialists became the special objects of antagonism, whipped up by Stalin, who did not trust them.[149] In the spring of 1928, Stalin mounted an attack on a group of some sixty engineers and foreign consultants in a coal-mining town in the Don Basin. He used the subsequent trial, the Shakhti trial, in a political attack on Bukharin and the Right Opposition.[150] The mistakes of the technical, managerial, and consulting personnel were portrayed as deliberate sabotage. Stalinists claimed that the right's advocacy of collaboration with bourgeois specialists was a dangerous and costly mistake which was slowing the development of industry. Indeed, counsels for a moderate pace of development were condemned as treasonable opposition to the faster pace which could be achieved if saboteurs, wreckers, and disbelievers could be eliminated. The Shakhti trade unions were accused of failing to control the specialists and administrators. The trial laid the ground for Stalin's attack on trade union leadership and the right's advocacy of a moderate pace of industrialization.

The growing antagonism toward specialists naturally found an echo at Dneprostroi. Specialist-baiting, *spetseedstvo*, had existed at the site from the start and was revived as a result of the Shakhti trial. Evidence suggests, however, that the trial did not seriously change patterns already established—namely, a persistent mistrust of "bourgeois spets." Engineers in management positions had perforce been educated in the imperialist period; it was assumed that they were not socialist. Senior engineers received high pay and other privileges.[151] Many acted in a traditional manner, aloof from the workers. *Dneprostroi* accused engineers at Dneprostroi of sitting apart, in their offices, and acting despotically, charges that were brought against them by their American consultants as often as by the trade union or party.[152] Other more serious charges must have been made, for one foreign visitor observed that a year after Shakhti, morale was so fragile that engineers hardly dared discipline workers for fear of retaliation.[153] On the other hand, the local press carried many articles supporting the authority of the technical staff, and the party was congratulated at the end of the year for its good work in controlling spets-baiting.[154]

Even while they tried to control the bourgeois specialists, the party and trade unions strongly supported the training and promotion of new specialists who would replace the suspect bourgeois spets. They established technical courses in order to develop the necessary numbers of highly skilled workers. "'Red spets,' we call our spets, *our* in the full sense of the word, fed with the ideals of socialist construction and interested in the success of this construction."[155] Some of these new cadres were moved into responsible positions, but the promotions were not always successful. In a number of cases, a new graduate was demoted to work as an unskilled worker because of departmental personnel reductions, because his specialty was not needed by the department to which he was assigned, or because he did his work poorly and no one wished to spend the time to train him further.[156] The party became concerned by the complaints of misassignment made by graduates of the Dneprostroi and other technical high schools. It polled the graduates to find out how they were used—"to run errands" or in technical work.[157] Although the results were not published, the subject became a matter for debate in the newspapers.

The party and trade unions also strongly supported promotion from the ranks.[158] These promotions (*vydvizhenie*) had ideological significance stemming from Lenin's notion of the marriage of physical productive work and administration and the eventual interchangeability of physical and intellectual jobs.[159] But it was difficult to find candidates to promote. The problem was not simply that workers were not promotable; the administration had planned from the start to train and promote workers and regularly advanced them.[160] The problem was to find politically reliable candidates who were also technically competent. For lack of their own candidates, trade unions claimed as *vydvizhensti* workers promoted without their help (*shtempel'nye* or rubber-stamped) because they had certain quotas to fill.[161] The trade unions also promoted workers who had insufficient knowledge or experience for their jobs. "X was promoted only because he attended more meetings than anyone else."[162] The trade unions recognized that sometimes individuals were promoted with insufficient qualifications. They saw, further, that *vydvizhentsi* failed to receive the support from their promoters that would have helped them survive the transition. They also noted, however, that *vydvizhentsi* got no help and even enmity from their colleagues. Finally, the political significance of having promoted workers in administration was not always acknowledged by workers who did not hurry to study for these jobs. When skilled workers, promoted into administration, received less pay than they had received previously, they asked to return to their better-paid production jobs.[163]

Vinter and the scientific-technical staff as a whole resisted sharing authority with new cadres who were pushing for faster promotions.[164] Engineer Salov voiced the engineers' complaints: "The question is, can and should Soviet construction accept its graduate students as a special, privileged stratum in comparison with the remaining mass of technical personnel?" No one, he wrote, denied the value of "red spets" and the necessity of new cadres, or that specialization was interesting, attractive work. But, he argued, production is not that alone; it includes other work. Learning to pour one type of cement is not enough; one must learn work discipline to become a useful worker in any shop. "Education does not end with school or a year later."[165] Salov pointed to the disastrous collapse of a water tower as an example of what happened when inexperienced graduates built without supervision.

Defenders of the graduate students argued that the old engineers were prejudiced against the new, simply because they were new.[166] Students, argued one article, deepened their learning in a post of responsibility; promotion was one of the best methods of preparation. Criteria for promotion should be readiness to work and technical fitness, not number of years of "sitting" in school. The older engineers should cooperate more with the new and help them find jobs and learn their new responsibilities.[167] Salov answered that in the companies in the United States, interns did hard work, passing through departments in sequence or serving as apprentices. There were no shortcuts or privileges; one learned by doing and only gradually received work with an element of responsibility. "We should learn," wrote Salov, "the young should work where they can improve steadily." Astutely, he argued, "Stalin said it was our shame that our *spets* are *spets* out of books, they lack practical experience."[168] He also accused the graduates of wanting exemption from labor rather than actively seeking to do their share; they were inactive in their community duties such as lectures in barracks and participation in voluntary work brigades.[169] The administration preferred one candidate to another and complained: "if I promote him, it's protectionism; if it's your choice, it's promotion from the ranks [*vydvizhenie*]."[170] The conflict was not resolved at Dneprostroi. The party and trade union continued to press for more worker promotees, and the experienced engineers continued to regard them as poorly qualified professionally and also as "opportunists and careerists."[171]

Conclusion

Vinter's first years at Dneprostroi were important in the development of management policy. Arguing that the local power, the chief engineer, needed authority over labor, appointments, supplies, and technical decisions, Vinter succeeded in changing the original appointment statutes and within the year rid himself as well of the board of directors. In so doing, he reduced both party and central control over his actions. Free of direct supervision, Vinter controlled the subcontracting for the site and shaped its financing. Moreover, he controlled the technical decisions, overriding the foreign advisors and Technical Council, even taking control of the council in January 1928. Under Vinter's influence, collegiality gave way to one-man management. Vinter justified his authority by asserting that in the face of the deadlines set by the Politburo, he could only compensate for the absence of machines and material by concentrating authority among specialists enjoying wide powers of command over men and resources. The party-industrializing faction found a strong ally in the ambitious enterprise manager.

Further, by making the decision to use men instead of machines, Vinter definitively shaped the evolution of management-labor relations on the site. His policy was imitated on the successor *stroiki* and by his assistants in their later positions, with a decided influence on the emerging socialist society.

The other major presences on the site—the party and trade unions—did not match Vinter's authority. The party leaders lost their direct control when the board of directors was dissolved. With the victory of the Stalinist industrializing faction at the end of 1928, the central financial and planning offices were less interested in establishing controls than in setting high production targets, further freeing Vinter's hands. Vinter's interests in managing a project, expanded to include enlarged power capacity and the rushed construction of an industrial combine, were compatible with the Stalinists' ambitions for a powerful industrialized state. They acceded to his gathering in power on the site as the price that had to be paid for efficiency. Their relationship with Vinter prefigured the emergence of one-man management (*edinonachalie*) which was so important in the 1930s.

The local party organization, the Dneprostroi collective, was occupied with establishing control over its members and recruiting. It found it difficult to attract new members or to "establish its influence" among workers. The bureau argued that it was hampered by the diversity of the work force, its physical dispersion over the site, and labor turnover. It noted also the difficulty of proselytizing hungry, tired, underpaid workers, of trying to interest them in the goals of the project when they were interested in bettering their harsh living and working conditions. Unable to find the kind of recruit who had typically supported the Bolshevik revolutionaries in the past, yet anxious to increase its representation among the growing work force, the Dneprostroi party compromised on the level of understanding and achievement expected of new and candidate members. It recruited workers with little experience, education, or knowledge of party ideology.

The trade unions were also occupied with establishing themselves, attracting new members, and winning support for the party line. Members and elected delegates protested living and working conditions, and their leaders supported and publicized their complaints but were able to achieve very little. Workers were or became apathetic and disillusioned about trade union support for worker demands. A mark of their alienation was that only about a third of the members attended election meetings and participated in elections.[172] The new members of the unions were inexperienced workers, with no background in trade union work and no programs or strategies of their own to offer in competition to their leaders or employers. With little support from the party leadership, the Dneprostroi trade unions did not have the power to challenge the priorities of the chief engineer.

General view of cofferdam construction in the middle Dnepr channel.

Col. Hugh L. Cooper and Aleksander V. Vinter consulting with other engineers.

On the site.

Zhenia Romanko's award-winning concrete-pouring brigade.

The American dance. A women's brigade stamping the air out of freshly poured concrete.

The cafeteria. This promotional picture belies the reality of food service during construction.

On-site schooling.

Women at work.

The administration building. This building today serves as the administrative center for the six Dnepr hydroelectric dams. It also contains a historical museum.

The spillway. The Vladimir Il'ich Lenin Dam across the Dnepr river from the left bank.

4

The Labor Force and
Labor Policy

We are advancing full steam ahead along the path of industrialization—to socialism, leaving behind the age-old "Russian" backwardness.

We are becoming a country of metal, a country of automobiles, a
country of tractors.

And when we have put the USSR on an automobile, and the
muzhik on a tractor, let the worthy capitalists, who boast so much of
their "civilization," try to overtake us! We shall yet see which countries may then be "classified" as backward and which as advanced.

Stalin, "A Year of Great Change," November 3, 1929

The Bolshevik leaders embarked on their mission of rapid industrialization with few guideposts to help them. The decision makers among the
industrializers—party members and those outside the party—had only
some comprehension of the complexity of the job ahead and little idea of
the difficulties that were to thwart their hopes of building a centrally
planned, rationally administered socialist economy.

The development of the labor force and its recruitment, training, and
employ were particularly difficult tasks in the early years of the plan.
Supervision of the workers on the site was, according to statute, the direct
responsibility of the chief engineer, and authority over them was his. But
the party and trade union organizations had their own claims to working-
class leadership. They expected to ensure that party labor policy directives were followed. To the extent that they shared goals, there existed a
potential for collaboration between the administration and the official
community organizations. And to the extent that their goals differed,
there was a potential for conflict. Moreover, party and trade union
leaders did not all think alike. What were these differences between party
and nonparty authorities and among the Bolshevik leaders themselves

91

concerning labor policy? How were labor policies affected by the political struggles between the Stalinists and opposition groups?

Policy development did not take place without an object. The role of the working class in this development is a topic that has been largely ignored or misunderstood; the undifferentiated working class is usually portrayed as passive, acquiescing to loss of rights and liberties, acted upon rather than acting or interacting with the party-state. Who were the members of this working class? Their personal gains and losses influenced their responses to work, social, and political incentives in different ways. Through the Dneprostroi experience, we can explore how worker reactions, even passivity, affected policy development. It is important to analyze the interactions among the administrators over Dneprostroi and the rank and file and among the various community organizations there, for it was during the first Five-Year Plan that the fundamental relationships among party, trade unions, and the fast-growing work force were established. Dneprostroi was the forerunner and model for the *stroiki* which funneled millions of old and new workers to jobs in industry and administration.

Bolshevik policymakers responded differently to the difficult political situation in the first decade after the revolution. At that time, the creation of a stable, politically supportive labor force was a priority project. Since only the existence of a proletarian class would legitimize the Bolshevik claim to leadership, the Bolsheviks were alarmed at the postrevolutionary decrease in the size of the working class and the decreased percentage of experienced workers. The small size of the work force was symptomatic of the relative backwardness of imperial Russia. On the eve of World War I, there were 9.8 million workers within pre-1939 borders (11.4 million in contemporary borders).[1] The small number of industrial workers further decreased during the civil war, and the New Economic Policy (NEP) period and only in 1928 surpassed prerevolutionary levels.[2] Even then, the composition of the new labor force was mixed. Most skilled and experienced workers had been mobilized and many killed during the European and civil wars. According to the Bolshevik leader G. Zinoviev, speaking in 1922, many of the workers in 1922 in the factories were "déclassé":[3]

> The best, revolutionary part of the proletariat, the young workers, have migrated to villages, or found occupation in the army and in the state administration. Many of them have perished. We have now in our factories the backward part of the proletariat; we have the petit bourgeois elements who went to the factories during the war.[4]

In the years of the NEP, the work force began to grow again—from the low point of 5 million in 1920 to 11.4 million in 1928 and 24.2 million in 1932.[5] This was much more than economic planners had foreseen. They had estimated that the maximum expansion of the total work force would be only 15.8 million during the years of the first Five-Year Plan, that is, between 1928 and 1932.[6]

This chapter will study how the labor force grew at Dneprostroi as former workers returned from the countryside and new workers joined their ranks. It will discuss labor policy in 1927 both as an ideal and as it was practiced in the creation of working and living conditions, especially as the party-state struggled to use the work force efficiently and, at the same time, to train, motivate, and incorporate workers into administration. It will examine how and why policy changed during the first years of the project, from 1927 to 1929. The chapter ends with 1929 because during that year the changes that had been accumulating—in party policy, within the labor force itself, and in the all-union environment—became irreversible. A new period began for the industrial labor force in 1929, when the purged party forced the tempo in collectivization and industrial construction.

Hiring

The appropriateness of the party's labor policies for the fair allocation and utilization of labor was tested early in 1927. Vinter hired a core of about six hundred skilled workers from Shatura, Volkhovstroi, and the Khar'kov Dom Promyshlennosti site, projects that were nearing completion and reducing their staffs.[7] The president of the all-union construction workers' union and member of the Dneprostroi directorate, N. P. Bogdanov, led the effort to find experienced workers elsewhere as well. Dneprostroi tried to exercise its "right to the best" as a project of all-union importance and raided the staffs of state "trusts" and industrial conglomerates over the objections of these organizations.[8] Some skilled workers came at the written invitation of department heads, and their expenses were paid while they visited the site. Some were recruited by friends and family.[9] Such recruitment was, however, irregular.

The bulk of labor allocation was the responsibility of the Commissariat of Labor's network of Labor Exchange Bureaus. The Zaporozh'e Labor Exchange Board, appointed by the Commissariat of Labor, represented official state policy, trade union policy, and local interests. In theory, it guaranteed equal access for workers applying for work and facilitated the matching of skills and opportunities for employment. Practically, it had the obligation of coping with local unemployment. As soon as rumors of the projected dam construction circulated, the town and region began to receive job-hunting unemployed.[10] Despite newspaper pleas to workers not to come there, the Zaporozh'e Labor Exchange Board registered some seven hundred new unemployed in 1926, making a total of 3154 unemployed. More kept coming: in early 1929, the number of unemployed, which had steadily risen despite the employment of many on the site, reached over ten thousand in a population of 94,175.[11] The Labor Exchange Board was able to send some of these to Dneprostroi.

As the number of unemployed continued to grow, however, the Zaporozh'e Labor Exchange Board found itself in increasingly acrimonious debate with the administration. It argued that Dneprostroi had a special obligation to help reduce the unemployment resulting from the great influx of workers often too destitute to pay for their journey home. The Labor Exchange Board also complained that unskilled workers were going directly to the site, bypassing the proper procedures, and getting jobs out of turn. The Dneprostroi administration retorted that the Zaporozh'e Labor Exchange Board had an overlong and bureaucratic system of processing applications; that it sent improperly qualified workers to fill specialized jobs; that since it lacked skilled laborers, the administration had to act directly to find its own workers. There were also accusations that the labor board members behaved improperly by promoting individual workers at the expense of others.[12] Dneprostroi received the right to hire skilled labor if such was unavailable through the labor exchange, but complaints of protectionism continued through the years and poisoned the once cordial relations between the exchange and the administration. The argument was submitted for arbitration to the Worker-Peasant Inspection, but as the need for qualified labor continued to grow faster than the supply, the labor exchange was never able to assert control over the administration. Rottert, deputy in charge of construction, reviewed the matter realistically: "to build the bridges we need to favor Volkhovstroevtsi, to build housing we need to godfather housebuilders." The necessity to "get the job done" justified the irregular recruitment procedures.[13]

For the same reason, Dneprostroi paid little attention to official labor policies regarding class aliens, women, and young people. Because it needed their skills and labor, the administration did not probe too far into the backgrounds of applicants. As a result, it hired many "class aliens" (*byvshie liudi*). Many of these had to leave in 1929, when they were "unmasked" as "enemies of the state," but others, more successful in hiding their parentage, stayed on with a new legitimacy conferred by the trade union membership they acquired at Dneprostroi.

Women experienced more and longer unemployment than men and had difficulty mastering the skills that would have made them more employable. It was difficult, therefore, to hire men and women equally. The majority of the women were hired to work in the service occupations—as cleaners and food service and clerical help. Very few held high posts. One, Zil'berstein, an engineer, recalled how Vinter had refused to hire her when she applied. She appealed to Krzhizhanovskii (former chief of Gosplan and Vinter's superior), who interceded for her. Only then was Vinter prevailed upon to accept her.[14]

Young people also suffered high unemployment. The Commissariat of Labor set a quota for their hire which gave the administration considerable difficulty at first.[15] Most youths were unskilled, and simple physical jobs were better filled by adult men who were stronger and better able to tolerate the harsh conditions. In order to meet the quota, the administration sent some youths to the construction school on the site. Other hiring practices were also influenced by special conditions. Red Army veterans received preference in official labor boards.[16] The trade unions insisted that their members receive a further priority.[17] Finally, as mentioned above, the Zaporozh'e Labor Exchange Board, with limited success, tried to win priority for local unemployed.

Among those who found jobs at Dneprostroi were the people whose stories follow. The names have been changed, but the accounts otherwise follow the memoirs of former Dneprostroevtsi.[18] They illustrate the variety of new recruits to the working class and the social revolution that was taking place.

Sonia Alekseevna came to Dneprostroi in the summer of 1928 from a small town downriver. Her parents had been workers before the revolution, and her father had died in the war. Sonia knew of the coming construction of Dneprostroi from the newspapers and walked north to get a job. Her mother encouraged her to go; there was no work in their town, and Dneprostroi offered an opportunity to make some money and perhaps begin a career. She was literate and was hired to work in an office in the central administration. In comparison to what she could expect at home, Dneprostroi offered a favorable alternative. She was among the better paid; she was free to come and go when she wished. There were few women, and she had many offers of marriage and was able to choose a husband who immediately raised her standard of living since he was a foreign specialist and enjoyed many special comforts.[19]

Katrina Pavlovna also came to Dneprostroi because it offered her a chance to create a career. As the daughter of a former mill owner who, being a member of an exploiting class, had lost the right to vote, she was a class enemy and did not have the right to schooling beyond the seventh grade. Katrina's cousin, a specialist at Dneprostroi, had already invited his six brothers there, and when he heard of her plight recommended that she come to work, join a union, and thereby earn the right to go to school. She came at the age of seventeen and carried rocks and rails. After eleven months, she was permitted to join the union and entered the *rabfak*, or workers' school. She was transferred to the central warehouse, where she kept track of material supplies. Katrina studied to be an electrician, and after Dneprostroi was completed, she went on to a factory in the new combine, where she worked as a supervisor.[20]

Pavel Ivanovich's story is much like Katrina's. He had finished seven years of school and was not allowed to continue because of his parents' classification as class enemies. He came to Dneprostroi in response to a telegram from his brother, who was already working there. He was sixteen when he registered for the construction school. As a student, he received a low stipend, usually about one ruble a day, and a cot in a small room for six in a former factory which had been renovated as a dormitory. He was always hungry; his student's stipend allowed him little more than plain cereal. He did not stay long at Dneprostroi. When he finished the course after eighteen months, he went on to the coal mines at Donbass, where he could earn a better wage.[21]

Some of those seeking regular work were displaced farmers. Among them were local German Mennonites, whose land and houses had been condemned, for they were in the area to be flooded.[22] Many of them had already lost much of their land in previous land surveys and much of their wealth in grain and livestock requisitioning. They had families to support and an immediate need for a roof and wages. Some joined together in *arteli* (see below for further discussion of *arteli*). They worked hard and were among the best paid. Despite their productivity, they were only tolerated by the party because of their background; they were German, farmers, and religious, therefore suspect of harboring anti-Soviet feelings. They, in turn, tolerated the suspicion and the attacks on their religion because they needed the work and the access to food and housing.

In addition to those seeking steady work, there were seasonal workers, known as *sezonniki* or *otkhodniki*, familiar figures on the Russian labor scene. The seasonal worker was very important in the Soviet construction industry, which maintained only a small core of permanent workers and drew supplementary workers from among those who had alternate forms of employment.[23] Typically, seasonal workers came in April, after the spring sowing. Many went home in August for the harvest and returned to work until the cold set in, as illustrated by the movement of workers at Dneprostroi in Table 3.

Vinter and the trade unions tried to identify the most productive seasonal workers and contract for their return to Dneprostroi.[24] The trade unions also tried to use the departing workers to popularize the industrialization policy and especially to win interest and support for local projects. They tried to reduce turnover during the harvest season by restricting home leaves to emergency leaves, but individuals provided themselves with the necessary telegrams saying the wife was sick or the father had died, or they simply left without notice.[25] Because there were more workers readily available, on the one hand, and, on the other, many jobs kept opening up for those seeking work, enterprise and trade union strictures against such movement went unheeded.

Seasonal workers worked with picks and shovels, preparing sites for railroad tracks, workshops, factories, dams, and other works. Some supplied horses and carts. Carpenters built the coffer dams that held back the Dnepr river, the barracks, and administrative buildings. Important in construction, mining, and timbering, numbers of seasonal workers in industry increased from 3,437,000 to 3,932,000, or fourteen percent, between 1927-28 and 1928-29, according to the Commissariat of Labor.[26]

The size of the work force soon outstripped all estimates. Its rapid growth was not caused alone by the delayed arrival of the machines; it was also the result of Vinter's attitude that in the absence of skilled workers the same work could be done by unskilled workers, it would just take more of them. In 1927, the labor population on the site grew from the planned 2000 to 3000 to 13,000.[27] In 1928, in spite of the administra-

Table 3. Number of Workers, 1 April 1927–1 October 1928

Apr.	790	Oct.	13,347	Apr.	7238
May	2187	Nov.	12,982	May	8358
June	3210	Dec.	9000	June	9313
July	6110	Jan.	8889	July	9721
Aug.	8937	Feb.	9076	Aug.	10,287
Sept.	11,449	Mar.	7103	Sept.	11,316

Source: Informatsionnyi listok, no. 1 (December 1928):19.

tion's frequently repeated promises to avoid the mistakes of the previous year, the labor force jumped from the adjusted plan of 5000 or 6000 to 10,242. In 1929, there were 15,687 workers; in 1930, 24,000; in 1931 and 1932, there were 36,000 on the site, which now included the dam and installations and the first of five factories, added to the project in 1929.[28] This was a phenomenon of the time, repeated often in the next few years at Magnitogorsk, Kuznetskstroi, the Stalingrad factory, and many others. When machines and fuel were short, administrators hired more hands.[29] They thus tapped into what they and party political economists believed was a state labor reserve of infinite capacity. Few ever expected that the unemployment problems of the 1920s would turn into a labor shortage in 1931.[30] Table 4 shows the unplanned growth of the labor force.[31]

As a result of these hiring practices, a critical element in planned development was ignored: the paced expansion of a work force in step with funds for wages, training facilities, and housing development. The increased number of seasonal and unskilled workers necessitated more training than planned and contributed to lower productivity. More workers meant greater pressure on finances, material resources, and services. These resources were limited, and the presence of more workers contributed to the deterioration of working and living conditions.

Table 4. Number of Workers: Planned and Actual, 1928–1932

	General Employment (in millions)		Industry (in millions)		Construction (in thousands)	
	Planned	Actual	Planned	Actual	Planned	Actual
1928–29	11.7	12.2	3.6	3.8	745	818
1929–30	13.3	14.5	3.9	4.2	1239	1321
4th qtr. 1930	—	—	—	—	—	—
1931	16.3	19.0	5.2	5.7	2100	2549
1932	21.0	22.9	6.6	8.0	2719	3126

Sources: Kontrolnye tsifri po trudu na 1928–1929 god (Moscow, 1929), pp. 70–71; *Kontrolnye tsifri narodnogo khoziastva na 1929–1930* (Moscow, 1930), p. 487; *Trud v SSSR* (Moscow and Leningrad, 1936), pp. 10–11; *Planovoe khoziastvo*, nos. 10–11, 1930, p. 343; ibid., nos. 6–7, 1932, p. 152; *Narodnoe khoziastvo SSSR* (Moscow, 1956), p. 190. Cited in Eugene Zaleski, *Planning for Economic Growth in the Soviet Union 1918–1932*, trans. M. C. MacAndrew and G. W. Nutter (Chapel Hill, N.C., 1971), pp. 360–61.

Wages

At Dneprostroi, at its inception, party wage and incentive policy reflected the compromise position of the reconstruction period and the adjustment of theoretical principles to practical realities. One distant ideal was an equalization of wages. Another was the involvement of workers in the work at hand because they understood its importance, associated themselves with its goals, and prepared themselves to administer it. But, for the time, while building socialism, the party only proposed to minimize wage differentials, to reduce the differences between mental and physical and urban and rural labor, and to support the advancement of workers into positions of responsible management. The Commissariat of Labor together with the Trade Union Council set the wage rates and linked them to norms established by labor representatives and management. The latter signed a collective agreement with the workers, *koldogovor*, which covered worker benefits and obligations. These negotiations reflected complex issues. Were the Dneprostroi workers due a certain level of pay? If so, how was it to be determined? To what extent were wages to continue to be used as a productivity incentive in this model enterprise? To what extent could the gaps between the best- and least-paid workers be overcome?

At the outset, the parsimony of the original project planners held sway. The Ukrainian Economic Council, arguing for the project, had counted on paying lower wages than those proposed by Gosplan planners.[32] The workers' earliest contracts had been negotiated by N. P. Bogdanov, construction union president, in conjunction with the local unions, represented by the Zaporozhe District Trade Union Council, OSPS. It would appear that he negotiated with too much attention to the interests of the administration and a low wage bill.[33] The Zaporozhe OSPS complained that the pay scale was too low. The chief of the Ukrainian construction union, Chaiko, went to Moscow to seek redress, and the pay scale was somewhat improved immediately thereafter.[34] A month later, the Rabochkom presided over a stormy trade union meeting in which the workers again expressed dissatisfaction with their wages and living conditions.[35] The average unskilled worker's pay rose from 1.54 rubles a day in April to 3.20 rubles in June.[36] Nevertheless, worker-administration conflicts multiplied; by late June 1927, already some three thousand had been registered.[37] During the summer, the Rabochkom helped negotiate new collective agreements, with improved pay and allowance for housing and travel; fuller enumeration of the administration's obligations to provide baths, medical services, and schools; and reiteration of the administration's obligation to hire through the labor exchanges where union members had priority.[38]

Productivity remained very low on the site, however, and responsible administration, party, and Rabochkom officials became increasingly concerned with high labor costs and the slow pace of construction in late 1927. As incentives to better work, the administration offered premiums for work done above the norm, for machines kept in top order and fully utilized.[39] It also tried to limit overtime, because even with a low base rate, workers did not increase productivity but worked longer hours to improve their earnings. But, most important, the administration, encouraged by the American consultants, expanded the piece-rate system. Opposing piece rates, the Rabochkom argued that piece workers tended to come and go when they liked and to work quickly but badly; it was better to mechanize more, train workers to use machines, and cultivate in them a knowledge and advocacy of the goals of the construction and thereby increase productivity.[40]

In spite of trade union opposition, the piece-rate system grew. While in 1927 and 1928 more of the lowest category of unskilled laborer worked by day, by 1929 most were paid a piece rate. In the first year, the unskilled worker earned 1.72 rubles a day or an average of 2.51 for piecework; in 1928, he earned 2.00 rubles a day or 2.02 for piecework. In 1929 and 1930, there was the difference of about one ruble between the two rates, more workers (1.6:1) chose the piece rate. Among the diggers, stonemasons, and carpenters—the largest categories of semiskilled workers—workers clearly preferred piecework. In the same period of time, these workers averaged about one and a half rubles more at the piece rate than the day rate. By 1929, there were ten diggers paid at piece rates for every one at the day rate. These workers earned an average of two to four rubles a day.[41] (See Table 5.)

Among the higher ranks of skilled workers—the electricians, locksmiths, fitters, and lathe operators—wages were higher and the difference in day and piece rates greater. (See Table 6.)

The technically trained personnel were paid by day and by month. Their pay was consistently higher, and the best-paid earned four times as much as the lowest-paid day workers and approximately twice as much as the lowest-paid pieceworker. (See Table 7.)

In 1928, a temporary control commission committee studying labor productivity and overall costs at Dneprostroi made an important recommendation respecting wage policy. It declared that the *artel*, or work group, was an unproductive method of organizing work which interfered with the use of wages as a productivity incentive.[42] Since the *artel* was the dominant organization among seasonal workers, especially in construction work, the results of the Dneprostroi investigation had far-reaching implications.

Table 5. Workers' Average Wages

	1927		1 Oct. 1927–1 Oct. 1928		1 Oct. 1928–1 Oct. 1929		Feb. 1930–May 1930		During 1931	
	piece	day	piece	day	piece	day	piece	day	piece	day
Unskilled	2.51	1.72	2.00	2.02	3.12	2.00	2.37	1.98	3.41	2.13
Digger	3.28	1.91	3.44	2.46	3.65	2.20	3.58	2.26	4.19	2.34
Stonemason	3.64	2.02	3.72	2.83	3.81	2.81	3.48	2.26	5.30	2.45
Carpenter	3.64	2.58	4.04	3.15	4.29	2.52	4.33	2.59	4.14	2.37

Sources: *Informatsionnyi listok Dneprostroia*, no. 6 (November 1929): 78–110; nos. 8–9 (June 1930): 549–57; Louis Puls, "Dneiprostroi," unpaged draft report.

Table 6. Wages of Skilled Workers

	1 Oct. 1927–1 Oct. 1928		1 Oct. 1928–1 Oct. 1929		Feb. 1930–May 1930		During 1931	
	piece	day	piece	day	piece	day	piece	day
Electrician	6.04	5.05	6.56	2.67	5.96	2.14	6.14	2.03
Locksmith and fitter	6.53	4.05	6.95	4.06	6.42	2.78	7.66	3.82
Lathe operator	7.41	4.34	8.31	2.81	8.53	2.38	7.85	2.03

Sources: *Informatsionnyi listok Dneprostroia*, no. 6 (November 1929): 78–110; nos. 8–9 (June 1930): 549–57; Louis Puls, "Dneiprostroi," unpaged draft report.

Table 7. Average Wages of Technically Trained Workers Paid by the Month and by the Day

	1927	1 Oct. 1928–1 Oct. 1929	1930	Feb. 1930–May 1930
Excavator operator	9.50	9.53	9.31	9.41
Steam crane operator	8.60	8.41	8.80	8.02
Compressor operator		5.99		6.23
Locksmith and fitter		5.51		6.07

Sources: Informatsionnyi listok Dneprostroia, no. 6 (November 1929): 78–110; nos. 8–9 (June 1930): 549–57; Louis Puls, "Dneiprostroi," unpaged draft report.

An *artel* consisted of peasant-workers who had come together to seek work. They usually shared a skill and were accustomed to working together and living together. They chose a leader who negotiated their hire, assigned the work, and supervised the pay. Together the members of the *artei* hired a cook who also took care of their laundry and often other household chores as well, including "serving as their wife in turn."[43] Before the revolution, seasonal labor *artel* members counted on their leaders to find jobs and negotiate pay. At Dneprostroi, the leader was not able to negotiate the pay scale, but he could influence the assignment of jobs both for the *artel* as a whole and within it.

There was some initial official regional party support for *arteli* as a means of mobilizing and organizing workers and providing them with an elementary welfare basis; the group was responsible for its members, and the *artel* cook looked after them all. Coming from the same village, members supported one another psychologically as well.[44]

As labor productivity became increasingly important in 1928, however, the *artel* came under attack.[45] The administrators desired to control the individual laborer's work but were blocked by the *artel* elder who interposed himself as an authority figure between the job supervisor and the individual workers. The elder could screen a poor worker and keep him on the payroll in spite of the group.[46] Further, the *artel* system did not permit the grouping of workers by qualification but mixed the experienced or able with the less able. *Artel* structure prevented administrative-technical personnel from becoming well acquainted with their workers; the leaders stood between them. The *artel* interested itself in the quantity rather than the quality of work and did not interest itself in the saving of materials. Finally, as in the mess-plate (*kotel'noi*) system, each worker received an equal share of pay, and the stimulus for raising the quality and productivity of labor was muted.[47]

Arteli were becoming less useful to the administration in other ways as well. With the opening of the factory kitchen and cafeterias, it was no longer absolutely necessary to count on workers to have their own cooks. There was less need for the social support offered by the village group because many workers could come with their families, which Dneprostroi officials hoped would act as a stabilizing influence.

As a result of the 1928 study, Dneprostroi officially opposed *arteli*. *Arteli* were not hired as such, nor were workers paid through *artel* elders. The administration and trade unions approved of cooperative group work and group assignments but created brigades of individuals who could then be moved at the supervisor's pleasure and paid, each according to his work.[48]

Wage policy was but one aspect of Soviet labor policy. Worker contracts with the state employer included other rewards and benefits, such as housing and access to food, goods, and services. How did the party's attitude to the allocation of these benefits evolve, and how were the workers affected?

Housing

In 1927, there were plans for housing an expected work force of two to three thousand workers. As the administration began its move to Kichkas, a number of town dwellings and factories were converted into housing for the workers.[49] At the same time, a number of houses were built. According to the plans, there were nineteen special designs, including permanent housing, semipermanent structures, and temporary barracks for seasonal and temporary workers.[50] In the houses and barracks, each individual, whether living singly or with his family, was theoretically allotted nine square meters with electricity, drinking water, and sewer facilities. Toilet, bath, and kitchen facilities were allotted (although not available) for every two families. Most buildings were heated by stoves, although a few dormitories and individual houses in the village especially constructed for the Americans had central heating.[51] Space was allotted for cultural affairs, both within the buildings and in additional structures planned for theaters and clubs. Landscaping was carried out in the American village and around the major administration buildings but lagged elsewhere. The barracks were encouraged to help with planting, and prizes were offered for the "greenest barracks."[52] Trees were planted on May Day and to commemorate marriages and births, a custom still honored today.

In spite of the generous designs in the plans, a housing crisis began early and intensified in following years at Dneprostroi. As a result of the decision of the Council of Labor and Defense to begin immediately in February 1927, many workers and employees were rushed to the site. Offsite housing for the latter was expensive—thirty rubles a month for a room for a worker whose average pay was one hundred rubles. Often five to seven shared a room.[53] The construction of houses and barracks proceeded rapidly, but numerous errors were committed. Chief of these was the location of some housing, including some semipermanent housing and the summer theater, in the flood plain. As a result, money was wasted and some six hundred family members, one hundred sixty individuals, and eleven organizations had to be relocated in 1929. Most of the houses had been built with one floor, a design later criticized as inefficient.[54] Construction could not keep pace with demand; buildings were crowded, dirty, dark, and noisy. Several hundred workers were housed under tents in 1927; this number passed one thousand in 1928 and 1929. Some workers slept under the open sky.

Built rapidly and with poor materials, the buildings were often shoddy. This was particularly apparent in the winter. Many of the buildings designed for summer use were converted to winter use. Roofs leaked, and wind and snow seeped through the walls. Windows lacked *fortochki*, the small windows that admitted air for ventilation when the main part of the window was sealed against winter drafts. Since many of the foremen lacked experience in constructing stoves, and since many of the stoves were damaged by the weather during a summer of open-air storage, there were many fires in winter.[55] Electricity, water, and sewers were only slowly supplied to the various settlements. Fuel was supplied at cost, but the stealing of lumber for fuel became rampant in the face of rising costs.[56] Distraught by the appalling living conditions, one commentator voiced his "song of sorrow." He did not want to dislike his neighbors, but he was worn out by surrounding disorder, insufficient water, too few garbage cans, shoes on the bed; trifles, most of them, but they mounted up; they occupied the mind.[57]

Conditions inside the barracks varied. The cleanliness and order in the premises occupied by Old Believers was described in admiring detail by the local press (admiring in spite of the fact that the party was strongly antireligious).[58] Not only was their dormitory clean and neat, it was also quiet. People were reading, and there were no cards and no alcohol. They had hung posters which admonished, "No swearing, no spitting." There was also particular praise of one women's barrack, where clean cloths adorned the bedside tables, and the beds and floor were neat and clean. Extra clothes hung from pegs.[59]

These pictures were contrasted to conditions elsewhere. The seasonal workers lay on their beds, still wearing their dirty boots, loudly arguing, playing cards, drinking. Bits of food—herring and cucumber ends—accumulated on the floor. Dirty footcloths and towels were stuffed under the mattresses. The loud arguing, swearing, card playing, and especially the drinking among workers were constant concerns of the party reporters on housing. They castigated such acts as uncultured and wasteful behavior and as a bad example for and influence on the children who lived in close proximity to their elders.

Some housing provisions were specifically designed to promote socialist ideals through communal living. Certain multifamily buildings provided communal cooking, washing, and living areas, with only separate sleeping quarters. Workers ignored the trade union's assignment of space, however, a German correspondent noted in 1928. Each family arrogated to itself its own space and slept, ate, and rested apart from its fellows, thereby refusing to participate in the socialist experiment.[60] Moreover, according to the general conception of the new environment, it was supposed that almost all workers would eat in cafeterias, that home preparation of foods would be minimal. Therefore, there was no space for food preparation or storage and no provision for the disposal of waste.[61] Cafeterias were slow to be built, however, and even after some cafeteria spaces became available, many workers preferred to eat at home where food was tastier.[62] The inadequate cooking, storage, and waste disposal facilities were overwhelmed and the barracks dirtied as a result.

The Dneprostroi workers were not alone in suffering congested living in bad housing, innocent of most amenities. All over the country, housing deteriorated. From 1926, it began to receive public attention. The Seventh Trade Union Congress heard: "We live in huts, cowsheds, in barns, . . . in the summer we live simply under the trees"; and in the Urals, workers had the "coffin standard" for living space.[63] The worst recorded was in Vladimir province, where some textile workers had only 1.8 square meters. In the Urals, at some factories, living space had fallen to 2.0 meters per person.[64] At the Eighth Trade Union Congress, workers reported that they lived in cellars, broken-down wagons, caves, buildings without roofs, and under the open sky. The state's inaction on housing is explained by the priorities of the Soviet leaders—industrial development and food production came first. The development of resources and the construction of factories absorbed available investment funds, materials, and much of the seasonal labor traditionally occupied in building. Workers flocked to industrial jobs and crowded into the existing housing, much of which was in bad repair caused by the ravages of time and weather and a decade of neglect.

One can well ask why the workers tolerated such cold, damp, dirt, and crowding. The explanation lies in the fact that the number of workers in search of employment kept growing, ensuring sharp competition for jobs. In light of such competition, it is not surprising that workers tolerated execrable conditions which gave them the means to earn a living and access to food, which was increasingly limited from 1928 on. It must also be emphasized that crowding and dirt were not unfamiliar to Soviet workers. Prewar factory housing and peasant huts were notably mean—dark, uncomfortably hot or cold, and crowded. Even wealthy peasants lived together in one room. Wartime conditions had accustomed the populace to even greater deprivation. Further, workers could and did exercise an option to leave bad housing, seeking other jobs or returning to the country. The hope of improved living conditions was, in fact, one of the most important causes of labor turnover. But as long as more workers were available, the enterprises ignored these departures. Planners gave serious attention to improving housing only when labor began to run short in 1930.

Workers and industrial planners and managers did largely agree on one point, which had and has continued to have important ramifications for the interrelationship of the work force and the employers. Both regarded the provision of housing as the employer's responsibility, as it had often been in imperial Russia. In its broadest interpretation, this expectation included responsibility for a broad range of services and amenities in addition to housing.

This patriarchal view saddled industry with planning, building, and paying for a social infrastructure at the same time as it was trying to develop and manage an industrial enterprise in as cost-effective a manner as possible. In discussing the comparative costs of Soviet and U.S. industrial construction in 1929, Vinter pointed out that in the United States families did not live on the sites with the workers and that there were no communal services. He tried repeatedly and without success to pass the responsibility for decent living conditions, light, water, roads, schools, and medical and cultural services on to Glavelektro.[65] As funds, materials, and labor became short, housing and the service sector offered opportunities for cost cuts whose consequences would appear only in the long term. At the same time, control over access to housing and services gave the enterprise an added instrument of power over the workers; improved living conditions could be used as a work incentive.

Food

The procurement of food was difficult from the start at Dneprostroi. At first, the difficulties were largely those of distribution. *Artel* cooks and two private cafeterias supplied the workers with food.[66] Food and supplies could also be bought in Zaporozh'e, twelve and a half kilometers away. In June 1927, a cafeteria for twelve hundred was opened, controlled by the Dneprostroi administration but administered by the Zaporozh'e Central Workers' Cooperative.[67] The cooperative also opened a store in Kichkas and promised shortly to open more cafeterias.[68] Although the food was insufficient and boring, the cafeteria was in demand because it had cheaper food than the market, whether one bought directly from the cooperative or from private traders.[69] But the cafeterias had inadequate facilities, and at the end of the year, it was estimated that they fed only twenty percent of the workers; the rest had to prepare their own food at home or rely on the *artel* cook.[70]

It was hoped that the food situation would be vastly improved with the opening of a much-touted "factory kitchen." The design of this up-to-date, highly mechanized cafeteria attracted the interest of many concerned with Dneprostroi. Food production was to be done by machines imported from Germany. Eight thousand meals could be prepared and served in one day in clean, pleasant surroundings. After many delays, the new cafeteria finally opened on June 19, 1928.[71] The grand opening was marred by confusion; the staff was inexperienced and unskilled. In particular, it was unable to use the highly publicized mechanical equipment that was to have given this cafeteria its special character. Disorder and long lines continued throughout the year. All cafeteria food, including that of the factory kitchen, continued to be very bad at all prices—twenty-two, fifty, and ninety kopecks.[72] Scarce food even spoiled in the new imported ice boxes because of improper meal planning.[73] In September 1928, after a prolonged attack in the newspaper and in public meetings, the chief administrator of the factory kitchen was removed.[74]

For the many workers who could not be served in the cafeterias, and for their families, food shopping took a considerable amount of time. The construction site was very large—twenty-five kilometers square. Many workers lived far away from any convenient shopping places, and some had to make extensive detours to find a bread kiosk.[75] Because of the irregular hours kept by the stores and the poverty of their supplies, the worker was never sure that any shopping trip would be successful. Frequently, bachelors and women who regularly did the shopping for their families had to resort to private traders, who were more reliable and who gave credit.

Food became increasingly scarce from 1928 on. The grain problem was especially acute in the Ukraine, where bad weather conditions caused crop failures. Bread and other foods were already in short supply in late 1927, and many towns experienced chronic shortages. In the winter months of early 1928, those in many areas, including the best-supplied Muscovites, complained of gray bread. Some villages at Dneprostroi had only frozen potatoes. In the spring, long lines appeared, and in June in the Ukraine and in July in the Urals, bread was sold only to those with ration tickets. Rationing spread as supplies grew short everywhere.

The shortage of food was caused by a combination of factors. Bad weather and distribution problems contributed, but the chief cause lay in the dislocation of the market. Less grain was marketed in response to the low price of bread grains and the absence of goods to buy; farmers had little incentive to give up the grain they had.[76] Further market factors were the higher prices paid for cash crops, which drew farmers to plant them rather than grain, and for animal products, which encouraged them to feed grain to the animals rather than marketing it and to plant fodder. Finally, peasants used grain to make alcohol, which also commanded better prices than the grain.[77]

As early as December 1927, party leaders became aware of the pending grain crisis, and, as we saw earlier, argument raged in 1928 over development strategy, in particular over the rate of investment in capital industry. Because of the growing dominance of the industrializing Stalinist faction, concessions to the peasant were too little and too late.[78] They failed to increase the grain supply, which continued to deteriorate throughout the year, as will be discussed later.

Local authorities attempted to improve workers' access to food. Early in 1928, the Zaporozh'e party decided not to allow grain to be traded outside the boundaries of the district and ordered local bread factories to be built. The Zaporozh'e and Dneprostroi party press attacked the director of the cafeteria, carrying daily stories about mismanagement, long lines, dirty environment, and bad food. They also attacked the food cooperative, complaining about branch store hours, supplies, the absence of credit, and rude personnel.[79] The Dneprostroi press made persistent efforts to improve supplies by describing the minimum food necessary to the site's population and comparing it to what was sent out and to what was held up in Zaporozh'e instead of being sent on to Dneprostroi. The worker's poor diet was publicly blamed for turnover and poor productivity, a potent argument when reported to party leaders interested in production results.

Workers were short not only of food but of goods of all kinds. Industrial sites and the cities received the best of whatever was available, but that was little enough. The absence of warm gloves and overshoes was particularly serious for construction workers, miners, and lumberjacks who worked in subzero temperatures. The shortage of work clothes was the special concern of the labor inspector at Dneprostroi, appointed by the Commissariat of Labor and usually a member of the Rabochkom. He complained in the press, and trade union and party reports to the center spoke of the problems caused by the shortage of protective clothing, but goods remained in very short supply.

Safety and Health

The labor inspector in these early years of industrialization actively investigated and reported on numerous safety issues. He looked into light, heat, and ventilation, and at Dneprostroi he was responsible for reducing the shift time in the rock-crushing factory, where continued exposure to rock dust was deemed injurious.[80] He also reviewed norms and pay scales but was not able to change them when he found workers rushing their meals so as to be able to work overtime.[81] He investigated sanitation but was not able to force correction of the violations he found.

The labor inspector also reported on health matters—mother and child care, venereal disease, and alcoholism. This last particularly interested other site officials because of its influence on productivity. The party and trade union supported the struggle with alcoholism and regularly mounted campaigns publicizing the evils of alcohol, including mild offenses such as swearing, loud arguments, and brawling and more serious crimes such as wife beating, murder, and—no less serious—lateness, sloppy work, and absenteeism.[82] While the party officially regarded alcoholism as characteristic of cultural backwardness specifically associated with peasant life, it also made a limited effort to treat it as a disease.[83] Clinics for alcoholism were opened, and various remedies, including electric shock treatments, were tried. Home visits followed, and the whole family was enlisted to prevent the backsliding of a cured alcoholic.[84] Alternative activities such as reading, movies, and sports were energetically promoted.

The party also restricted access to alcohol. The sale of vodka was forbidden on the premises.[85] It was, however, readily available in the nearby villages, where it was produced in home stills. Wine and beer were available in the state-owned stores offering an alternative to the harder liquor and, coincidentally, a way to absorb cash.[86] Drunks were also given reprimands, fined, or even dismissed on account of outrageous public behavior or when their work performance was demonstrably poor. But party policy toward alcoholism did not become fully defined during these years. Drinking was so widespread and socially accepted that party efforts to treat it seriously as a physical or social disease and evidence of peasant backwardness had little success.

General health services were typically supplied by an enterprise as part of its overall responsibility to the worker. At Dneprostroi in March 1927, the medical staff consisted of a chief doctor and his deputy, a gynecological surgeon, two doctors of internal medicine, a dentist, and a doctor specializing in sanitation. There were also periodic visits from regional doctors in various specialties. The construction site was served by a hospital, a dispensary, and several medical stations and polyclinics.[87]

The staff practiced preventive medicine, requiring disinfection baths and physical exams before workers were assigned to dormitories, particularly if they came from areas where there was typhus. There were also inoculation campaigns.[88] The medical staff distributed circulars and organized lectures and exhibits in the barracks and clubs on sanitation, hygiene, proper diet, and mother and child care. The newspapers often carried articles on health and sanitation. Of course, because of the food shortages, not much could be done about diet. Moreover, it is difficult to evaluate the effectiveness of the publicity on sanitation. Some barracks were very clean, especially the women's; most were dirty. In the frequent absence of soap, towels, and sometimes running water, it was difficult for the sanitation inspector or building supervisor to require any set standards. As the administration had difficulty in completing the sewage system, polluted water caused typhus and various gastrointestinal diseases. It was only in 1929 that even fifty percent of the workers' settlements had sewage lines.[89] Finally, the quality of the medical services provided by the doctors in emergencies, in the mobile clinic, and in the hospital is difficult to evaluate. The doctors were frequently criticized for arriving late to accidents, and the medical department regularly berated itself for its inadequacies. Yet the site was free of major epidemics in spite of primitive sanitary conditions, and the department saw and treated some 77,385 medical cases in 1928, the one year for which there are statistics.[90] Two factors, however, impeded the delivery of adequate health care. One was the rapid, unplanned expansion of the numbers of workers. There were never enough doctors or medicines for all the sick and injured. The other factor was the unmeasured toll on health of cold, noisy, crowded, unsanitary housing and inadequate nutrition.

Labor Discipline and Training

The harsh living and working conditions of workers in 1928 caused the party and industrial leaders concern because they fell so far short of the minimum material level aspired to. They also contributed to labor turnover, absenteeism, and slow and faulty work, particularly in construction, in the mines of the Donbass, and in the metalworking plants. Turnover was high, particularly in seasonal work such as construction. At Dneprostroi, the work force turned over three times in 1928, and the average work span was three to four months.[91] Most workers worked less, and only a small core of workers remained on the site throughout the year. In addition, absenteeism was a serious problem. The average number of days lost per worker per year was ten and a half.[92] In a calculation in 1928 of lost time, the trade union presented the figures in Table 8 comparing 1927-28 and 1928-29.

The development of productivity was, from the start of the industrialization drive and the inception of the Dneprostroi project, one of the crucial components of labor policy. Productivity could be raised, argued many, not just by good labor discipline of labor intensity but more especially by the training of workers in the use of machines.[93] In fact, Lenin's vision, accepted by those who followed him, identified the rapid introduction of the most advanced technology as the key to industrialization. Lenin, as we saw earlier, passionately advocated electrification. For him and his successors, Dneprostroi was to be the model of mechanized work, proof that the Soviet Union could pass its exam in the application of the most modern technology.[94] The Dneprostroi administration and Rabochkom planned from the beginning to train many workers, particularly as they were importing machines never before used in the Soviet Union. Officials realized that with few skilled workers available, training tasks loomed large. As one reporter visiting Dneprostroi wrote, workers stood with their mouths agape, watching wide-eyed as large steam derricks swung huge loads through the air.[95] In the same vein, Cooper reported that during the first year half the derricks were fully occupied picking up the other half, which had tipped over under unbalanced loads.[96]

At the most elementary level, the rural worker needed education in a new way of life. His very participation in Dneprostroi accustomed him to seeing masses of workers, as anonymous as he, working on parts of a whole, the final sense of which was as yet unclear. He became used to seeing machinery and eventually to using it. He learned that he was expected to come and go to a given place at a given time. He had to collect and return his tools in an orderly fashion so the members of the next shift could find them.[97] Accustomed to chatting with a fellow farmer as they both worked on a task, he learned that such private conversations were not allowed during work hours, and rest, smokes, or trips in search of materials had to be sanctioned by bosses and taken only at appointed

Table 8. Average Distribution of Time for One Worker

	1927–28	1928–29
Number of days in the year	366.00	365.00
Number of days worked	266.00	270.06
Nonworking days	67.00	65.00
Vacation	10.00	10.23
Communal obligation	1.50	2.13
Illness	10.50	10.71
Absences: excused	1.00	1.47
unexcused	10.00	5.40

Source: *Informatsionnyi listok*, no. 2 (February 1929): 94.

times.[98] In the same way, changes in the plan of work could only be made by those with the proper authority. The worker's supervisor, except in the case of *arteli*, was generally no one he knew outside of the world of work and a person with whom he developed no personal ties. His relationship to his supervisor and, through him, to the administration was governed by a new set of rules rather than by patriarchal tradition.

On the job, the worker had the opportunity to learn about tools and machinery. Some workers, usually young ones, were brought together in student brigades and assigned an instructor. In February 1928, 132 of the 202 young people on the site were in such brigades, studying twelve different specialties.[99] There was difficulty with this procedure; tools, machinery, and bench space were short, and instructors were reluctant to take time from piecework.[100] New workers also had manuals describing the procedures to be followed. The one for dump-car operators indicates the level of detail necessary—the instructions recommend that the operator look down the track before setting the car in motion, to make sure the path is unobstructed.[101]

Informal circles and formal classes supplemented on-the-job training. The most basic course offered was a literacy course, usually organized by the trade union committee. In 1927, there were five literacy circles.[102] Forty-five students graduated at the end of the year, but 145 more had left before finishing. Sometimes it was impossible even to recruit students, as, for example, in June 1928, when there were teachers being paid but no courses run.[103] The known number of illiterates fluctuated with the season. In August 1929, a trade union reporter found 400 illiterates,

200 of whom were in school; another found 200, 120 of them in study circles.[104] During the summer, the number of students kept increasing, and some graduated,[105] but many students signed up who never attended or attended only irregularly and left before finishing the course. Even among those who finished the course, many forgot what they had learned, a situation lamented by the party organization.

For the literate who wanted basic general schooling, a seven-year school opened on the site in September 1927 with thirteen groups of 520 students.[106] In 1928, there were 890 students seeking entrance, but there was money enough for only 200.[107] Not all the students were young; half of the 120 students in a general-education night school during the winter were between the ages of thirty and forty.[108] More applied, but there was no room.[109] There were also 120 students studying on their own.[110] Because of the expense of these schools, the Dneprostroi administration sought to transfer responsibility for general education to the local government and succeeded in doing this in late 1929.

Both the administration and the trade union committee took serious interest in the preparation of skilled workers. In January 1928, a construction school was opened with 50 students; by September, there were 120. In April, the first 18 students graduated, but in May they were working as unskilled laborers, being unqualified for existing openings for skilled workers.[111] In spite of this bad record, the number of students kept increasing. In 1928, there were 80 students, and in June 1929, 120 graduated. In August, 14 graduates went on for higher education, but 42 others failed to qualify.

One explanation for the school's poor achievement record was the shortage of workshop space and tools for the students to get practical experience. After four hours of studying theory, they were free.[112] Some wandered about the site, studying the machinery on their own, and most also worked on a shift later in the day.[113] As late as the fall of 1929, the construction school had no permanent building. Its students were crowded into a dormitory, fifteen to twenty in a room, and lived on so small a stipend that they could barely afford to eat.[114]

The many short courses offered by the trade unions and the administration, and sometimes by the foreign consultants, did not achieve significantly better results. Some courses were very specific, such as the seminars for the rationalization and mechanization of construction which held weekly meetings for two months. Others taught special skills. In August 1928, there were 133 students in such technical courses.[115] There were courses organized in the trade union's "red corners," but they received "little help and rose and fell spontaneously."[116] Some 300 students were registered in seven evening professional schools in August. By the end of the year, there were 620 workers in technical courses and 120 in professional schools.[117] Six individual Dneprostroi departments organized training in different specialties in October 1928 but produced no graduates by the next summer.[118]

All the schools lacked materials. The new machines the students were supposed to learn about were needed on the site. It was not until mid-1929, for example, that a derrick crane was set aside for trainees.[119] Both teachers and students were late to classes, and attendance was irregular. There were also discipline problems. Students were rude to teachers and walked out of class. They stole school materials and instruments.[120] The poor training left students and specialists dissatisfied. The students complained after graduation that they were not hired to work in their specialties, and their supervisors complained that the new graduates needed experience before they could assume responsible posts.[121]

The central party called for more trained workers in recognition of the country's growing demand for scientifically prepared administrators for industry. The specific party resolution in December 1928 had no direct impact on the training institutions at Dneprostroi during the next year; the number of students continued to grow slowly. In 1929, as the need for specialists became more urgent, the party announced plans for the location of new polytechnical institutes on the sites of major industrial enterprises, where students could learn theory and practice together. The first of these institutes opened at Dneprostroi in December 1929. It was soon embroiled in a jurisdictional dispute which exemplified the struggle between those who advocated training a few with depth and breadth over an extended period of time and those who wanted fast, specific training of multitudes. Those impatient to accelerate the tempo of industrialization carried the day, and the longer training was replaced by narrowly conceived, short courses taught at an accelerated pace. The ensuing institutional development properly belongs to the next chapter, however, for the institute was a casualty of the accelerated tempo whose results it felt as 1929 ended.

It is difficult to estimate the full effect of the training policies promoted by Dneprostroi and general onsite training by late 1929. As a result of the achievements there, the Dneprostroi administrators and RKI inspectors became convinced in 1928 that more skilled workers would greatly speed construction and cheapen it, by improving machine utilization and cutting down on material waste and machine repair. The construction school, evening schools, and technical courses, moreover, were contributing to greater productivity, as was experience with machine operation and maintenance. Productivity among drill, excavator, and crane operators began to rise in 1929. Dneprostroi workers in particular were sought elsewhere and invited to teach on other sites. The schools, however, were not meeting the site's needs; most of the graduates were too poorly trained, and they were too few in number. The record at Dneprostroi contributed to the party leaders' growing concern about training workers, a concern which led to the founding of the polytechnical institute in December 1929, increasing party propaganda promoting technical cadre preparation, and finally, in 1931, to a solid financial commitment to widespread technical education.

Both the party and the trade union pursued yet another approach to raising productivity. By providing exhortation, information, and leadership example, they sought to mobilize the workers and inspire them to put forth their best efforts. The Rabochkom did most of this work. The trade unions sponsored all-site and workshop "production information meetings," defined as the vehicles through which the trade union would introduce the masses to the problems and the progress of the Dneprostroi project.[122] The party taught that when they became knowledgeable about the overall direction, the Dneprostroevtsi would better understand and value their own contribution to the project and to the goal of Soviet industrialization and, therefore, would maintain good labor discipline, improve productivity, and study to improve their skills.[123] These efforts to associate workers with management and to persuade them to identify with management objectives did not succeed; workers did little more than attend meetings, and then only when it was absolutely necessary. Many meetings, including an all-site meeting, were called off for lack of attendance.

The trade unions also attempted to involve workers in the problems of administration through advisory and review commissions—the Temporary Control Commissions or VKK. The first of these commissions was appointed in March 1928 to investigate labor productivity and to make recommendations. The commission was staffed by technical persons and failed to attract nonspecialists or to arouse any interest in its report among the workers.[124] Four later commissions did valuable work and received better publicity but failed to function as a means of drawing the average worker into administration.[125]

The Party Struggle Reaches Dneprostroi

Notwithstanding their cooperation in labor recruitment and training, the party and trade union and, to a certain extent, administration members found themselves in 1928 differing over labor policy and even economic goals. As discussed earlier, party and trade union factions at the all-union level differed over the rate of industrialization, the means of accumulating funds for investment, and the role to be played by the trade union, the traditional intermediary between employer and employee. As we saw in the previous chapter, these differences came to a head in 1928 and led to the crisis that ended with the defeat of the right in the Politburo and its members' loss of authority. The differences existed at the local level as well as among the leaders, dividing cells during 1928 and affecting their work. How did the programmatic and power struggles bear on the effectiveness of the local party cells? Did they influence the direction or evolution of party policy?

The Dneprostroi party began as a part of the Zaporozh'e district. It had a difficult time getting established because of the novelty of the assignment, the size of the site, the speed with which the project grew, the great variation and dissimilarities among the workers, and the party's inability to attend to workers' demands concerning living conditions. Its growing pains were further complicated by the internal party struggle.[126]

Already in 1927, the local party cells at Dneprostroi were affected by differences over two major issues: workers' interests vis-à-vis state enterprises and grain policy. In the earlier discussion of wages, we saw how the party members acceded to the introduction of piece rates while continuing to agitate for higher daily wages and better living conditions. There was less unanimity over the grain issue. As early as November 1927, the district meeting had discussed the effect of low grain prices and had, at that time, been seriously divided over policy.[127] The party press reported the scarcity of food and the resulting hunger, discontent, and even alienation of workers, matters also reported by the Dneprostroi party and trade union to the party personnel bureau.[128]

During the first six months of 1928, the party collective at Dneprostroi held one hundred meetings, fifty-four of them closed to nonparty participation and devoted to serious intraparty debate.[129] The local party was concentrating on politics and the grain crisis. Concerned by its lack of visibility and minimal mass activity on the site, the Ukrainian Central Committee chastised the Dneprostroi collective for its lack of training and discipline, for its failures to establish a tightly organized system of lower cells or energetically to promote party work among engineers and technical personnel. The cells were criticized for referring important questions to the higher collective instead of encouraging workshops to take responsibility.[130] In an April 1928 drive for greater involvement of both party and nonparty workers, the Ukrainian Central Committee directed the Dneprostroi collective to sponsor action in workshops based on workers' suggestions and to "create in the small cell that sense of duty, responsibility, and achievement that would encourage regular participation."[131] New bureaus were elected in April, reflecting "internal democracy," suggested the party paper, but probably also reflecting a calculated change in personnel relating to the factional struggle. Sometime between April and June, the party secretary, Pozdniakov, was replaced, although his reassignment was only announced in September. It is likely that he was removed in connection with the argument over agricultural policy, perhaps because of too close a relationship with Onishenko, the Zaporozh'e district secretary, who had been removed a few months earlier.[132]

Party reports indicated that the Dneprostroi cell continued to experience difficulty during the summer. Party schools were poorly taught and poorly attended.[133] Few workers joined the party in spite of membership campaigns (which stressed quality, then quantity, and then quality again).[134] Growth occurred, but new members were sent in from outside the district rather than coming from the site itself.[135] Party members neglected their economic work as well, "which in the interest of the construction must be rectified." Only ten percent of meeting time had been spent on questions of construction, labor, and living conditions and had produced no resolutions for specific work.[136] The district party committee told the party cell to pay more attention to rationalization, reduction of costs, and work discipline.[137]

In recognition of the increasing difficulties on the site and because of its physical size and importance, the Ukrainian Central Committee granted Dneprostroi's request for higher status, guaranteeing it more personnel and financial support. On September 12, 1928, it announced the designation of Dneprostroi as a *raion*, or county, and its reorganization.[138] The sectors became more important than the workshops once again, but the job rather than the geographic principle for the assignment of personnel was maintained. The goal of this reorganization was to stress the principle of cohesion among the physically scattered party members without losing the orientation to production questions given by the workshop-based network. To give better direction to the lower cell network, the party bureau formed an instructors' group. The cells were directed to follow the party notes in *Dneprostroi*, the newspaper. The cell secretaries were encouraged to visit and learn from one another. On the other hand, cell directives were differentiated for the first time, focusing party members' attention on specific production problems.[139]

The first county conference took place in November 1928. It recognized the difficulties caused by the very rapid expansion of the project, the housing crisis, and the shortages of bread and other foods.[140] In general, however, the resolutions expressed confidence that the collective was doing a good job and knew where it needed to concentrate its efforts for the future. They emphasized production issues—reducing costs, raising productivity, mobilizing party and nonparty masses for finishing the work on time, and reducing administrative staff. The conferees also specifically asked the party to assign a party member as deputy chief engineer.[141]

The tone of these resolutions and the organizational changes at Dneprostroi coincided with and reflected the changing emphasis in union-wide party activity and reflected the victory of the Stalinists. Whereas previously the party had, in general, held its organization a little apart from the jobs done by the administration, now the party organization at all levels concerned itself more directly with costs, with labor, and with management. During the Thirteenth District Party Conference in December 1928, the linkage between the construction of socialism and the economy was worded in a new way. The conference emphasized that Dneprostroi's energy would facilitate the reconstruction of the economy: it was equally important as a "school for the masses who work there" and the "technical organization of work."[142] After discussing both the importance of the project and its novelty, O. G. Shlikhter, member of the Ukrainian Central Committee, pointed out that the position of the construction administration was particularly difficult: "The establishment of normal ties between party and executive is one of the most serious tasks of the party on Dneprostroi, . . . the party should not forget the importance of faith in the administration."[143] The sense of the meeting was that administration goals were identified as party goals.[144] It reflected the spirit of the Eighth Congress of the Trade Unions of the USSR which had met earlier in the month. The congress had voiced the same support of administrators of productive enterprises and, furthermore, had acquiesced to the industrial wing's purge of Tomskii, president of the trade union council, rightist leader, and past defender of the workers' interests. The Stalinist faction and the others in favor of rapid industrialization had been pursuing their goal relentlessly because they were convinced that the creation of heavy industry, defense, and national stature were indissolubly linked. Enthusiastic reports from enterprise chiefs encouraged them to believe that they could achieve more than they were already doing. They also counted heavily on growth based on mechanization and the rapid, broad application of inanimate power. They were confident that they could explain low productivity on the basis of labor turnover, workers' ignorance of goals and therefore poor motivation, and insufficient training—and that they could improve labor discipline and raise productivity. They were thus convinced of both the importance and the feasibility of rapid industrial development. When the Stalinists accomplished the political defeat of the Right Opposition in November 1928, they removed the last barrier to raised Five-Year Plan targets.

Problems of Labor and Cost

Party officials in charge of the economy introduced numerous measures to raise production in 1929. One such measure, the hiring of extra workers, evolved from policy associated with other programmatic goals—full employment and the reduction of working hours. In the fall of 1927, both the Supreme Economic Council and Gosplan had linked the introduction of three shifts with the reduction of unemployment and an intensified use of equipment. In 1928, the three-shift day was introduced in the textile industry.[145] Encouraged by the rise in production, the central government decreed that three shifts should be introduced into industry as rapidly as possible.[146] This policy suited the Dneprostroi administration. Vinter was anxious because work had fallen behind schedule at the beginning of the 1929 season because of the late spring. Fears for the future schedule contributed to his decision to intensify production by introducing the three-shift schedule and uninterrupted week (work did not cease on Sundays) and even a four-shift schedule in some departments.[147] As a result of the new policy, Dneprostroi hired thousands of new workers. (See Table 9.)

The policy of employing more workers presented problems for the new workers moved frequently and worked irregularly. (See Table 10.) Poor living conditions contributed to the high rate of turnover. The food situation at Dneprostroi had deteriorated steadily during the winter, reflecting the harvest failure in the Ukraine as well as the negative results of the grain price policies of the central government. Local grain collections in December 1928 were only 36.7 percent of plan,[148] and in March plan fulfillment fell to 7.4 percent and even 3.1 percent.[149] Workers lined up for hours in the cold for bread and scanty supplies. Frozen potatoes and, in the cafeteria, skimpy, tasteless dishes boasting only fancy French titles were available, but meat, milk, and fuel ran short.[150] The party distributed some goods as part of workers' pay in recognition of supply problems.[151]

The housing situation was no better than the food. Barrack dwellers complained of snow drifting through rooms.[152] Tent dwellers endured temperatures below −13 degrees C in the winter, and tornado-strength

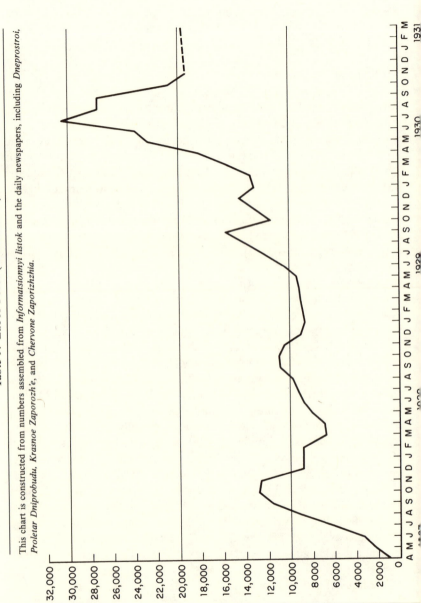

Table 9. Labor Force (in thousands)

This chart is constructed from numbers assembled from *Informatsionnyi listok* and the daily newspapers, including *Dneprostroi, Proletar Dniprobudu, Krasnoe Zaporozh'e,* and *Chervone Zaporizhzhia.*

Table 10. Workers Hired (----) and Workers Departing (——) April–September 1928

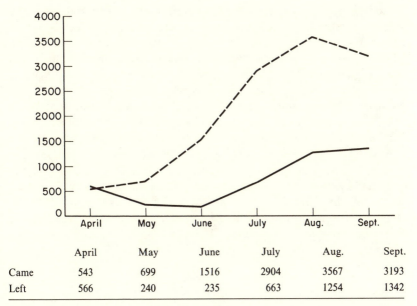

	April	May	June	July	Aug.	Sept.
Came	543	699	1516	2904	3567	3193
Left	566	240	235	663	1254	1342

Source: Informatsionnyi listok, no. 1 (December 1928): 87.

winds whipped tents away in the summer of 1929.[153] Crowding, dark, and noise were endemic. Toilet facilities were inadequate and frozen in the winter months.

In spite of the harsh conditions, turnover abated somewhat in the early months of 1929. This is probably explained by the absence of jobs in the countryside. In 1928, nearly two thousand workers left the site for the spring sowing; in 1929, only three hundred left.[154] Few farmers were hiring extra hands because of the party's agricultural policy which discouraged the expansion of an individual farmer's enterprise by taxing his land and stock, by paying low prices for his products, and by strictly limiting the employment of farm laborers.[155] During the summer, forceful grain requisitioning sent even more peasants flocking to seasonal work.

The large labor force worked with little discipline. A report by the Dneprostroi administration in March 1929 showed that on a given day, three and a half percent of the workers were absent without excuses, one percent arrived late or left early, fifteen and a half percent went off to fetch materials, thirty percent were smoking or resting, and only fifty percent worked at capacity.[156]

Addressing this problem, the Dneprostroi party bureau sent a strongly worded directive to all cells, all fractions, and trade union members.[157] It attacked alcoholics, absentees, loafers, slackers, and those producing work of poor quality. It urged all supervisors to take strong measures, up to and including dismissal of workers for poor discipline or poor work. Echoing their December meetings, the party and trade union committees reminded members that they should help the enterprise even if norms were raised more than workers liked. They also pointed out that party members should receive no special treatment; in the matter of work discipline, no difference should be made between party and nonparty, a clear indication that members in the past had received special treatment.[158]

Strict laws to deal with truancy were publicly supported by Kuibyshev and other party leaders as early as November 1928 and approved by the Supreme Economic Council in March. They were published in April after the party plenum meeting. The new regulations established two categories of punishment, reprimand, or dismissal.

> Lateness to work or early departure twice in a month—reprimand; repetition—discharge; regular—discharge.
> A worker more than ten minutes late may be refused work until after the break.
> Absence without permission twice in a month—reprimand; repetition—discharge; regular—discharge.
> Idleness or distraction of others from work—discharge.[159]

The strict laws did not, however, solve the problems. New workers might be hired easily, but there was no guarantee that they would be any better than those they replaced. Moreover, the laws did not deter workers; they easily found jobs at other expanding enterprises. The construction union was more concerned with keeping workers on the sites than with finding legal means for firing them.[160]

Party leaders explored positive incentives for workers. Moral appeals had existed from the time of the civil war, when workers had worked extra hours without pay, particularly on Saturdays. Such volunteer labor was used to encourage extra effort in overcoming lagging production or to surmount unexpected difficulties. There were also competitions for nomination as the best worker and the title "Hero of Labor" was created in July 1927 to honor public service.[161] The Order of the Red Banner of Labor, instituted in September 1928, recognized individuals, groups, or whole enterprises.[162] The party encouraged competition for the best performance and for voluntary extra work, a kind of competition that had been sanctioned by Lenin in *State and Revolution* (1917) and further described by him in the article "How to Organize Emulation" in January 1918. On January 20, 1929, *Pravda* printed this article, describing socialist competition (*sotsialisticheskoe sorevnovanie* or *sotssorevnovanie*), an ostensibly voluntary activity for the benefit of all society. Individuals or groups, even whole enterprises, called one another out in competition to see which could best reduce costs, raise productivity, or meet certain production deadlines. Competition among groups for the good of the whole was legitimate.[163] It gave an outlet to the more energetic and able, who did not then amass wealth or position which could be used to exploit another. Honors, fame, and sometimes material prizes went to the winners, but these were not designed to be commensurate with the total gain to the enterprise. The glory of working hardest for socialism was to replace material incentives.

Introducing socialist competition to Dneprostroi in April 1929, a special issue of *Dneprostroi* proclaimed the goal that every worker should understand and take part in *sotssorevnovanie*. Every worker, every brigade and department, every group and enterprise was to challenge a peer to see which could improve itself more, reaping its reward from having eliminated waste, overcome inefficient practices, or found better ways to meet production goals. The larger whole—the group, department, enterprise, the whole country—would benefit from the fact that all competitors were working to improve production.

Sotssorevnovanie, however, did not accomplish the high goals anticipated. At first, its organization was largely on paper. "From the outside," a reporter commented,

> it looked wonderful, a staff was formed, radio lists of competitors published, mountains of paper were produced, the party, trade union and administration were all collecting material for a long report. However, on the sectors, many knew nothing, masters and young engineers often do not know who of their workers are competing.[164]

The party noted that new workers were slow to join in socialist competition. It agitated among them and among the youth, who had also not shown a marked proclivity for competition.[165] By the end of the summer, socialist competition campaigns focused on reducing absenteeism. These campaigns showed significant results.[166] This may have been because the penalties for continued absenteeism—the loss of the job and therefore a food card—were less easily suffered by workers and their families then thronging the construction sites in escape from collectivization.

While *sotssorevnovanie* may have occasioned genuine rivalry or a desire to set records, such situations were in the minority. It was difficult to create and maintain enthusiasm about daily and ill-compensated hard labor. Workers disliked the system because bonuses for winning were balanced by penalties for losing; one contracted to do extra work if one lost. In addition, norms were raised in light of records achieved, so that all workers had to meet higher expectations as a result of a record set by competitors. Finally, it quickly happened that failure to enter into competition made one liable to dismissal.[167] As a result, *sotssorevnovanie* had a decreasing impact on production, because the unwilling competitors learned to set goals that had already been achieved or were within easy reach. On the other hand, it provided the party with an important way to require extra work.

Another effort to raise productivity and accelerate construction with little expense was a revival in the use of free time for volunteer work, Saturday work, or *subbotnik*. Under party leadership, a workers' group would donate a day's work for the success of the project, to ward off the imperialist threat, to honor the revolution, or to erase a penalty for losing a socialist competition. As with socialist competition, *subbotniki* were only officially voluntary; nonparticipation was culpable.[168] Although it was asserted that "voluntary" activities saved the project thousands of rubles, they were difficult to plan, organize, and incorporate into the body of planned work. They had a short-term effect, a "shock" or *udarnik* character.[169] They did not have much effect on work discipline or the development of sustained good work habits. Their chief production value was that some work was done at a reduced per diem cost. They also served as a negative incentive, allowing the administration and the party to pressure the worker, because not only was failure to participate in *subbotniki* and socialist competition grounds for dismissal,[170] but it was also interpreted as passivity on the job and hostility to the socialist goals of the party and state—in other words, class enmity and an anti-Soviet attitude.

Still another measure was the encouragement of shock workers or shock work brigades, especially among the younger workers. *Udarniki* were those who volunteered to do dangerous or extra work to finish a special project on time, intervene in a crisis, or simply set an example for faster or better work in a sector where productivity was low. Because such work was recompensed with bonuses and prizes, it attracted participants. *Udarnik* brigades often set records, such as the world concrete-laying record of September 1929. Together with socialist competition and *subbotniki*, shock work provided added impetus for the work completed at Dneprostroi, helping to compensate for the weakness of other incentives.

The cost of the large numbers of workers hired in the drive for production created difficulties for the administration. Vinter attempted to raise productivity by more efficient use of machines. Engineers kept full records on machine operators and workshop mechanics, rewarding them differentially for good work in the operation, maintenance, and repair of machines. Courses were organized to increase the number of skilled operators. Finally, numerous studies were made of the utilization of different machines so that the organizational bottlenecks could be removed and machine use broadened.[171] The administration gave renewed attention to the assignment of the correct machine for a particular task and its full support with experienced personnel, necessary materials, and supplementary machines. Realization of the potential of this kind of planning resulted in the Stakhanovite movement of the mid-1930s, discussed below in Chapter 5.

Trying to evade some of the soaring costs of the project, Vinter faced up to a problem common in Soviet industry. Comparing the costs and the length of time for construction at Dneprostroi with similar construction sites in the United States, he pointed to the extensive services supplied by Dneprostroi and expected by the workers, the unions, and the party. In the United States, he said, there were two guards, one during the day and one at night, instead of a many-numbered army. No American sites maintained factories, workshops, elaborate material depots, or the administrative apparatus to manage them or the capital construction to house them; supplies were simply ordered by telephone. The workers lived on the site, but their families did not. There were no communal services and little medical help. The American sites used a simple financial system: daily internal records and weekly reports which were generally approved with certain limits. Specialists were not on the site but concentrated elsewhere. Detailed drawings were made before work was begun, and necessary changes were fixed by telephone. Chafing at the financial supervision and interference with his authority, Vinter suggested an end to the outside review commissions. He also suggested that it was time that Glavelektro took financial and managerial responsibility for living conditions, schools, medical services, culture, roads, lights, water supplies, and all such matters.[172] Vinter succeeded in shedding some of these last duties. The town council of Kichkas had long accused him of interference in matters of public domain. In July, the Ukrainian government and Kichkas took responsibility for health services and schools and relieved Dneprostroi of a fraction of its costs.[173]

Dneprostroi's high costs concerned party leaders in the Supreme Economic Council. In response to their request, the Worker and Peasant

Inspectorate sent a commission to examine site operations. Such commissions were common in 1929 in industrial enterprises, and their reports were widely published and discussed. This inspection commission, planned in 1928 and assigned in early March, arrived on the site June 1, 1929.[174] Under Z. M. Belen'kii, a commission of seventeen worked with several local elected and appointed groups for about a month, soliciting worker comments and comparing plan estimates and achievements. It reported its results in July to the Ukrainian party, to the RKI commissar, and to numerous central state organizations.[175] Belen'kii focused on the lack of financial order, the expenses beyond the budget, and stockpiled materials. He attributed them to hurried planning and the substitution of hand labor for machinery, and he recommended rigorous economy.

Belen'kii also commented on the high turnover and low productivity of the work force.[176] In 1928, the average worker spent only three or four months on the job and worked only seventy-five percent of the time. Workers did not try to learn to run the new machines. Because much hope for lower costs had been based on the efficient use of a greater number of machines, Belen'kii suggested more attention to this area. He advised a big cut in administrative expenses and, echoing the Central Committee's decision at the November plenum, recommended replacing some technical personnel with young specialists, preferably Communists. The implication was that young, dedicated specialists would build more daringly and more cheaply, but no justification was offered for the recommendation. Finally, Belen'kii also noted that foreign consultants were insufficiently utilized. Other party members had noted the same problem.[177] The American consultants occasionally remarked on the reluctance of Soviet engineers to take their advice, and the rivalry between pro-German and pro-American Soviet engineers also interfered with effective consulting.[178] Belen'kii suggested that the consultants should be sought out more often and their advice followed.[179] The information gathered by the Belen'kii commission resulted in discharge of 399 persons from the administration.[180] The policy of using masses of workers was not questioned, however, nor was Vinter challenged.

The Party Purge

The RKI's call for better administration, stricter attention to costs and schedules, the overthrow of old procedures, and the resulting review of administrative personnel coincided with the political purge at Dneprostroi. After the Thirteenth District Party Conference on January 12, 1929

Mark L'vovich Leibenzon, president of the Zaporozh'e District Party Control Commission, announced that party and state control commissions would review the local party members and enterprise executives and purge the unfit.[181] The official purge began only some months later, but some investigations began forthwith. The papers carried news of expulsions and firings through June.[182] In instituting this purge, the Zaporozh'e district was carrying out the orders of the party plenum of November 1928 and setting a precedent for the unionwide purge formally announced by E. M. Yaroslavski, chief of the Central Control Commission, three months later.[183] It was associated with the expulsion and silencing of opposition to Stalin and his faction.[184] No clear evidence directly links the political and the economic investigations, but their aims were fully complementary in June when the investigations began.[185]

The goals of this administrative purge were, as Leibenzon said in January, to ensure support for the general party line and ideological unity and to expel the Right Oppositionists and remaining Trotskyites. At the beginning, the party tried to create a positive, nonthreatening atmosphere for the investigations.[186] Yet in the investigations of administrative personnel, "dangerous" class origins—noble or landowner—were ample cause for dismissal.[187] Other administrators were discharged or reprimanded for illegal behavior—protectionism, drunkenness, or false representation of qualifications.[188] In the review of party personnel, a party spokesman wrote, "the tribunal should demand that the question be about what is a good Communist, it should be about how he should act."[189] This goal was often missed, it appeared, for the author admonished that using the purge for personal vendettas was clearly wrongful, and it was also incorrect to emphasize only revolutionary biography.[190]

The first reported investigations tended to emphasize the good qualities of those selected to serve on the purge committee; they were steadfast workers, responsible in both their party and communal work. After them, the rank and file were checked. In mid-June and in July, members received reprimands and sometimes expulsions for extreme and unexcused passivity (failure to pay dues or attend meetings), self-serving membership (joining to get better housing), or open labor indiscipline, usually associated with drunkenness. The most serious, of course, were the political errors—factionalism, support of Trotsky or the Right Opposition, Ukrainian nationalism, or anti-Soviet statements.[191] Later in the summer, the party purges became more clearly defined as a struggle with the Right Opposition.[192] Maintenance of the party line, proper execution of party directives on grain collection, and the correct interpretation of the slogans of class were the chief subjects discussed. Whenever Right

Opposition attitudes were uncovered, expulsion was decreed, with reprimands being given for lesser crimes.[193] The attack on the right continued throughout the summer and culminated in a closed meeting for the activists on September 24.[194] They discussed the mistakes of the Zaporozh'e district organization and the tasks of the Dneprostroi organization. In conclusion, they passed resolutions identifying the party organization's failure to put pressure on *kulaks* to improve grain collection and their own duty to speed the tempo of collectivization.[195] As a result of the purge, 174 persons were expelled from the party.[196]

New appointments to Dneprostroi were made in Moscow. Vasilii Mikhailovich Mikhailov became deputy chief under Vinter.[197] Mikhailov was an old Bolshevik, who had served as one of the first party secretaries with Stalin from 1921 to 1922. He was elected member of the Central Committee at the Tenth Congress but demoted to candidate member at the Eleventh. He served in the Moscow party organization and in the Moscow trade union organization.[198] Because Mikhailov had favored reconciliation with the Right Opposition, his appointment to Dneprostroi was probably a form of exile from Moscow.[199] At that time, Soviet leaders regularly appointed those who were politically out of favor to distant posts, safely away from the political center but usefully employed.[200]

Mikhailov's appointment as deputy chief fulfilled the local party's two-year-old request for a party representative in a top administrative post. As an engineer, Mikhailov had some technical qualifications for the post as well. In the following year, he accompanied Vinter onto the newly created staff of the Dneprostroi combine, as the enlarged project of the hydroelectric dam and its accompanying factories was called. At that time, he became deputy chief of the combined construction as well as acting head of Dneprostroi.[201] With this appointment, the Central Committee looked to strengthen administrative control over the Dneprostroi project.

Conclusion

These political and administrative changes at the end of the economic year 1928–29 marked the beginning of a new epoch in Soviet industrialization. After three years in industrial reconstruction and expansion, administrators at many levels had accumulated experience and new knowledge about organizational matters, applied technology, labor organization and training, and a host of other issues related to management, labor policy, and production. Industrializers developed new resources, introduced new technology, and rationalized existing procedures.

The work force grew vigorously, and new workers were gaining experience in an industrial setting. But these new workers were not working under the conditions anticipated by the protagonists of Dneprostroi and the authors of the *Electrification Plan*. Working and living conditions had deteriorated rapidly. Discriminatory hiring and firing, promotions, and recompense favored fast producers. Equal opportunity, equal effort, and equal pay were forgotten in the drive for tangible progress. Workers' demands for lower norms, better wages, housing, and services were refused. Complaints or defense of worker demands were associated with enmity to the state and party and became dangerous to pursue.

Some of these developments are explained by the situation forced on the administration by the party's command to meet the original completion date, even in the absence of the planned-for and necessary machinery and the consequent substitution of men for machines. But other factors were also important. The enthusiastic industrialists and party idealists overestimated the potential interest and commitment of workers to the goals of the revolution and their willingness to work for low pay in harsh conditions. Hungry, cold, tired, and crowded, workers left the site as eagerly as they had come seeking jobs. Turnover rates grew steadily as workers hunted better conditions. Absenteeism rose.

Moreover, there was a shortage of both skilled labor and experienced managers. The administration had overestimated the availability of skilled workers and underestimated the difficulty of organizing complex enterprises and that of training the necessary staff.

Efforts to raise productivity through piece rates were effective. Trade union protests ended with the defeat of the Right Opposition. Workers acquiesced as the majority, the unskilled, could not live on day wages. But incentive funds and goods were in ever shorter supply as the party encouraged new and expanded construction and production.

The calls for voluntary work and socialist competition, introduced by the party as an alternative to paid work, had very limited success. When shock work (*udarnichestvo*) was rewarded with special pay or benefits, such as extra food rations, there were active volunteers, many of them young and representative of the 1929 influx of young workers. They threw themselves at challenges and set records, doubling the production of the rock-crushing factory and pouring concrete in record-breaking quantities.[202] But participation in socialist competition did not make a significant contribution to production, however, until it became "required."

Yet, in sum, visible progress was made. Construction continued in spite of obstacles. The work force developed in numbers and productivity as more workers gained experience in the operation of machines. Encouraged by signs of growth, some party leaders in the central administration, some in regional areas, and nonparty industrialists as well came to believe that the country's problems of industrial underdevelopment were overcome and that the Soviet Union was ready to catch up to the developed industrial nations and even ready to bypass them. Under Stalin's leadership, they forced through a program of accelerated growth. Development plans claimed to balance competing demands for supplies and growing shortages in all but agriculture. However, the acute crisis that developed in agriculture in 1928 and early 1929 threatened the newly expanded industrialization program. The Stalinists reacted with forced collectivization. The unnecessary and premature acceleration of these two programs in 1929 slowed the development of both agriculture and industrialization and did irreparable harm to the populace and society.

5

The Expansion
of the Work Force

Hundreds of hands.
Thousands of hands.
There
  a chain,
Here
  a circle.
Hundreds of hands.
Thousands of hands.
On the left
  a friend
And on the right
  a friend.
Rain in the face.
Wind in the face.
No one will break
From out the ring
Of men.

A. Bezymenskii,
Tragediinaia noch', 1930–1963

Vociferous campaigns in the party press announced the new tempo of industrialization and forced collectivization in the fall of 1929. They gave official recognition and confirmation to the acceleration already introduced piecemeal during the summer. The new tempo resulted in the construction of more than a thousand new industrial enterprises.

The same combination of forces which had contributed to the 1928 expansion of the Dneprostroi project contributed in 1929 to the approval of the plans for *stroiki* at Magnitogorsk, Kuznetsk, and Stalingrad and the huge factories at Zaporozh'e, clients for Dneprostroi's power. Chief among these forces was the ambition of Stalin and his supporters to develop industry as rapidly as possible, using all the advantages of modern technology, the economies of size, and the availability of a large labor force. The ambitions of the party leaders in the capital were shared by local leaders who, like Chubar in the Ukraine, sought local investment and, like Vinter, had the confidence in their technical and managerial skills to push for ambitious industrial projects under their own direction.

Imbalances aggravated by the uneven fulfillment of the 1928–29 plan caused serious concern among economic planners, especially the right wing of the party.[1] Already in the first year of the first Five-Year Plan, production had substantially risen in metals and mining, reaching 97.5 percent of plan in coal and 112.9 percent in steel, for example.[2] Serious strains in the economy, however, were not overcome because demand for certain products increased faster than the supply.[3] The party right wing, seeking to revise and restrain the industrial plan, presented moderate programs in 1928 and particularly in 1929, tying industry to achievements in other sectors.

The Stalinist wing responded by intensifying its efforts to expand the industrial base. The party approved a 48.9 percent increase in investment for heavy industry, accelerating schedules for existing construction and approving new factory construction.[4] In contrast, investment in consumer goods industries was lowered by 6.8 percent and total agricultural investment was raised by only four percent.[5] The existence of imbalances and deficits within the plan itself were recognized but addressed only indirectly; for example, the industrial sector as a whole was advised to use short materials more efficiently and to improve technology.

Agricultural policy was harnessed to the same Stalinist objectives and was more extreme. In order to control existing agricultural production and in hopes of expanding food supplies, Stalin announced the acceleration of collectivization on November 7, 1929. He announced that a "great turn" had already taken place, that the peasants were joining collective farms by whole villages and even districts.[6] Decrees announcing the revision of collectivization goals appeared in December 1929 and the early months of 1930. During the intensive campaign between November 1929 and February 1930, the number of households collectivized reached 15 million, or 59.3 percent of the total. Collectivization and de*kulak*ization were accompanied by serious and even armed opposition.[7] Peasant hostility and resistance were so severe that Stalin interrupted the campaign, blaming local officials for undue militancy in his March 2, 1930, letter to *Pravda*, "Dizzy with Success." He affirmed the principle of free choice for peasants with respect to joining collective farms and advised party members to help the peasants, not persecute them, and persuade, not force, them to join the farms. The number of collective farms dropped rapidly. "Paper" collectives disappeared, and peasants left the collectives as quickly as they had joined them. However, in October the drive for collectivization began again, and by December more than a million households were collectivized, and the goal of at least fifty percent collectivization of all peasant farms was set for 1931.[8]

It has long been recognized that agricultural production dropped as a result of collectivization and that, in the Ukraine, a terrible famine resulted, but what of collectivization's effect on industrialization? Clearly, many peasants fled the rural areas. The hostility of the newcomers to the communist authors of their plight contributed to a growing morale problem in the industrial work force as well as in the countryside. Moreover, the influx from the countryside changed the characteristics of the work force. The changes, many of which we can measure, are important to an understanding of the evolution of labor policy.

We can study the special character of industrial development by looking closely at the *novostroiki*. The policies party members implemented there directly affected not only the construction labor force but all those thousands of workers who passed through construction on their way into industry. This chapter will examine the effect of the drive for accelerated tempo on the progress of the work being done at Dneprostroi, the development of the work force, the evolving relationship between management and labor, and the party's changing social objectives. It will examine the legacy of the "great turn" for the working class through the close study of the developments at Dneprostroi and other construction sites.

Labor for the Stroiki

The expanded targets in industrial construction created a labor crisis. In their efforts to meet production schedules, individual enterprises hired more and more workers. The number of workers in industry, construction, and transportation grew rapidly. As can be seen from Table 11, construction grew especially rapidly. Developmental plans, however, had not encompassed so great an expansion.[9] The minimum goal for 1931 to 1932 was 1,378,000 workers, the maximum 1,662,000. The minimum target for 1932 to 1933 was 1,527,000, the maximum 1,883,000. The actual number employed in 1932, 3,126,000, was 166 percent more than the largest number planned.

In spite of this enormous expansion in the number of workers, all the construction sites regularly reported serious labor shortages, as did the industrial branches competing with construction sites. In addition, the enterprises of secondary importance were stripped of workers to meet the insatiable demands of the priority projects, including Dneprostroi and the other giant *novostroiki*. Clearly disorder was growing on the labor front.

In 1930, the central planning organs in Moscow and local officials recruited forcefully for the *stroiki*. They urged labor boards in the large cities to act and fulminated against individual boards for their failures. Workers sent to help collectivize the farms in 1929, the twenty-five thousand-ers, were urged to recruit farm workers for the construction season. The Supreme Economic Council searched for reserves to replace "deserters" at Magnitostroi and attacked the commissar of labor for underestimating the need for workers across the union. Construction needed "two million workers . . . but last year's lessons were not learned," claimed *Za industrializatsii*, the organ of the Supreme Economic Council—"there's a mess again, . . . raiding, . . . local patriotism, . . . fruitless agreements."[10] Collective farms were reluctant to let workers go, needing them for the spring planting. Some farms sent workers but made "unheard-of demands" for compensation and used the "shortage of unskilled labor to strengthen their own financial position."[11] Clearly, no central plan was functioning in the allocation of labor.

The situation at Dneprostroi reflected the turmoil caused by the accelerated tempo. The number of workers on the site in 1929 passed the peak of 11,600 employed in 1928 by 5000.[12] Numbers dropped sharply in October, then rose again, dropping only slightly during December and January, the usually low periods for employment. In May, *Postroika*, the construction union's newspaper, reported that Dneprostroi was short 8000 workers.[13] In June and July, the labor crisis intensified. The labor force shrank when it was supposed to increase. It went down at Dneprostroi from 23,219 to 21,803. In one five-day period in June at Dneprostroi, 256 workers left; at the end of the month, 300 a day were leaving. In July the labor force grew again, reaching 31,000 as work was begun on the Dneprostroi combine. During that month, however, sixty to eighty percent of the force left and had to be replaced by new workers.[14] Even when numbers dropped in November and December 1930 to 19,000, they remained far above the 1928 high of 11,600 and even above the 1929 high of 17,000. (See Table 12.)

The shortage among all enterprises using semiskilled and unskilled labor worsened in July and August as the farms made their claims on

Table 11. Average Annual Number of Workers in Industry, Construction, and Railroads (thousands)

	1928	1929	1930	1931	1932	1933 (preliminary)	1934 (preliminary)
Industry	3096.0	3365.9	4263.8	5483.3	6481.3	6222.1	6528.0
Construction	723.0	917.8	1623.4	2548.9	3125.8	2343.5	2475.0
Railroads	971.0	984.0	1084.0	1320.2	1526.5	1473.7	1610.4

Sources: "Sredne-godovaia chislennost' rabochikh i sluzhashchikh po otraslam truda, 1928–34," *Sotsialisticheskoe stroitel'stvo* (Moscow, 1934), 474–75.

Table 12. Workers on the Combined Site (thousands)

	Jan.	Feb.	Mar.	Apr.	May	Jun.	Jul.	Aug.	Sep.	Oct.	Nov.	Dec.
1928	8.6	8.6	6.7	6.8	7.9	8.6	9.0	9.6	10.6	11.6	10.2	8.7
1929	8.4	8.6	8.8	8.9	9.1	10.1	12.0	13.7	15.7	16.0	17.0	14.3
1930	13.0	13.2	15.5	17.9	22.5	23.5	31.0	24.0	30.0	21.5	19.0	—

Sources: Table numbers drawn from local newspapers and site journals, including *Dneprostroi, Proletar Dniprobudu, Krasnoe Zaporozh'e, Chervonne Zaporizhzhe, Khronika Dneprostroia,* and *Informatsiomnyi listok.*

labor for the harvest. Magnitostroi, Kuznetskstroi, and the other *stroiki* also regularly reported labor shortages. The Donbass mines, which also used unskilled workers, reported a shortfall of fifty thousand workers. After the high point of the crisis in August, shortages continued through-out the season, but on a lesser scale as the demand for unskilled labor fell with the onset of cold weather.

It was clear from the beginning that many different factors were contributing to the labor shortage. For one thing, the *stroiki* were not very popular among workers who could find other jobs. Workers pre-ferred city jobs near their homes and families to the *stroiki* barracks, which lacked most amenities, where often there was no room for families, food was short, and the work was hard and poorly paid. Further, the demand for labor was increasing faster than the supply. The more than a thousand new and expanded construction projects approved as part of the accelerated Five-Year Plan competed for labor. Workers continued to leave one site for another despite prohibitions, as will be discussed below. Plan expansion generated demand for workers in jobs supplementary to industrial work as more housing, cafeterias, medical centers, schools, and shops became necessary. Labor for such work added to the existing demand.

Labor Recruitment

In order to guarantee all industrial projects with workers, the party launched a major campaign in the spring of 1931. Two million new permanent workers were to be recruited, more than half of them trained.[15] Some seven hundred thousand were to enter the labor force through the industrial schools. A particular effort was made to recruit women—1.6 million in that year. In addition to this force, nine million seasonal workers were to be recruited. This major campaign was neces-sary, because labor estimates in the plans had been based on the planned replacement of labor by machines, but such substitution had not taken place. On the contrary, as at Dneprostroi in 1927 and 1928, machines had been replaced by labor.

The very organization of recruitment proved to be difficult. The labor boards tried but failed to mobilize and assign labor in anywhere near the quantities demanded. The enterprises bypassed them, hired workers who came on their own (*samotek*), and even began to recruit on their own. For a time, the party upheld the labor boards' control of labor resources. In December 1930, they had forbidden direct recruitment by enterprises.

Perhaps because of the difficulties the labor boards experienced, perhaps because they were already being circumvented by desperate employers, and perhaps because the central economic organizations decided that direct trading between enterprises and collective farms would make labor recruitment more efficient, in March 1931 such direct engagement was permitted.

Seeking to guarantee themselves large numbers of workers, the enterprises recruited individually in the provinces assigned to them. Dneprostroi recruited in its assigned areas in the Ukraine, the central Black-Earth district, the western provinces, and the Tatar republic. Between January 1 and November 1, 1931, the administration concluded 546 agreements for 11,180 workers.[16] Some labor boards refused to respond; in January, the labor board of Smolensk province "refused to allow any recruitment of labor, whatsoever, without the conclusion of a specific agreement."[17]

During 1931, recruiters for some of the largest *stroiki* competed in the same territories for new workers. They visited the collective farms and made individual arrangements with them, promising to repair machines and help with the sowing and harvest in return for workers.[18] Dneprostroi set a significant standard with a recruiting campaign which included agitation work and traveling movies.[19] It overfilled its plan of 6990 and recruited 8527. Soon Magnitostroi, Kuznetskstroi, and other *stroiki* produced competing films.[20]

These programs regularly ran into problems because one or the other partner in the agreement failed to uphold his bargain. Sometimes special arrangements were written into contracts stipulating housing and special clothes for the recruits. However, often it happened that when workers arrived, they found there was no work or no work for people of their skills, and they could earn nothing; frequently, no housing or food was available. Others came and worked but were bitterly disappointed by the absence of the good things that had been promised to them.[21] Returnees described the absence of amenities and the falseness of such promises as "[T]here you'll get linen, felt boots, higher pay."[22] Another complaint was that "Recruiters don't know norms and inaccurately represented the work required."[23] Some left immediately, others stayed to the end of their contracts, but many stayed because they had come with their families in search of a life better than what they could find in their villages. Nikolai Nikolaevich came in 1931 in response to a recruiter who had shown a movie of Dneprostroi and told of the living, working, and schooling opportunities. He was disappointed with what he found yet could not leave, for he did not have the money to transplant his wife and baby a second time. Further, he had nothing to return to—no roof, no job, and no special skills to help him secure a living.[24]

The *stroiki* were not the only ones guilty of irregularities. Some recruits signed up for work or courses with the Commissariat of Labor and got permission from their local councils to leave the countryside, but they quit within a week. Upon learning of the shortage of workers elsewhere, they would try again for a better situation. Workers often went elsewhere than assigned, hunting for better conditions. Labor recruiters had to deal with broken promises of both parties. Sometimes the recruiters contributed specifically to the problems. Anxious to meet their quotas and earn premiums—usually fifty kopecks per recruit[25]—they continued to promise more than the enterprise could produce and to accept laborers who were unfit. Many recruiters did not know the norms of the work they were recruiting for. Others were illiterate and incompetent, remarkable for their drunkenness, embezzling, and inaction. Recruiters spent heavily—twelve hundred to two thousand rubles a month—and at Magnitostroi, recruitment costs were nearly double the plan.[26] Recruitment costs rose over the years, and in 1933 they reached an average of between one hundred and one hundred sixteen rubles per recruit. Some recruiters charged for lodging, wine, and fine food, as well as multitudinous telegrams, costs amounting to one to two thousand rubles a month.[27]

To help the enterprise managers, the party and state organizations, particularly the TsIK and SNK and party plenums, passed laws and directives. Beginning in 1930, when the enterprises had been allowed to recruit directly in a given area, bypassing the local labor boards, there evolved a policy which came to be known as organized recruitment (*orgnabor*), the recruitment of labor from the collective farms. A speech by Stalin to the industrial managers in June 1931 marked its official birth. The laws in 1931 and 1932 supported the industrial drive for workers by giving privileges to collective farmers who took seasonal work; by forbidding farm managers to penalize them with taxes, land, or crop share loss; or by taking measures against their families.[28]

Orgnabor did not work. It did not provide workers to meet industry's needs. Neither industry nor collective farms used it. The state urged enterprise managers to use it because, they were told, it would provide more disciplined workers; workers could be easily "thrown from one sector to another; there would be group harmony in the barracks."[29] (Similar arguments could have been made about the *artel*, attacked in 1928 and in official disfavor thereafter; see Chapter 4 above). Enterprises continued to prefer workers who came on their own—it was cheaper; it avoided contractual obligation for housing, goods, and services; and workers could be assigned individually to brigades. Many discovered their labor needs only as the year progressed, in any case, and were in no position to make contracts with farms ahead of time. Finally, contract labor did not necessarily come or go as promised by the contracts, so the enterprise gained little by agreements.

The collective farms, moreover, did not embrace the idea of contracting out their able-bodied during the busy seasons. It regularly happened that they restricted the movements of members seeking work in industry. Some refused to cooperate with the Commissariat of Labor or individual enterprises, sending only incompetent and unfit workers. "We have no extra workers," one farm answered to Magnitostroi, "and even if you find one, we'll only send you drunks, boozers, and parasites."[30] Farms made "impossible demands" for in-kind payments in goods.[31] The farms also made life difficult for the migrant workers' families or took a percentage of the money the migrant earned in industry.[32]

Outside the contract system were those collective farmers who sought work on their own. Although party leaders sought to centralize labor allocation, their ultimate goal was to provide the labor to industry. To this end, they required collective farms to permit the *independent* departure of members seeking work in industry. They recognized that such departures were taking place, that they could not effectively control or end them, and that such departures did serve the prime purpose of getting labor into industry.

The majority of new recruits to industry did go "on their own" (*samotek*), as they had in the 1920s. The enterprises preferred to hire "at the gate," workers they could see and put to work rather than workers on contract whose strengths and professions they would not know till later. Most collective farm peasants preferred to come on their own because they could choose where they went, the time of their departure, and the length of time they contracted for. Recruits coming on *orgnabor* were promised rights and privileges, but in practice existing rights were shared by all workers, and privileges were most frequently assigned on the basis of productivity, length of time at work, and participation in community work, such as party and trade union.

Changes in the Labor Force

The character of the labor force was changing as a result of state hiring policies. Of course, there had always been a strong connection between construction work and the countryside. There was a qualitative change, however, in 1930. Whereas in the beginning of the first Five-Year Plan period seasonal labor from the farms were older, experienced workers with skills in carpentry, masonry, and other construction work, the new workers were younger, inexperienced, and lacking the skills their predecessors had possessed. In 1930, thousands were peasants interested only in fleeing the anti*kulak* campaigns. Many left later in the year, seeking to assert their claims to homes, land, and animals. Forced away from the countryside again, peasants returned to industry in 1931 with new imperatives. Some of them came as seasonal workers, but many sought permanent jobs as family farms were broken up and conditions in the countryside worsened. The rise in the number employed in 1931 was also a result of the urgent persuasion of recruiters promising regular wages, food, housing, and access to goods. The construction sites, and especially Dneprostroi as the first of the giants, prefigured these changes in the composition of the work force which then later occurred in the industrial plants and factories.

The trade unions documented and studied these changes. They concerned themselves with who these workers were, their social backgrounds, education, experience, and skills. Already in 1928, the Dneprostroi Rabochkom had argued that its members had to know who was on the site in order to know how to plan campaign appeals. In May 1930 and in March 1931, the Combined Construction of Dneprostroi conducted a census of all workers on the site to gather the necessary information on the length of time workers had spent on the site, time in a department, and changes in rank. Such censuses were regularly conducted on other enterprises as well.

The increased number of peasants at Dneprostroi is reflected in Table 13, based on censuses taken on the site among the workers and employees then registered at work. Analysts of the 1930 census noted at the time and again in 1931 that the peasants underreported themselves. The editors of the administrative journal *Informatsionnyi listok* attrib-

Table 13. Social Origins, Percentage of Labor Force

	Peasants		Workers		Employees	
May 1930 N: 16, 940	4121	24.3%	12,532	73%	287	1.7%
March 1931 N: 19,499	12,694	65.1%	6591	33.8%	214	1.1%

Source: Informatsionnyi listok, nos. 8–9 (1930): 683; nos. 10–11 (1931): 212, 216.

uted the increase to the proportionate growth of construction work, the expansion of Zavodstroi, and the underreporting to the hostile atmosphere of collectivization, the fear that peasants had of being associated with the *kulaks* under attack by the state.[33] They estimated that the peasant proportion in 1930 was about fifty percent.

The new recruits were also younger on the average than their predecessors. The decrease in the average age of workers throughout the Soviet Union was a trend that first appeared among construction workers. (See Table 14.) The average age was actually lower than reported, the census takers suggested, because of the way the numbers were rounded.[34] In 1930, the average age was 28.69; in 1931, it was 27.4.[35] Some labor analysts blamed young peasants for poor productivity, arguing that they did not produce as much as their predecessors, the older, more skilled workers who had formed the core of the workers in the first year of the first Five-Year Plan.[36] Others claimed that young workers were a positive addition to the work force, that it was easier to accustom them to technology, new political thinking, and enthusiasm for the construction.[37]

At Dneprostroi, the core had come from the central Russian provinces and had been made up of workers accustomed to hiring out to construction work. Between 1930 and 1931, a change, already begun in 1929, accelerated. More Ukrainians came to the site, outnumbering the Russians. (See Tables 15 and 16.)

Finally, the census date at Dneprostroi and similar investigations of *stroiki* population and trade union membership attested to the mobility of the young workers. The new recruits seemed to remain on the site only a short time, and the average stay was even shorter in 1931 than it had been in 1930. This may have meant that habits and skills learned at Dneprostroi were being carried to other sites, but it was also true that the high rate of turnover meant that the site was always in danger of not having as many workers as the administration wanted.

Table 14. Distribution by Age of Workers, United Dneprostroi Construction, 1929–1931 (percentage)

	1929	1930	1931
Up to 23	33.6	37.0	45.4
24–30	NA	30.3	28.8
31–40	NA	18.9	13.6
41 and older	NA	13.8	12.2

Source: Informatsionnyi listok , nos. 10–11 (1931): 212, 217.

Table 15. Places of Origin (percentage)

	1930	1931
Ukrainian	60.2	62.3
Russian	32.1	30.8
Tatar	—	1.7
Other	—	5.2

Source: Informatsionnyi listok , nos. 8–9 (1930): 682, nos. 10–11 (1931): 216.

In an effort to control labor turnover, the party mounted a campaign to win worker acceptance of work books in which a worker's employment record, experience, and skills would be listed together with explanations of any job changes. These books, it was suggested, could practically replace the tens of other documents currently in use—trade union records, ration cards, birth certificates, military records, and others.[38] Production records in the books were to ensure as well the proper reward of "true" shock workers, the party press argued, recognizing that shock-work payments and privileges were going to the majority of workers and losing their potency as incentives to leadership acts of extra work. No worker was to be employed without his or her book, and an incomplete record was to deter a future employer, so the books were to end unauthorized job transfers. The books became a reality in August 1931.[39] However, because the labor shortage continued to be acute, workers continued to get jobs without the so-called required documents and papers.

Forced labor played an important role in the industrialization of the Soviet Union. It was less important in the years of the first Five-Year Plan than later and does not seem to have been a crucial factor at Dneprostroi. On all the *stroiki*, there were workers who had lost their rights, sometimes only temporarily—criminals, class aliens, or anti-Soviet peasants. Sometimes these workers came from the site itself. In minor civil actions, they had temporarily lost their "rights" for causing an accident, stealing, or breaking some other law and had been sentenced to continue at their work for a given time without pay. Many peasants, forcibly evicted from their farms during collectivization, were sent to the *stroiki* to work under guard.

Dneprostroi had some of these workers, although probably not in the numbers found on *stroiki* which were started later. Some of the peasants under sentence lived in special barracks and were marched to work under guard. Such people without rights (*lishentsi*) were assigned to work in the rock-crushing mill, where the conditions were among the most unhealthy

Table 16. Permanent Home (percentage)

	1930	1931
Ukrainian	68.1	76.3
Russian and others	27.9	21.3
Tatar	4.0	2.4

Source: *Informatsionnyi listok*, nos. 8–9 (1930): 682; nos. 10–11 (1931): 216.

on the site.[40] The Dneprostroi newspaper was proud of the site's participation in what it considered reeducation of those whom the party prosecuted. In "corrective colonies," the editor wrote, those

> deprived of rights are indeed reeducated and become even accustomed to useful work processes, after which they return to working society. . . . We have construction colonies where those deprived of rights take active part in the construction of the giants of industry. To the worker of Dneprostroi such participation is especially well known.[41]

Women in Construction

An important aspect of the labor recruitment program was the party's concentrated effort to incorporate women into the work force. It served the party's immediate aims of development of the working class and industrial production and the long-term goals of economic self-sufficiency for women and their liberation from male dominance. The employment of many thousands of women during the first Five-Year Plan was cited as proof of a new role for women in society. The evidence from Dneprostroi and the other *stroiki*, however, suggests that the picture was a very complex one, fraught with problems for women and challenges to traditional social practices.

Collectivization in 1930 and the intense recruitment of women workers in 1931 brought many into the industrial sector throughout the Soviet Union. Many of those who came were escaping collectivization and the violence in the countryside. Some were seeking alternative ways of making a living, having lost their farms and husbands. Others, like some of their predecessors from farm and village, were simply seeking work, both permanent and seasonal.

Of the 1.6 million women to be recruited in 1931, the party planned to send 167,000 to construction. An additional 329,000 were to be recruited for industrial schools, whence they could be expected to move into the work force.[42] In response to the aggressive hiring policies and because of their own material needs, the number of women entering the work force as compared to men grew dramatically in 1931 and 1932, rising from between seven and eleven percent to forty percent in industry as a whole, and from between five and nine percent to approximately thirty percent in construction. A glance at statistical data (Table 17) gives us an idea of the developing trends.

In construction, the percentage of women workers rose from 6.3 percent in October 1928 to 16 percent in January 1933. In the summers, when more unskilled workers were used, the percentage of women was even higher.[43]

There were considerable differences in age among the men and the women. According to trade union census data of 1932–33, the average age of women was four and a half years younger than that of men. The majority were under thirty years of age, and more than half were under twenty-three.[44] This topic needs further investigation, particularly as it affected the worldview of a generation—the generation of women who lived on through the terror, war, Stalinization, and de-Stalinization, and brought up the generation which established itself in power in the 1980s.

At enterprises near the forcefully collectivized countryside or among those hiring workers with low skills, the number of women workers rose quickly. At Dneprostroi, the numbers rose from 656 in 1929 to 2776 in August 1930; 1639 were working directly in construction, 447 of them skilled.[45] In December, the number rose to 2934, and women constituted 5.6 percent of the work force. In February 1931, there were 4836 women; in April 1931, 4030; in December 1931, 6815,[46] and in February 1932, on the eve of the production of electricity, 7075.[47]

Women were still entering the work force at the bottom, as they had in the beginning of industrialization. They continued to work largely in service occupations. Some, particularly those with children who could not manage employment away from home, made special clothes for the site's workers, sewing mittens and protective overalls. Some, especially the young, came as unskilled and learned a skill in a special course or technical circle. Among the women who were able to enter school, the majority were in the lower classes, acquiring skills in the more or less traditional fields, such as food service and bookkeeping. In 1930, among the 680 in higher education, 67 were women.[48]

The average work experience of women was two or three years less than men, and more of them were concentrated in the lower ranks. This

Table 17. Women Workers in Industry

(Jan. 1)	1928	1929	1930	1931	1932	1933
Workers in industry	2531.9	2788.7	3116.2	4252.4	5271.3	5139.7
Women in industry	725.9	804.0	885.0	1271.5	1735.4	1826.2
Women among workers	23.7%	28.8%	28.4%	29.9%	32.9%	35.5%

Source: Georgi Serebrennikov, *Zhenskii trud v SSSR* (Moscow and Lenigrad, 1934), pp. 64–66.

was true even in those fairly new professions that they entered at the same time as men, a phenomenon explained by one observer as evidence of the continued prejudice against women workers.[49] A few, still about ten percent of the student body, were enrolled in higher education at Dneprostroi, but most women lacked even minimal requirements for upper-level courses.[50] Of the nearly five thousand women workers in February 1931, only 8.26 percent were skilled.[51] Even this number is misleading, because the skills included very low-ranking domestics and construction workers (*zemlekop*). Women made up 46.9 percent of the newest and lowest-ranking white-collar employees and 76 percent of the young service personnel (MOP), the lowest-paid rank of all except for students.[52] In industry as a whole, 93 percent of the women were clustered in ranks 1 to 3.[53] There were no special plans for promoting them, and the very speed with which they were being absorbed into the work force militated against their getting the training required for promotion on the basis of specialized knowledge.

Interviews with these women reflect their surprise that they had gotten so far, rather than distress that they had not gone farther. They came from the countryside and expected very little. The fact that they had made the first step, gotten a skill, and were earning without harassment seemed to be enough for them.

Some of the older women who came to the site at the beginning prepared the way for their successors.[54] Ekaterina Filimonova, who said she had never dreamed of having any skill, became, at age forty, an assistant stove builder and repairer. Ekaterina Romanov was a poor peasant (*bedniak*). "It was hard," she said, "at twenty-nine to start a new life." She was content with her position as an assistant metalworker, where her fellow workers "treat me as an equal comrade." Nadezhda Zhdanovich began as a barracks cleaner and worked her way up into the sanitation department. She transferred into construction and became an assistant fitter and finally a machine operator. Evdokiana Kolombet began by oiling machines and moved on to work with them as an assistant metalworker. These women proved that women could do these jobs and created new career patterns for working women.[55]

Numerous women who came to Dneprostroi as unskilled workers moved into the ranks of the skilled. Elena Puzanova had begun work at age thirteen in a factory where her father worked. She went to the factory school and trained as an electrical machinist. She came to Dneprostroi on contract and "earned the reputation of knowing her work best in the mechanical workshop."[56] Maria Petrus, orphaned by the war and revolution, grew up in a children's home. She worked as a hired laborer (*batrak*) in a village. At fifteen, she went to the city, where she did housework and then entered a factory where she learned to read and write. She studied while working an eight-hour day as an unskilled worker. She became assistant to a crane machinist and was quickly promoted through a range of courses. Such student-workers "were always in short supply, so the best were promoted."[57] Oleksandra Tkachenko was not so fortunate. She and other members of her brigade were sent to Leningrad to learn to be electrical technicians. When she returned to Dneprostroi, she and the members of her brigade where "thrown into the breach," cleaning snow in the central channel, paid *groshi*, or pennies, and refused work in their new specialty.[58]

The severe labor crisis and the urgency of the work at Dneprostroi hurtled some women to the forefront. Zhenia Roman'ko, a worker's daughter born in 1910, a member of the Komsomol, came to Dneprostroi in 1929 as an unskilled worker. In 1930, she organized the first women's brigade and took a leading role in concrete pouring. She organized socialist competition between her brigade and others. Her outstanding record earned her many honors, including the Order of Lenin in 1933.[59] There is, however, no record of Roman'ko's professional advancement. Some such heroes of labor did, in fact, have tragic careers. In reward for their physical exploits, they received city apartments and generous allowances. They did not know how to make use of their time and wealth, and some became unhappy alcoholics.[60]

A very few women held professional positions at Dneprostroi. Among them was V. D. Iastrebova, one of the first graduates of the Higher Women's Polytechnical Course, in 1915. After having worked at a number of other *stroiki* as an engineer, she came to Dneprostroi as the wife of the chief engineer, B. E. Vedeneev. As she wrote in an autobiographical sketch, she tried to retire and become a full-time wife but missed her work. She learned a new specialty, that of assembly engineer, and went back to work.[61] Shulamis Aronovna Zil'berstein, born in 1903, joined the party in 1924 and graduated from the Odessa Polytechnical

Institute in 1927. As mentioned earlier, she found it difficult to persuade Vinter to give her a position at Dneprostroi but succeeded with Krzhizha-novskii's assistance. She received many medals for her work as an engineer on large hydroelectric projects, the first of which was Dneprostroi.[62] These two women were part of a small minority at Dneprostroi, where in 1931 only 8.26 percent of the women had any skills at all.

The labor ministry created commissions to investigate job possibilities for women in individual enterprises. These commissions reported potential openings to enterprise managers, but they were little used, and the planned quotas were not met.[63] The notable exceptions were in fields in which women already worked in large numbers, such as textiles and the food industry. At Dneprostroi, of the 1764 in food services, 1342 were women in 1933. Among them there were thirteen department heads.[64] In general, however, men did the hiring, and they preferred to hire men. "We are not interested in women workers," the deputy chief of construction workers at Magnitostroi said.[65] As one woman wrote, "The question of women's work is being left in the hands of men. It is time to end this conservative and limited procedure."[66]

At a time when party membership was extremely important to advancement, proportionately few of the new women workers entered the party. Women, therefore, lacked representation in the network most likely to have promoted their goal of equal rights, especially after the 1930 demise of the party's women's organization, the *zhenotdel*. Newspaper stories rarely carried party reports signed by women or quoted any women identified as members. Yet some women clearly demonstrated organizational capacities. Fifteen domestics, for example, organized a commune and elected their own council. They shopped with one communal book; they all entered literacy, general education, and vocational courses. Others displayed political activism as they built day-care centers, such as at Magnitostroi, and demanded cultural services.[67] At Dneprostroi and on the other *stroiki*, women organized to demand fair wages, equal to men, as well as nurseries, schools, and cafeterias. A high percentage of working women participated in shock work when it was becoming the practice of the party to recruit heavily among shock workers. Nevertheless, there were few women joining the party. Of the more than five thousand party members in 1933, only 524 were women.[68]

How does one explain the low profile of women in the Dneprostroi party? Is it enough to say that they had little education and few skills and could not rise in the party? Or that they were busy with their engineering professions, as were Iastrebova and Zil'berstein, or housekeeping and children and had no time for party affairs? Perhaps if we can someday probe the archives, we will find explanations for women's low profiles. Perhaps there were male taboos keeping them out; perhaps, they had no interest in the party because it offered nothing to women.

The rapid and greatly expanded participation of women in the work force changed the composition of the working class. It brought many young women into contact with new ideas and customs. The party welcomed the new over the old, encouraged the young to adopt the ways of the city, to value the machine, and to be progressive. Change took place at many levels. Women moved about in the country; some left their home villages forever. Their dress and hairstyles reflected the influence of the city. Many learned to read and to work in new professions. The numbers of women and their proportional representation in industry continued to grow in the years after the first Five-Year Plan period, particularly during the war. Some shared with men in the increasing opportunities for education and upward mobility but were constrained by the absence of community support from turning these opportunities into professional careers. Most women, however, stayed on the outskirts of change, as is so often shown pictorially in the news photos of the first Five-Year Plan. Women were not significant contributors to political organizations or activity.

Women's roles were limited by the traditional values of the society, common among the male revolutionary leaders and among party members and common among the majority of women as well. Women were not particularly respected as workers. For every woman who did a job well, there were more men praised as models. Articles on skilled women workers often referred to them by their familiar names, while men's surnames were used in similar articles, marking a clear difference in status. The fame of Roman'ko's brigade, known for defeating a "boys' brigade," reflects the unspoken superiority claimed by men and boys, for what boys' brigade ever celebrated beating a girls' or women's? Women who did good, fast work were admired more as freaks than as models to be emulated. And even the best of them tended to get attention only on March 8, International Women's Day, as one female correspondent to *Dneprostroi* pointed out.[69]

Underlying this attitude toward women workers was the dominant view that the first duty for women was the care of the household. Some efforts were made by the party to aid women in this regard, but they were little and late. For example, a children's school (*detploshad*) was opened in 1933 for one hundred children, most of whose mothers were single.[70] Eleven *iasli* took 1100 children, and kindergartens took another 1600. But the facilities were in no way adequate for the need. At the time,

13,000 women worked on the site, and 9049 of them had children of kindergarten age.[71]

In spite of the difficulties they encountered, millions of women responded to the party-state recruitment—some of them directly, some through the schools, and even some through seasonal work. The party did tend to direct women into traditional fields, and women, choosing perhaps the jobs with low supervision and irregular hours, acceded to or chose these jobs as well. The trade union commissions' studies of jobs that women might profitably fill were probably less important in making appropriate jobs available than the party and trade union responsibility to file reports that a certain number of women had been hired and promoted.

The party offered a number of arguments for continuing to promote the hiring of women. Women were deemed less likely to move than men. Labor turnover records demonstrating this were not critiqued in light of what job changes were available for women, the effect of their family responsibilities on job changes, or variables associated with the ratio of men and women in the work force; it was assumed that it was the inherent character of women to be more quiescent and responsive to guidance from above.[72] Further, both men and women were thought more likely to stay put if they had jobs and housing in the same area. A further side effect anticipated from the hiring of workers' wives was an increased family income, itself another incentive for stability. Wages for the majority of workers—the unskilled workers and those in the lower ranks—were so low that an increasing number of families had to have two members working. Statistics in 1929 and 1932 reflected this. In 1929, 1.26 members of a family worked; in 1932, 1.53.[73] The party welcomed these statistics as proof that more women were working, theoretically earning their own income and no longer financially dependent on their husbands or families. They also welcomed them because it meant that family units were earning enough to live on in spite of the high cost of food and goods.

The relative importance of bringing women into the work force, however, was defined by the demise of the *zhenotdel* in 1930, when production was enthroned as first priority, and all else was subsidiary. Such a priority meant, of course, that day-care centers, kindergartens, and cafeterias were of low priority. Laws to protect women at work and the opening up of new professions were also of low priority.

The women responded to the falling real wages by continuing to look for jobs—any job, even low-paying, was better than none. Why the young women who came in such numbers in 1931, 1932, and 1933 did not compete, at least not successfully, with their male peers is a topic for further investigation. Were their personal aims or values more important to them than commercial or political success? In sum, however, a pattern was built; women acceded by default to the party's emphasis on production. Their energies seem to have gone into the work of simply surviving.

Living Conditions

Party leaders frequently discussed the high turnover and measures to combat it. They identified the deteriorating living conditions as the major cause. Construction of permanent housing could not keep up with the influx of workers, so the latter simply crowded into existing barracks and tents. Average living space was reported to be 3.89 cubic meters in 1929 and was expected to drop to an average 3.6 cubic meters per person in 1930.[74] The misery caused by crowded conditions was aggravated by damp and cold, especially during the winter months when the wind blew snow through the cracks in the hastily built barracks.

The party encouraged local worker correspondents (*rabkory*) to write in about leaky roofs, molding walls, the absence of potable water, broken sewers, cockroaches, and vermin. The local and national press reported on squeezed living space, the crowded barracks, the renting of a corner of a room, and living quarters in sod huts and caves. "No provision is made for the arrival of the seasonal workers," the national press chided. The press gave examples of contract labor who arrived from a distant province, found no housing, and went home again.

In their efforts to improve the situation, party and trade union officials directed barrack commanders to expel those not directly employed in the work of the site from site housing and to forbid families in barracks for single men. Activists were told to lead in battles against bugs, beetles, and vermin.

Housing was not the only crucial problem. Workers suffered constantly from food shortages. The harvest failure of 1929 contributed to the shortages that plagued the site. Collectivization caused even more turmoil in the markets. The site was so large that it was very difficult for workers to reach the central cafeteria or its branches. There, too, food was scant, and, in addition, the lines were long, causing workers to waste potential work and rest time. The surroundings were dirty, and tableware of all kinds was in very short supply. The party press rebuked the cooperative for its failures in organization and operation and the absence of shock work and self-criticism. The national construction union paper reported that the Dneprostroi cafeteria fed only four thousand of the thirteen thousand there in January 1930, that quality and sanitation were extremely poor, and that prices were high. Examples cited by the article include pieces of galoshes mixed in with food and inflated prices for tea, sold for 5 kopecks when it only cost 1.3 kopeck. The cafeteria service was contrasted with that of better quality and greater efficiency provided by *artel* kitchens.[75]

Already in March, when the number of workers had risen to seventeen thousand at the dam site, the cafeteria could handle only fifty-five hundred, or 32.4 percent. *Artel* kitchens in the barracks fed another 16 percent. That left more than 50 percent of the workers to "eat as they can."[76] The paper, warning that the absence of inexpensive cafeteria food contributed to instability in the work force, argued that the Rabochkom should supervise the cafeteria, especially in time to be ready for the expected influx of twenty-two thousand new workers in April, of whom fifteen to seventeen thousand would be single. It also recommended that the Commissariat for Food bring in better, trained workers and supply more food.[77] The Rabochkom argued regularly with the regional cooperative organization, pointing out that Dneprostroi did not get its allotted ratio of what came through Zaporozh'e and that the town was better supplied than the construction site.[78]

The cafeteria food worsened during the spring of 1930, and in June "there were neither calories nor vitamins."[79] Even in August, as the summer gardens ripened, the cafeteria could not serve adequate meals at a reasonable price: one small portion of tomato, cucumber, and onion cost twenty kopecks; a portion of eggplant with one slice of tomato cost twenty-five kopecks; there is no record of meat, eggs, or cheese being served.[80]

A commission, including representatives of the Worker-Peasant Inspection, Rabkrin, and the Commissariat of Trade, investigated Dneprostroi conditions. It reported that while told "everything was fine," it had found one meat store inoperative, another so small as to be nearly useless, and vegetables very scarce—and this at the height of the harvest. No sugar had been available for a month, and only a third of the daily requirements for potatoes, milk, eggs, and oil came to the site. Worst of all, bread was available only to those who stood in long lines, and in three of the sectors of the site, bread was available in the stores only from twelve noon to one o'clock P.M.[81] Many preferred not to go to the cafeteria to wait an hour in line for a limited menu, search for utensils, and eat off a dirty table, itself set on a filthy floor. Others could not get in. Some living together hired their own cook. Such cooks and individual families bought their food in the cooperatives and bazaars, where prices were higher, supplies were also limited, and lines were long.

In July 1931, yet another committee was established to study and alleviate workers' problems.[82] A survey of the cafeteria indicated the low level of food available. The general calorie level was 259 to 710 per day, without bread. The meat cutlet was supposed to weigh 110 to 125 grams but weighed only 80; bread supposed to weigh 180 grams weighed 125 to 150.[83] There was "no choice" and "poor taste"; everything was "below all criticism." There were insufficient vegetables. Salt cabbage was served in the fall when fresh was available.

Individuals and organizations tried to respond to the gross failures of the central supply system. Their initiatives to increase the local food supply were favorably reported in the press. One cafeteria planted its own vegetable garden; another raised its own pigs. These efforts became increasingly important as food supplies dwindled. In early 1932, they were presented as useful models for emulation. Attacks on workers who spent time on a melon patch or raising chickens were a thing of the past. Volunteer labor in truck gardening was highly praised. Ground and seed were set aside for enterprises and departments. The *raion* party committee even encouraged workers who wished to set up individual gardens and animal husbandry.[84] In spite of these efforts, the food situation did not actually improve. It deteriorated.

Acute food shortages threatened the future of the industrialization plan; it was clear that workers could not produce without food to sustain them. Decreased production in the collectivized areas affected all of the Soviet Union. Famine in the Ukraine peaked in 1932 and 1933. Its effects were felt more in the countryside than on the industrial sites, but even there it was devastating to the health of the population. The bread ration dropped as supplies dwindled. At Dneprostroi, of the 250 grams due a worker in the cafeteria, only 100 grams were served.[85] People had to leave work to shop for the few foods available and stood in long lines in the shops and cafeterias. Food cards were checked and rechecked, and periodically those with extra cards were handed over to the militia. Grain deliveries had to be made at night under armed guard. Bakers were accused of selling bread on the side and arrested.

In an effort to create new sources of food, the local party committee required individual departments and sectors to act as patrons to collective farms in the area. In February, Dneprostroi was patron to some eighty collective farms, and the current slogan was "Every worker must be a patron to a collective farm."[86] They helped with the sowing, weeding, thinning, replanting, and harvesting. The farms sought extra workers, and special food brigades were formed to help with their work. One had its picture taken, proof of its organization and goodwill—but did no work![87] Komsomol members were sent to help a collective farm build a dam, bringing both labor and materials.[88] The party took control of fishing on the river; there was a fifty-ruble fine or seven days' work for those who fished illegally. The trade union sponsored the raising of rabbits for food and better care of cows and horses.[89] At Dneprostroi, specific departments were assigned to certain garden hectares to raise food.[90]

Did these measures improve the food supply? Some vegetables were produced, especially potatoes, but food remained desperately short. Seed grain was lacking, as were horses to pull the plows. In 1933, the calls for workers to help out in sowing were more strident than those in 1932 and aroused less response. Workers could barely do the work absolutely required without turning out for extra meetings and extra labor. A 1933 survey reported that a bookkeeper spent 2000 calories, a metal worker 3000, a blacksmith 4100, and a rockbreaker 4800, when the cafeteria meals provided 300 to 600 calories, not counting bread, and the bread, approximately 100 grams, provided about 210 calories.[91]

Poor nutrition contributed to the general ill health, as did the intensely crowded living conditions in poorly built barracks. The summer of 1930 saw an increase in smallpox, scarlatina, and typhus. Tuberculosis, gastrointestinal disease, typhus, and typhoid were serious concerns, the latter aggravated by inadequate sanitation, the absence of sewers in some areas, and the absence of potable water. Venereal disease increased sharply. Free vaccinations and consultations for the healthy as well as the sick were made available as the medical services tried to hinder the spread of infection. Doctors even advertised their services and clinics in the newspaper to alert workers to the availability of medical help. The water system suffered filtration problems, but the most important factors in the spread of disease were the overloading of existing sanitation facilities and their absence in the areas of new housing.

The dangerously poor health of students was blamed for their low attendance and achievement in school. The health of babies and children became so much of a problem that special diet centers were established where children could get milk and diet supplements.[92] Industrial accidents increased in number and were related to the accelerated tempo in the face of increasingly harsh living and working conditions. Medical services could not keep up with demand.

A discussion of the cost of illness is remarkable in its absence. Much attention was given, particularly in the spring months, to measures to combat epidemics of typhus, spotted fever, and small pox, so one must conclude that the number of deaths and the time lost were so great that they could not be revealed without discredit. The disorganization of medical services was last reflected in a report on Dneprostroi in 1931. It remarked on the crowded conditions, bedding of the sick with the healthy, beds placed in bathrooms and corridors, the absence of emergency care and transportation, the doctor seeing an average of seventy to eighty patients a day instead of the norm of thirty-five.[93] The article also pointed out the comparably worse conditions in surrounding villages and called for water pipes, the repair of sewers, and construction of additional medical facilities.[94]

The chief concern of the party and trade union, however, was not the fading of the goal of the workers' good life but rather the negative effect of these conditions on labor discipline, especially on the stability of the work force. In the early period of construction, living conditions were discussed in terms of the workers' interests and regarded by the trade unions as an area where the workers' and state-as-employer's interests might diverge. But after 1929, party and union policies treated housing and food as instruments in labor discipline and ultimately production growth rather than essentials in the workers' well-being. Living conditions could have been improved only by the slowing of the pace of construction—a choice not considered by the industrializers.

Conclusion

The accelerated tempo of industrialization and collectivization had an irrevocable influence on the development of the labor force. The forced pace was set by the self-confident and ambitious Stalin and his faction and was supported by many regional leaders and enterprise managers with coinciding goals. As Vinter had done in 1927, these industrializers substituted men for machinery as what had begun as a temporary stop-gap measure became policy. Justifications abounded. Machinery was not immediately available; it was costly, especially of foreign exchange, which was in short supply. It put available resources—human beings—to work instead of delaying their employ or waiting for scarce resources for productive purposes. Such productive full-time employment of labor in state industry and its transfer out of agriculture, private, and semiprivate sectors was desirable for both political and economic reasons.

Collectivization and the mass mobilization of labor caused significant social change in the latter part of the first Five-Year Plan. A massive transfer of population occurred as many peasants left their rural agricultural life for an urban and proto-urban industrial one. The violence of collectivization and the deprivations of rural life drove peasants from the countryside, bitterly antagonistic to the party which had appropriated their lands. Demoralized, they came to work which they had not chosen and for which they had no training. At the same time, the upheaval associated with collectivization disturbed patterns of seasonal labor, some of which dated to much earlier in the imperial period. The absence of seasonal laborers in 1930 contributed to the labor shortage.

The policy of unrestrained labor recruitment of 1931 caused serious problems. There were no plans or organizations for mobilizing workers in the needed numbers. The ad hoc measures developed—enterprise and state recruiters and *orgnabor*—added to the competition among enterprises and contributed to turnover without meeting the demand for labor.

The violence of collectivization and the deprivations of rural life drove peasants from the countryside at the same time as the industrial sector recruited workers with promises of better living conditions and career possibilities.

The composition of the enlarged work force changed. The party recruited first among hereditary workers' families—hiring wives and urban domestic workers and signing up workers' children in the factory schools—but these population sectors were soon exhausted. After 1930, the typical recruit was a young, unskilled, inexperienced peasant, as likely to be female as male as the supply of young males began to run out. Finally, there were changes in the domiciles as numbers of non-Russian, non-European, and, ultimately, non-Slavic workers were mobilized in the Ukraine, Siberia, and areas of Central Asia.

This new heterogeneous work force of rural origins, crowded and hungry, did not fit the model planned in the earliest stages of the first Five-Year Plan. In 1927, party and trade union officials had been writing about creating a sense among workers of unity and commitment to the construction project at Dneprostroi, but during the next year and thereafter, their reports reflected the difficulties of communicating with workers of a wide variety of backgrounds and interests, dispersed on a large site in diverse types of work, with goals increasingly at variance with those of their employers. Certainly the harsh living conditions contributed to the labor turnover and therefore to the labor crisis. Further, the party's unwillingness to provide for improved living conditions soured the prospects for cooperation between it and the majority of workers. Nevertheless, party leaders were determined to meet the goals of the accelerated plan. Reaching for the Five-Year Plan targets, the party looked to its training programs and tried a range of positive and negative incentives to stimulate productivity.

6

Production
and Productivity

It would be foolish to think that the production plan is a mere enumeration of figures and assignments. Actually the production plan is the living and practical activity of millions of people. The reality of our production plan lies in the millions of working people who are creating a new life. The reality of our program lies in living people, you and I, our will to work, our readiness to work in the new way, our determination to fulfill the plan. Have we that determination? Yes, we have. Well then, our production program can and must be fulfilled.

Stalin, speech delivered to a Conference
of Business Executives, June 23, 1931

The party gave top priority to meeting production targets while cutting costs in the latter years of the first Five-Year Plan. The party leaders knew that more workers alone could not achieve the expanded targets of the first Five-Year Plan and the goals of future growth. As total production rose too slowly to meet planned targets and costs soared, party leaders realized that they had to develop policies to cut expenses and utilize scarce resources more efficiently than before.

Total production had risen, but it was largely a result of the expansion of the work force. The number of workers doubled during the first Five-Year Plan period, growing from 11.5 million to 22 million, 162 percent more than planned. The labor force in construction grew even faster. It quintupled; the numbers grew from 623,000 to 3,126,000, 226 percent over plan. The costs of production, moreover, rose steadily. Productivity was to increase 85 to 110 percent according to the Five-Year Plan.[1] Industrial costs, however, actually rose during the period by at least 2.3 percent according to Soviet statistics, and more by Western estimates.[2]

When party leaders addressed plan targets, they were more concerned with achieving a level of production than with its cost. From the beginning, party exhortations extolled cost containment only in a general fashion, while exuberant praise went to those who fulfilled and overfulfilled production targets. Discussion of cost-saving techniques was unspecific. Savings were supposed to come from improved administration, from such items as the better work resulting from the work force's growing experience, and from use of the most progressive technology.

As costs continued to rise, however, party leaders and enterprise managers addressed the problems of productivity with increasing attention. At Dneprostroi, the party district committee and trade union committee resolved in 1930 to raise production twenty-five percent and to cut costs fifteen percent.[3] This resolution was passed in spite of the fact that serious cost overruns had occurred the previous year. Productivity had failed to rise the mandated thirty to forty percent.[4] Campaigns to cut costs followed one after another with increasingly modest goals, from twenty-five percent to ten percent.

The managers and party officials at Dneprostroi and throughout the industrial sector experimented with different policies to raise production while cutting costs. For example, state agencies and the trade unions promoted training programs. The party-state appointed investigative commissions, passed laws attacking problems of administrative mismanagement and labor force indiscipline, and introduced important incentive pay schedules. This chapter will discuss these policies and others and their results—their effect on productivity and on labor attitudes toward work. Moreover, it will consider the long-term significance of the measures, particularly as they influenced labor-management relations.

Upgrading the Skills of the Work Force

At the time of the acceleration of the industrialization tempo, technical training at Dneprostroi was at a turning point. The administration had successfully handed over many of the general education responsibilities to the local city council so that enterprise resources were available for the more specialized training of the work force. A network of informal study groups had been supplemented by the enlarged construction school and the establishment of a polytechnical institute. The training provided and accumulated experience had contributed to increased productivity among certain skilled workers.[5] The majority of the work force, however, was still unskilled.

Some workers were still so new to industrial working and living conditions that they needed very basic information about health, especially sanitation, and literacy. Mikhailov, the deputy chief engineer, said that many needed agitprop pep talks about the importance of industrialization, the project, and each worker's obligation to maintain labor discipline.

Skills training, however, was most important to the government. The Commissariat of Labor supplied funds for some courses. Others were established under the aegis of the trade unions, the Commissariat of Education, and the administration.[6] The most prestigious technical institution at Dneprostroi was the polytechnical institute, founded in December 1929 and scheduled to prepare graduates in 1930. Its opening was delayed, however, first by disputes over the type of education to be offered,[7] then by lack of funds for buildings, teaching materials, and teachers. The administration allocated some funds, but even then professors refused to move to the site and courses were further delayed. By 1931, the construction faculty was the only one operating. It regularly trained about six hundred students. This number grew by the end of the year to one thousand. The students found classroom space where they could; there was no school building until 1932.[8] They combined work and study with difficulty. Many left home at four A. M. in order to be on time for their jobs and returned only at six P. M.[9] Many in the engineering profession raised questions about the suitability of the schedule which tried to combine so much practical work with professional training. They protested strongly when the term was shortened in 1931, complaining that the students were too young and ignorant.[10]

Already in the fall of 1930, moreover, serious doubts were being raised about the success of the schools and the quality of the technical training that workers could claim. Not more than half the students registered were actually attending courses.[11] The courses were very short and taught at a very low level. In the increasingly crowded conditions of 1930, the party meeting spaces ("red corners"), where the basic literacy classes and basic "Technology for the Masses" courses were held, were being taken over for sleeping accommodations. They were not free for lecture and study. Further, the short-term worker had little time or opportunity to learn new technology on the job or to join a course and stay with it long enough to learn anything. Even if a seasonal worker were inclined to make the effort to attend a class after an arduous working day, he, and especially she, found it difficult to get into classes which discriminated in favor of the urban, so-called permanent workers with worker origins and against those from the countryside. Workers with appropriate social origins did not have the educational background necessary for more formal education in technology and engineering. Some of them entered special preparatory courses and went on to technical institutes, but the extra schooling delayed their entry into the ranks of specialists. Other candidates were drawn from the white-collar classes, a solution the class-conscious party officials did not welcome. Finally, workers who acquired new skills often found it very difficult to use them. Workers were assigned in massive numbers to specific jobs as they needed doing and as the workers became available. The newly mastered skill was not necessarily the one needed just then, so the worker often had to work and earn as an unskilled worker.

The poor levels of production and the falling growth rate in 1931 stimulated even more interest in labor training.[12] The trade unions opened courses and encouraged everyone to enroll. Thousands of workers signed up; by mid-October, there were some 22,000. By November, 31,733 of 36,360 were in some kind of school.[13] More students attended the workers' evening school and the higher technical courses (VRSh, VTK). According to a site study published in January 1932 at Dneprostroi, some 3500 studied in the workers' evening schools in 1931.[14] In accordance with current party policy, most of those admitted had a worker background (84 percent worker, 17 percent peasant, 4 percent employee). There were a few women, 12 percent, up from none to 5 percent in 1930. Few of the students had much earlier education: 71.3 percent had learned to read and write at home; 24.7 percent had finished four-year school; 4 percent had attended seven-year school.

The work of the school during 1931 was increasingly linked to the daily work of the site. It combined lectures and brigade work, group work in laboratories, offices, and with master workmen. The teachers, largely the engineering-technical personnel of Dneprostroi, attended teaching conferences, where they discussed how to combine onsite instruction and more traditional study. But results were poor. The work of teachers and students was highly vulnerable to turnover. In 1931, twenty percent of the school body left and was replaced by new students. When a teacher left, the replacement was likely to start the course over again from the beginning.[15] There was no school building. The courses were held in dark, crowded, and freezing quarters. "Boredom makes nervous those left very tired by the working day; and whole groups throw their studies up entirely."[16] The lecturers were equally badly off as responsible members of the already-burdened, small, technological intelligentsia. "The *stroika* had first demand on their time," and they felt the frustration of being asked to do the impossible.[17] Transfers meant that even eager students and teachers left the system.

The higher technical schools with fifteen hundred students in 1931 suffered from similar problems. They offered courses designed to meet the immediate needs and resources of the site. But there was often no way of knowing exactly which specialty would be needed or in what numbers. Absenteeism was a problem; 6 percent of the students on an average on a given day were at work on the site, 15 percent were at community duties, and 2.5 percent were ill.[18] Illness among students became a matter of increasing concern during the year.[19] There was no building, and teachers were overworked. Finally, the students took the shorter, easier courses. Graduates were increasingly hard to place.[20] The chief emphasis in the schools came to be on raising productivity on the job, and prizes were given to those who could work fastest. A contemporary slogan alleged that shock brigade work habits would carry over usefully into education: "Shock work—productive practice to shock study."

Some workers arrived with training by Ustanovka, a training organization working all over the Soviet Union. Ustanovka sent more than three thousand workers and teachers to Dneprostroi between January 1 and June 1, 1931, including carpenters, bricklayers, fitters, concrete pourers, plasterers, and pipe layers. Their skills were so poor, however, that further training had to be hurriedly organized: "They didn't deserve to be called skilled and drove all to wring their hands. Wherever they worked there was constant conflict." They did nothing of quality or on time. Fully discredited, they came to be used as unskilled workers.[21] Reduced so in rank, they earned "miserable pay," and forty percent of them left after having had expectations of being paid as skilled workers.[22]

Matters did not improve in the following years. Some on-the-job training was done by older workers helping new ones.[23] Students were recruited to the factory schools (FZU), the evening factory schools, and technical circles, rather than directly to the job. Special efforts were made to recruit women. The Central Committee even sent specific directives to major *stroiki* such as Magnitostroi, outlining how they should train skilled construction and factory workers to meet their needs.[24] But the problems of the preceding years continued.[25] Inspectors of training found facilities at Magnitostroi wanting in space, equipment, and teachers.[26] In March 1932 at Dneprostroi, only thirty percent of the six hundred students passed the evening school courses, and the party complained that too few of the engineering-technical personnel were teaching.[27] Students continued to say that they felt pressured to "put away their courses" until the factories were built.[28]

Although the major problems of 1930 continued unabated, workers developed certain skills. Some earned particular praise and pay by learning techniques new to the Soviet scene, such as steam crane and derrick operation, pneumatic drilling, and mechanical dump-car operation. Moreover, on the basis of even limited technical skills and moderate experience, these workers became foremen and brigade leaders. Many thousands moved out of construction into the ranks of workers in the factories that they themselves had built.

Specialists

One of the special problems to be addressed was the attitude of the newly trained engineer. Party members hoped to be creating specialists who would be devoted to party goals. They found, however, that many engineers had their own goals. Some left their jobs because of harsh conditions or for higher pay. Laws forbade one enterprise to recruit from another or to offer a higher salary for a comparable job, in an effort to control such movement.[29] The party ordered individual enterprises to send quotas of specialists to other enterprises, but the evidence suggests that administrations and the engineers themselves found ways to circumvent undesirable assignments. For example, in July, Dneprostroi responded to an order to send twenty specialists to Magnitostroi by approving ten, a number later cut to six. Magnitostroi complained that it never received any. Too often, engineers refused to leave Moscow, Leningrad, or Kiev and to go where they were sent. In addition, those at the more established sites avoided service in the newer *stroiki* farther east.

Engineers were suspect in matters other than immediate pecuniary self-interest. "Were the new engineers not too much like their predecessors?" asked one reporter.[30] Did they not act as if knowledge set them apart? At Dneprostroi, the trade union reported in January 1930 that the engineer-technical personnel union club was inaccessible to the workers.[31] The accusation was repeated months later in December by *Postroika*, the construction union newspaper. It noted that the club had only six workers among its 463 members. The club counted forty-one party members and fifteen members of the Komsomol who might have been expected to encourage a higher number of worker members. The club's large library was technical and contained no political books. The focus in the club circles was "not on things that would interest a worker." The social division was evident during the holiday on December 7, the celebration of the concrete plan completion, when not one worker was present.[32]

Not only were some engineers dangerously close to setting themselves apart as an elite stratum, but some were insufficiently supportive of the plan targets in the eyes of the party leaders. In the early months of the year, party leaders reminded specialists that they could not be apolitical, that "those not with us are against us." Criticism of the accelerated plan was associated with conservatism, with Right Opposition, and with "political error," even political opposition.[33] Engineers and specialists in administrative positions were reminded that "objective reasons" for not meeting the plan were not acceptable. They were told, "enough talk about troubles, conquer them!"[34] In November, prominent engineers who had criticized development plans on the basis of their specialized knowledge were brought to trial as rightists, seeking to slow development, and as saboteurs of the industrialization plan. They were convicted and imprisoned, but numbers of them continued their professional work in confinement, under guard, and without pay. Many had been associated with the *stroiki*, including S. A. Kukel-Kraevskii, who had been involved in an argument over the construction of a transmission line from Dneprostroi to the Don Basin. This was a project often mentioned by Stalin and politically important to his supporters. These trials and sentences discouraged independent thinking and silenced expert comment by Soviet engineers.

Gearing Up to Improve Productivity

Dneprostroi fell farther and farther behind target in spite of the extra time and funds allotted in 1928 accommodating the enlarged project. A team sent by the central government's Worker-Peasant Inspection in 1930 reported that more than ten million rubles could be saved in administration, materials handling, and better use and assignment of labor and administrative personnel. For example, building iron was stockpiled at a time when iron was in short supply and expensive, extra (seventy-five percent above plan) special issue clothes were bought, certain skilled workers could have been replaced with rank-and-file workers, and extra labor was used to maintain tempo when more use of drills, excavators, and steam cranes would have led to work more efficiently done at less cost.[35] Instead of responding to such criticisms, Mikhailov, deputy chief engineer, gave his attention to the tempo of construction. He concentrated resources on concrete pouring in the dam foundations and ensured that the monthly plan was met. All other sectors, however—the locks, powerhouse, and rock excavation—fell behind schedule.[36] This last held a double threat: the rock which had to be removed so the foundations could be laid was a necessary ingredient for the making of concrete; a serious delay in rock excavation had therefore the potential of slowing other work.

The biggest production achievement at Dneprostroi, and one held up as an example all over the Soviet Union, was the record-breaking pouring of five hundred thousand cubic meters of concrete in 1930. It was achieved, however, only by the continued stripping of men and materials from the other sectors of the project which then fell ever farther behind plan.[37] In addition, productivity dropped overall on the site. Rock excavation, for example, fell from three and a half cubic meters to two cubic meters.[38]

Even the expanded use of machines did not bring costs down, although production totals rose in a few departments. At Dneprostroi in midyear 1931, *Postroika*, the construction union paper, reported that machines were only used at fifty percent of capacity in the first quarter and fifty-five to sixty percent in the second.[39] Even lower rates were reported for the newer *stroiki*; at Svirstroi the percentage use was twenty-five to thirty,[40] and at Magnitostroi reports ran as low as five to thirty percent.[41]

Site administrators moved from simply noticing that machines were not used to keeping records on their hours of use, productivity, the causes for their idleness, and the length of time they spent under repair. Records of hours of use and explanations of idleness directed attention to a number of other problems. Often fuel or water was absent. Sometimes skilled operators were missing, sometimes appropriate work. At other times, a machine remained idle because the department holding it had no immediate work for it but would not let it go to another department, or because no one claimed it for work, not knowing how to reorganize a department's work so as to apply machinery or enough about a given machine's capabilities to use it fully. At Dneprostroi, there was much publicity on the use of machines, their care, efficient operation, and the need to raise productivity with machines. National figures, however, showed a decrease in machine use during 1932 in spite of an increase in the investment in machines.[42] The 1931 plan had forecast a fifty percent use nationwide, but only about twenty-two percent had been achieved. Early in 1932, this percentage dropped even farther.[43] Breakdowns were an obvious cause of machine idleness. One author writing on the construction sector reported that breakdowns in excavators accounted for forty percent of their idleness in 1931 and seventy-five percent of their greater idleness in 1932.[44] He reported, however, that the greatest cause of idleness was the absence of need for their particular product. Machines contributed little to productivity, which was due to rise sixty-five percent but rose not more than fifteen percent.[45] The "machine park" was only half used, and instead of 6.3 million man-days saved, only 1.3 million were saved.

Almost as much was hoped for from rationalization of work processes as from mechanization. Party reporters claimed that the inefficient use of both skilled and unskilled labor impeded productivity. They variously ascribed it to the absence of materials, machines, transport, designs, and supervisory personnel. For example, "only twenty percent of the workers work a full day," a Dneprostroi reporter claimed.[46] At Magnitostroi, rock breakers were idle twenty-seven percent of the day and earth movers twenty-four percent because of poor planning by the administration.[47]

The use of skilled labor in unskilled work or in work other than that in which workers were specially trained was wasteful. As early as July 1930, in the coal mines, a special brigade of party workers and specialists taught brigades to organize their work processes and utilize assistants.[48] A party resolution in 1931 mandating the assignment of workers to those who filled their day best was not, however, heeded at this time.[49] At Magnitostroi, the percentage of their days that workers spent on work for which they were not qualified ranged from fifteen to twenty-six.[50] The Dneprostroi press regularly complained that skilled workers were working at unskilled work.[51] When a skilled worker loaded or unloaded materials because the unskilled worker failed to show up, he was wasting his time,[52] whereas with the efficient use of unskilled assistants, skilled workers increased production.[53] Also contributing to the "inefficient" use of workers, economists argued, was the growth in the average absenteeism of workers because of community obligations, which rose from 0.98 (1931) to 1.44 days (1932); the growth in the number of vacation days, from 7.17 (1931) to 8.88 days (1932), and the high number of days of absence with the administration's prior agreement, 4.56 days in both years.[54] Labor analysts argued that administrators were remiss in organization and could do much to activate reserves of labor, especially skilled labor, already on the site. However, frequent turnover among technical supervisory personnel hindered the development of such improved management.[55] Because of frequent job changes, supervisors found it difficult to know their assignments or their workers.

Party organizers supported administrative efforts for better plan fulfillment by sponsoring local versions of national mobilization campaigns. The party encouraged workers to sign contract agreements which obligated signers to pursue the goals of raising production and cutting costs. Party directives popularized the production-financial plan which outlined the financial targets set for the various tasks and urged workers to study, meet the targets, and even produce more within their limits. In recognition of hard currency shortages, they conducted campaigns against the too eager use and ordering of foreign-made materials and machines and encouraged workers to invent home-manufactured substitutes. To overcome supply bottlenecks, in 1931, the party introduced the "through" (*skvoznyi*) brigade to see that materials and machines ordered in one department or workshop were completed on time and delivered to their authorized destination.[56] A campaign introduced the tugboat (*buksir*) brigade, in which one experienced and productive brigade "took in tow" a less experienced brigade and helped it to improve its productive record.[57] Party activists promoted the introduction of technological improvements by encouraging workers' suggestions with contests and cash prizes. The party had a sort of populist attitude toward technology with the underlying assumption that all suggestions were equally valid—an attitude never welcome to the engineering-technical personnel (ITR) or their union. Engineers heartily disliked the necessity of reviewing the suggestions and did their best to pass them off to special commissions.[58]

Frequently the party mobilized workers for special tasks. Volunteers were drafted from among students, clerical workers, and townspeople for certain civic construction jobs at Dneprostroi. This work was not well organized, remarked one commentator, who saw the men doing the light work and the women out with the shovels.[59] The wrong tools were used, and people wore the wrong shoes. Workers got in one another's way.[60] City officials tried to help but without much effect. One correspondent noted that officials in line to pass shovelfuls of dirt in fact dropped the dirt in the first pass and simply passed an empty shovel.[61] In its zeal to draft extra laborers as volunteers, the party invested resources into getting numbers of workers out into the field but lacked management reserves for their proper direction. It accepted poor, token work in return for volunteers' participation in party-sponsored after-hour and free-day work projects. It expanded the scope of its demands over the population but wasted both managerial and volunteer time and energy.

Changes in the Pay Scales

The party tested numerous incentives to stimulate workers to extra effort throughout the first Five-Year Plan, not least among them piece rates and graduated pay scales. The poor performance of labor in 1930 in the face of the higher plan targets caused serious concern in organizations responsible for labor motivation. The indices in early 1931 looked even worse.

In January 1931, the trade union council reviewed the cost effectiveness of the "new, socialist" forms of work. Shock work and socialist competition brigades had helped raise production, but they were costly. The brigade system made it difficult to distinguish between good workers and bad, skilled and unskilled, and it was difficult, therefore, to encourage the good and the skilled. Further, costs were not counted, just the final product, so that efficiency and cost control were not promoted. The council also considered pay schedules, especially the use of pay rates to promote desirable behavior such as regular attendance, longevity, and improved skills. A party resolution (March 3) on labor included sections on norm setting and the broad expansion of piece rates. As in 1930, pay incentives and bonuses continued to be given to reward regular appearance at work over time. Nonfinancial incentives were offered as well. For example, to combat turnover: "Workers contracting to stay to the end of construction have the right in the first order to rest homes and sanatoria."[62]

Discussion of pay in June 1931 specified that pay and bonuses or prizes should interest the worker in raising output and cutting costs. This theme was struck by Stalin on June 23 when he listed six conditions necessary for the success of industrialization, including a new pay schedule. He attacked the equalization of pay, or *uravnilovka*, as opportunistic and recommended the differentiation of pay as a way to draw workers into jobs demanding more skills and training. He also advocated more attention to costs and more managerial responsibility for cost containment. Stalin's speech gave the seal of approval to a new direction in labor policy.

The new premium pay schedule introduced in August 1931 encountered serious opposition on practical and ideological grounds. As in most economies, workers and managers alike resisted the expansion of piece rates. The new piece rates and the prize system differentiated among workers by valuing types of work at different rates. Such task definition and the writing of norms was difficult in construction work. This was partly caused by the great variation in conditions on different sites and in different regions, the uncertainities of supplies, transport, and the weather. There was also a serious shortage of personnel capable of or interested in setting norms, tracking their achievement, or calculating the appropriate pay.

Further, historically workers had resisted piece rates and the pitting of one worker against another in quantity production. In the early days of Dneprostroi, many workers had accepted piece rates as the only available escape from the very low daily rates at which norms were already high. At first, they resisted doing the extra work demanded by shock work and socialist competition by ignoring the campaigns. Under heavy pressure from the party to conform, they joined in the competitions, setting the lowest possible goals and in such numbers that nearly all earned the associated rewards. The new 1931 extension of piece rates and the premium system for extra work beyond the norm was seen to threaten existing norms; record production feats were sure to be turned into new norms and more work for everyone for unchanged pay.

The new system was widely publicized during the fall months. It produced a range of new problems throughout the Soviet Union. Where there were no norms, the prize system simply raised the workers' pay; premiums for speed were paid for work below the norm without distinguishing work done above the norm, so no stimulus was given to counter "equalization"; the pay structure did not distinguish between useful and less useful work, nor did it acknowledge quality of work or material use. In construction, the most immediate result was that pay began rising faster than production. For example, at Zavodstroi (part of the United Dnepr Construction), pay rose six percent while production rose only three percent.[63] (See Table 18.) In another department at Dneprostroi, salaries gained one hundred twenty-seven percent while production rose only fifty-seven percent.[64]

As workers and production rates failed to respond to the new policy, party leaders looked to local party organizations and members for direct participation in the production process. Special committees of party members went into enterprises to form special accounting brigades, lead shock work, review living conditions, and energize the rank-and-file

Table 18. Production and the Pay Fund: Zavodstroi, 1931

	% Plan complete	% Pay fund paid out
April	0.90	100.0
May	0.95	104.0
June	0.97	107.5
July	103	112.6
August	103	112.6
September	101	113.6
October	102	112.6

Source: F. Zilberbrod, I. Dobzhinskii, E. Kochetovskaia, Tselmin, "Za nemedlennuiu realizatsiiu vtorogo ukazaniia t. Stalina na novostroikakh, *Voprosy truda,* nos. 2/3 (1933), pp. 2–3.

members. In their efforts to improve productivity by improving labor discipline, party members erected blackboards on which they inscribed the names of backsliders—those late and absent without leave, drunks, and careless and wasteful workers. One enterprise reported that blackboards had proved ineffective and ran show trials to make the point.[64]

In 1932, in order to force workers to use their time more efficiently, expand production, and cut costs, party leaders urged enterprises to implement aggressively the new progressive premium pay scale introduced in August 1931. Very few in construction (five to thirteen percent) had switched to the individual or small, one-rank group (*zveno*) piece-rate system in 1931.[65] Collective piece rates by rank (*razriad*) and brigade continued to predominate. Resistance to the progressive premium came from different directions. Some workers complained, "We don't want to work for individual pay; in the countryside we wanted to, and many were sent to Solovki. We don't want to be eliminated as *kulaki*." "We don't understand what's going on; in the countryside you're rounded up into collective farms, while here you're divided up as individuals." "I don't want to earn more; you'll just come to my home all the same and destroy me as a *kulak*."[66]

The new system was used by some for their own purposes. Brigade leaders who were advocates for their workers could use it to increase their pay. It was, for example, useful to a brigade leader to report fewer days and more work done in order to earn premiums.[67] There were no strict guidelines which made it possible to distinguish between useful and unprofitable work, so some performed the latter. And it often happened that hurried quantity work meant that quality was poor, and even that work had to be redone.

Authors of the premium system hoped it would draw able workers to learn skills and skilled workers into positions of technical supervision and managerial responsibility where they could earn more. This the system failed to do. It was still possible for an earth worker to earn more than a more skilled carpenter, a cleaner more than a skilled worker.[68] Because a brigade leader was usually elected by the brigade, members wanted their leaders paid the same as they were so that theirs and the leaders' interests would be the same. The leader was usually paid with his brigade, so it often happened that a brigade leader earned less than a worker in a nonsupervisory position being paid as an individual piece worker or working in another, more productive brigade. One suggestion made to counter this was that brigade leaders be paid separately as managers.[69]

Would the progressive premium system together with new norms and incentives for low-level managers promote greater production at less cost? It seemed to the party leaders and planners that something more was needed. At Dneprostroi, the party press urged all workers to form *khozraschet* brigades, which kept their own accounts and were responsible for keeping within the production and financial plan. Such autonomous accounting had been extended to individual enterprises in December 1929 as a part of the effort to strengthen the enterprise manager and to make him more responsible for the efficiency of his operation.[70] Special prework shift meetings were organized in 1930 and 1931, during which workers were to review the day's work in terms of costs as well as physical achievements. Stalin mentioned better financial accounting as essential in his speech in June 1931, always a sign of priority for party policy. In the early months of 1932, financial responsibility was shifted down. More was said about the importance of accounting and responsible leadership at the brigade level. Failure to participate made one an "opportunist"; *khozraschet* was "politically important," for "it involved every worker and manager" in lowering costs and raising production. But *khozraschet*, the object of a mass mobilization campaign in 1932, proved to have serious weaknesses. It controlled for meeting schedules and limiting waste, but it did not balance these with the cost of labor, raw and partially prepared materials, repairs, and supplementary services. Further, in response to party exhortations, many brigades were formed, but many were only on paper; they did not actually count costs and did not work to keep costs within the financial plan. Generally, the effort was unproductive.

The Role of the Party

The expansion of the party's role was the most fundamental development in party policy during the latter part of the first Five-Year Plan. The task of maintaining the tempo marked the party organization and its members, their definition of their role, and the manner of executing their tasks.

At Dneprostroi, as in the city factories, the local party organization was responsible for local collectivization. It had to popularize, explain, and win support for the decision. It recruited and sent out some of its most experienced and stable workers as activists or "25,000-ers."[71] In the barracks, the party strove to counteract the angry reports of the displaced, disenfranchised peasants who had fled the violence in the countryside.[72] It painted the war against the peasants as one against speculators and obdurate enemies of industrialization and the party government.

At the same time, it reported on malcontents to the next higher party organizational level.

As discussed earlier, the party played the leading role in collectivization. It also mobilized its own organization and masses of workers in a wide variety of campaigns promoting industrialization, such as subscribing to industrial loans, recruiting women to the work force, or submitting technological innovations. As seen above, the party recruited brigades to improve production levels and meet budgets and campaigned for shock troops and a stable labor force. Production-oriented party-sponsored campaigns intensified in 1930. The party turned to its members, to the Communist Youth League (Komsomol), and to the trade unions, telling them that production targets were their direct responsibility.

In spite of the fact that costs had been rising (twenty-five percent since plan acceleration), party directives mandated fifteen percent cost reduction in 1930 and an increase in productive work. The directives offered some guidelines. One was an increase in direct attention to the *stroiki*.[73] The Central Committee resolved that there were too few Communists directly involved in construction and announced the assignment by May 1 of twelve hundred Communists—half of a large town's quota was to go to nearby construction work and half to the large new *stroiki* in Siberia and the Urals. Each town was also to send two hundred workers for two-month stretches. Party cells on construction sites were reminded that the party membership included only one to two percent of the construction workers. Members were directed to strengthen their recruitment efforts. Party directives called for an organized approach to local party resolutions on socialist competition and campaigns to lower costs and raise quality, using models from Dneprostroi, Traktorstroi, Magnitostroi (Urals), Kuznetskstroi (Siberia), and Avtostroi (Gorkii) for production meetings (described above) and permanent cadre creation. Linking training to basic education, the Central Committee called for an end to illiteracy in two years. Finally, it ordered improved political work among seasonal workers so that construction workers would "initiate and organize" the socialist reconstruction of the country. The party also turned to the Komsomol and trade unions. The Komsomol was told to mobilize one thousand' volunteers. The construction workers' trade union was urged to increase its membership and to assign three thousand activists to work directly in construction. The open question was whether the assignment of hundreds of party and Komsomol members to Dneprostroi and the other *stroiki* would significantly affect production.

The party bureau campaigned against labor indiscipline, turnover, and absenteeism. It struggled to mobilize the mass of workers into shock work brigades and then to recruit the shock workers into the party, but with little success.[74] The Sixteenth Party Congress (1930) restructured the organization to bring the center of party activity to the basic production unit and to raise the personal responsibility of the individual party member for the quality of party leadership.[75] Even so, at Dneprostroi, the party members could not force workers to meet production targets. Plan completion fell from sixty percent in the spring to forty percent in some areas in August.[76] The struggle to complete the plan had to continue, the party press proclaimed, in spite of the Right Opposition and those who cited "objective conditions" as their excuse for poor performance.[77] The party press told the members "to stand firm in a bolshevik manner against interuption in their work," to mobilize the masses, and that "the party's most important task was to increase socialist competition and shock work."[78] In response to party pressure, a growing number of shock workers declared themselves. They went from 7.6 percent of the work force in January to 57.1 percent in March and sixty percent in September.[79] Failure to participate meant reduced wages and access to food.[80]

It was especially to the Komsomol that the party turned to mobilize young persons in the industrialization drive. Free of parental restraints; encouraged to criticize, investigate, and report on their elders and superiors as well as their peers; inspired by a popular dream of world revolution and social transformation, they were rewarded for their work, enthusiasm, and loyalty with training and advancement and access to whatever goods and services were available. As early as January 1930 and again in March, the Komsomol members lengthened their work days and in August gave up their holidays and days of rest. For two months, they took no time off so that the concrete-pouring plan might be met.

The Komsomol leaders publicized a portrait of the new socialist person through campaign speech making and newspaper vignettes describing contemporary heroes. These new heroes participated actively in community life and were careful with communal goods. They were active battlers for heightened productivity, creative in their search for the "new." Komsomol officials took a highly visible role in shock work, volunteer overtime, and socialist competition.[81] In February 1931, responding to the party draft for more technically trained workers, the Komsomol organized a campaign of members into workshops, with their "face to industry," and in two months some eighteen hundred students entered courses for machinists, electricians, foremen, and others. They signed up for shock work, production brigades, rationalization groups, and societies for carrying technology to the masses. They organized courses for themselves and others and read lectures in the barracks. They cleaned barracks, participated in sowing campaigns, and organized Pioneer brigades. In April, "they began the monthly battle with turnover, reviewed the condition of machinery, led a socialist hour, gathered up material endangered by flood conditions, and held meetings of the rationalization group and the Light Cavalier [a roving reporter "watchdog" group]."[82] They held public discussions on the role of the shock worker and the link of shock work with political and social work. They attacked absenteeism and high costs by organizing members of brigades to work collectively on these issues. They competed with older workers in mechanized work—to uncover and overcome "our Asiatic attitudes to machinery."[83] They organized courses to liquidate illiteracy and became patrons over nearby villages. In 1931, they reported sending out sixty-five Komsomol brigades for short periods of time, one hundred fifty members for full-time work as secretaries of village soviets, teachers, youth work, and collectivization, for a total involvement of one thousand fifty members.[84] It was in 1931 that the importance of the advent of the young worker became very clear. Because of their numbers, energy, idealism, ambition, and naiveté, the role of young workers was vital to the successful completion of Dneprostroi.

Much less successful in mobilizing workers and eliciting commitment was the trade union organization, so often considered the "school for communism" and a preliminary step toward party membership. In January 1930, 70.4 percent of the work force belonged to the trade unions, down from 81.6 percent in May 1929.[85] In September eleven thousand of the thirty thousand on the site belonged to the union, 37 percent.[86] The trade union officials blamed this lack of interest in part on changes in the work force itself, its large numbers of nonmembers, "the influx of *kulak*-type, self-seeking workers, experiencing a socialist environment for the first time."[87] The Rabochkom decided that it needed closer contact with the workers and resolved to achieve it by promoting more workers into trade union administration and placing them in newly created workshop bureaus.[88] In June 1930, the trade union organization was once again restructured, this time to move it away from a simple duplication of the administrative structure to functional organization, with different brigades of activists responsible for overseeing work with the countryside, the cafeteria, cadre training, culture, and production.[89] A 1930 survey of eighteen projects, including eight large industrial projects and among them Dneprostroi, produced the conclusion that the majority of the members were not interested in production, that the psychology of work was foreign to them, and that it was incumbent on the union to reeducate them.[90] The rules for entry into the union were revised and made very strict, and many members were expelled for improper conduct.[91] These new rules certainly reduced the membership numbers, but conditions on the site contributed as well. Most importantly, trade union membership was no longer necessary to those seeking work. Benefits for members only were few at a time when schools were seeking students, and extra food and services were earned by shock workers.

In spite of or perhaps because of the party and party-sponsored programs, economic problems multiplied. The plan shortfall and peasant resistance to collectivization had contributed to renewed dissension among party leaders in 1930. Some castigated the use of "shock methods," the unwillingness to face up to failure, and the fudging of results.[92] However: "It was a political error to think of reducing the plan" and rightist to ask "What if we can't do it?" the party press said, reflecting the Stalinist victory over those who had urged a slower pace.[93]

Many party members failed to be as active as the leadership demanded. During the summer and fall of 1930, the party press identified a serious discrepancy: while the number of participants in shock work and socialist competition had grown, many Communists and Komsomol were not among them. They were "not soldiers of construction but deserters!"[94] Party members were urged again and again to lead in the battle for construction. The best response, as we saw above, came from the Komsomol, whose members worked regularly in great numbers in their free time.

Doubt in the plan grew in the party, among party leaders and locally as well. Makar, secretary of the Dneprostroi party, who had railed against citing "objective conditions" as an excuse in April,[95] said at the end of the year that the record concrete pouring had been accomplished only by stripping all other sectors, and that near plan fulfillment was being achieved only through the substitution of a reduced plan for the original one.[96] Clearly, he no longer thought the plan was realistic. The trade union district committee had backed away from the forced tempo even earlier when it made the vital "political" error in July of advocating a lesser tempo.[97] In January 1931, the local *Proletar Dniprobudu*, "under the pretense of self-criticism," spoke out against socialist competition and the party organization of shock work and complained that nothing was working right, that there was no plan or perspective for the future.[98] Makar, although nominally responsible for leadership over the trade union and the newspaper, was not attacked for this slip-up. The central party leadership did, however, quietly transfer him. Perhaps he was saved from more serious punishment because of his effectiveness with the work force and his popularity.[99] M. L. Leibenzon, formerly chief of the regional (*okrug*) control commission, became the new secretary. The newspaper editorial board was changed, and *Pravda* called on the paper to correct its mistakes.[100]

The doubts in the plan expressed by committed party members were shared by the workers, many of whom were strongly antagonistic. Among these, of course, were the peasants driven from their farms. Many workers, too, felt the party was the enemy establishment, driving too hard and making conditions even worse than they had been under the tsars. "Communists are red exploiters," said one worker, who explained that he did not join the party because he wanted "to die an honest man."[101]

Moreover, the party membership included individual members and candidates who varied widely in their understanding and commitment to the leadership's goals. Already in April 1930, the party bureau recognized that it lacked authority over cell members. It attributed this to the fact that the five hundred new members just accepted were "little distinguished from other workers"; they needed lots of training.[102] This training was hard to organize as local party officials' and members' time was largely taken up with production tasks. "We'll pour cement, you [party educators] stick to your party studies. We have to use the season; you won't beat us if we don't form up five or six schools, but we'll have no peace if the concrete isn't attended to."[103] Less than half the membership subscribed to the local paper, the major source for the party line. Few attended the courses organized by party officials. Primary party schools were organized during the year, as well as six higher party schools and fifteen study circles.[104] But some schools never even started, and others closed as members and candidates failed to attend.[105]

In 1931, party leaders focused directly on party education and demanded that the local organization give it more attention. But their directives gave a mixed message, equating production achievements with ideological preparedness. Local party educators were told to prepare new party recruits from the best shock workers, *udarniki*, to develop an understanding of Marxist-Leninist theory and to combine it with revolutionary practice.[106] In response to two Central Committee decisions in March 1931, the Dneprostroi party restructured the school network so that workers could attend after their work shifts and carried out a monthly check on attendance and the quality of instruction.[107] Each cell became responsible for the schooling of its members. The network of schools which enrolled some twenty-eight hundred of the twenty-nine hundred party members in May 1931 included an evening communist academy, eleven evening Soviet party schools, nine Marxist-Leninist circles for activists, twelve circles of contemporary politics, thirty-five beginners' schools, and a number of other courses combining party and technical study such as those organized for the military and those within the VTUZ and evening workers' school.[108] These schools shared the problems of their nonparty counterparts. They were plagued by turnover, a shortage of instructors, and a serious absence of instructors who both knew the material and were able to teach. Finally, many cells were unable to produce an ideologically motivated rank and file, working not for their daily pay but for an undefined "socialist" future.

In July, the educational campaign had lost its momentum, and students had begun to drop out. The party committee tried to meet its obligations of publicizing the party line and mobilizing workers to support it by holding a one-day mass schooling. It organized shock brigades for special tasks, to make sure they were accomplished, and then recruited the most active and responsive workers directly into the party, sometimes a whole brigade at a time. Party education became more and more the study of slogans, especially the words of Stalin. Readiness for party membership was proven by participation in shock work, socialist competition, accounting brigades, and other activities that demonstrated a worker's or a group of workers' readiness to carry into action Stalin's prescriptions for greater production.[109] The impact on production continued to decline.

The party had moved to enroll whole brigades at a time in 1931 because party membership was not keeping up with the growth in the work force. It will be recalled that the Dneprostroi party grew initially by importing members from outside industrial sites. Then, between January 1929 and January 1930, it had doubled in size when 801 members and 446 candidates were taken in.[110] By May 1930, the number had settled at about 1850 members and candidates, about eight percent of the workers.[111] Of these, 1559 were workers, 161 peasants, and 150 employees in origin.[112] However, applications lagged in the first two quarters of 1931, and in the third there was none at all. Numerical levels were only maintained by extraordinary measures in the fourth quarter, when, in response to the party's energetic recruiting, one thousand candidates entered the ranks in the fourth quarter.[113] (See Table 19.)

Table 19. Membership in the VKP(b)

	Jan.	March	May	Sept.	Dec.
1929	831	—	722	1040	1144
1930	—	1247	1816	1800	—
1931	2108	1668	3000	0 growth 3rd quarter	3546

By the spring of 1932, the party had registered some important changes. It had increased in numbers and in proportion to the whole work force. There were 4937 party members, about 13.5 percent of 36,538 workers.[114] The overwhelming majority, 4316, were still of worker origin; 401 had peasant parents; 220 had clerical, white-collar parents. The number of women had grown to 418, approximately 8.5 percent of the party, about 10 percent of the female work force of 4030. The greatest national group was still Ukrainian; 2734 were Ukrainian, 1519 Russian, 292 Jewish, and 332 other; 897 were also members of the Komsomol, providing the leadership link between the party and the youth activists. However, more than half, and one source claims more than four fifths, were candidate members.[115]

The new members were chosen by the party recruiters for their activism in work and organization and co-opted to promote the leadership policies. They were not the experienced, skilled, and politically motivated workers on which the party had counted during its earlier years. With the large expansion of the work force, the ratio of prepurge and precollectivization to postcollectivization members dropped radically, particularly since one thousand had joined after the beginning of September 1931.[116] This meant that the party was relying increasingly on new members, politically naive, unfamiliar with Bolshevik history, especially its inner party struggles. Party recruiters sometimes signed up whole brigades at a time, so it is unlikely that the new candidates were making an ideological choice and more likely they were simply staying out of immediate trouble. The influx of new, inexperienced, unsophisticated workers had an impact on the party as the new members grew in proportion to the old and brought with them new career goals and new values.

The party turned directly to its members to press on with construction and industrial production in spite of the widespread hunger and demoralization. The central and local press carried speeches and stories which made clear that the model Bolshevik was enthusiastic about the plan, the work, the future. He came to work on time, worked full-time, and wasted no time. He made suggestions. He led his brigade in meeting the production and financial plans. He repaired machinery, trained tractor drivers, and helped the collective farm in whatever way he could. Biographies of model applicants to the party showed men and women who came to the site with peasant backgrounds, working, learning new ways, making suggestions for improved procedures, heroes and heroines in the common effort—and joining the party as their ultimate step. A Bolshevik "sang in the cold as if it were spring," his work gave him such pleasure.[117] Communists signed up in *khozraschet* brigades, socialist competition, volunteer work, civil government jobs, party schools, and antireligion circles.

Finding such a model Bolshevik was not easy, however. It was a particular problem in the construction industry, where the average party layer was two to three percent, although it was usually eight to ten percent on the giant *stroiki*. This self-selected group, moreover, harbored within its ranks those who were ignorant of or ignored some of the party's teachings and others who did not agree with the central leadership. Aware of the distress collectivization caused among its own party members, the Dneprostroi activists passed resolutions in January 1932 reminding its members what it was to be a Bolshevik. "Building socialism was not just industrialization, it included the reconstruction of agriculture," they wrote. And "class enemies" in the work force and in the barracks had to be uncovered and expelled. Class enemies were those who questioned the plan, collectivization, loan subscription, and the party line, even those who were apolitical. Further, "building socialism" necessitated the mastery of technical knowledge. Cadres, moreover, needed political training as well as technology in the schools. There they studied Marx, Lenin, Stalin, and party teachings in support of the monolithic party, antileft, antiright, antiopportunism and antispontaneity.[118]

But party members were not responding as hoped to the call for activists. At Dneprostroi, for example, among the skilled armature workers, there was no party work, even though twelve of the eighty were party members and all were trade union members. There was no Komsomol work, and only three of the eighty turned out for a "volunteer Saturday" that the majority had voted for. There was no Marxist-Leninist study.[119] For most Komsomol members, work on the construction was the sum total of their "duty."

It was not only for *khozraschet* that participation was on paper; this was true of socialist competition and shock work as well. Others followed the party directives but with no "ideological" commitment.[120] Party secretaries scoured their ranks for members to work with small groups of workers to improve production, to direct the work with young people and children, and to mobilize women to study, run for office, and participate in shock work and socialist competition.[121] The trade union committees were responsible for mobilizing workers to plant, care for, and harvest food for the enterprise cafeteria, but they failed to send workers on their days off as they were supposed to. Participation by party members in response to mobilization campaigns was little higher than that of nonmembers.

How was the party to succeed in carrying out its programs if its own members lagged in the campaigns or vacillated in their support of party resolutions? Clearly, it would be very difficult for waverers to assert leadership over the masses. The party leadership turned once again to put its house in order in 1932. Central party directives mandated the study, broad publication, and unequivocal implementation of its resolutions. The party members and affiliates were reviewed for loyalty and service. Membership documents among the Komsomol were checked in 1932; the administration and party at Dneprostroi were reviewed and purged in 1932 and 1933.[122] The targets of these purges included the malcontents, inactive members, nonpayers of dues, and poor administrators.[123] The purges also removed those who questioned the central party's methods and plans.[124] In the face of increasing hunger and distress at Dneprostroi and elsewhere, the party tightened its ranks and told each member to work and study and to remember "a Communist is not a rank-and-file fighter but a leader of the masses."[125]

In addition, moreover, the party managers in the field and the central policymakers adapted their strategy to the undeniable needs of the moment. Recognizing the great cost of labor in the overall production budget and concerned that workers were not able to produce more at less cost without attention to their needs and wants, the party devoted renewed efforts to increasing the food supply. It cut grain requisitionings and allowed some free trade in agriculture. Renewed public attention to cafeteria, housing, and certain goods and services signaled that some attention could now be diverted to these basic necessities. Funds, previously budgeted but never spent, were directed to safety, health, and insurance. Articles on labor safety and labor inspectors increased in number. Referring to the change in construction from a seasonal occupation, geared to the good weather, to a year-round one, a conference speaker remarked, "With the uninterrupted year, we forget the living person. Low temperature, wind, humidity affect not only construction materials but also the worker."[126] Administrators who held up or diverted social welfare funds were "unmasked." There was new attention to public services, sports, and even excursions for Pioneers and Komsomol. The party also officially limited the number of workers to be hired by tying their hire to the availability of living space and, more importantly, by requiring enterprises to reduce their labor demands and enforcing this by stricter wage fund control. In the second Five-Year Plan, the growth of the labor force ended its precipitous climb, growing thereafter at four percent annually. The rapid decline of the value of real wages leveled off, and the standard of living, at least on the industrial enterprises, began to recover.

Conclusion

The new tempo had a very negative effect on all aspects of Soviet development. As is well known, it led to near civil war with the peasantry; the death, imprisonment, and exile of many peasants; and famine in the Ukraine and other areas. The famine spilled over into industrial sites, where food was desperately short and workers always hungry. Peasants, escaping collectivization and its aftermath, flooded the construction sites and cities, looking for jobs, food, and security. Driven from their homes and lifelong employment, many of the older peasants hated the party, which they compared in its rapacity to its imperial predecessor. They bitterly resented efforts to teach them new trades and new goals. Many of the young peasant recruits, however, were more receptive to the party's mobilization campaigns. Most came to the *stroiki* with some elementary education and were soon enrolled in the many available short courses. Their readiness to learn challenged some party shibboleths about the inherent greater value of workers over peasants, for the young raw recruits regularly outlearned and outpaced the older workers. Brigade leaders and workers of all ages and skills signed up in mobilization campaigns, not because they accepted their premises but because they realized that they thereby improved their access to the limited goods and services. Their participation, however, was superficial, as was all too clearly demonstrated by rising costs and decreased productivity.

The party-supported training on the *stroiki* introduced technical training to the labor force. Many of the courses did little more than acquaint workers with rudimentary skills because of the lack of time, materials, continuity in the course of study, and appropriate placement procedures. The demands of the forced tempo meant that less money and time were given to advanced training courses as well, so partially trained workers had little depth in their training or basis for the accumulation of new or updated skills. The technical institutes had difficulty achieving a level of education adequate to the jobs at hand. The poor quality of their graduates forced a review of the institutions, their restructuring, and the return of many practices of prerevolutionary education. The prestige and rewards accorded the technical intelligentsia encouraged its members, old and new, to view themselves as a special group and helped lay the basis for a new elite, separated from the ordinary worker by its occupation in mental rather than physical labor, as in the prerevolutionary period. Nevertheless, party policy promoted widespread literacy, at least, and exposed workers to new ideas, industrial habits, and study in enough new techniques that they could move on to jobs elsewhere in industry, sharing the newly acquired knowledge with others.

The party had counted not only on the training of a corps of skilled workers for better production but also on increased use of machines. The difficulties they encountered in mechanization of construction can be attributed equally to the party's drive for speed and to the inexperience of the administrators and workers. Because of the pressure for results, enterprise managers tended to throw in extra workers in a massive attack on a particular task. It was easier to do this than to schedule the limited number of skilled workers, machines, and fuel; provide the supplementary equipment and materials; and have all this done and the task ready to be done. Such organization and rationalization of work took more time and experience than most administrators had. As a result, the industry did not utilize available technology.

Increased production and productivity, party leaders quickly realized, were going to take more than the training of workers and engineers. Pressure to recruit workers to socialist competition and shock work was increased. The expense and disruption caused by these campaigns, however, necessitated new ones—to unsnarl the disorder created by priority tasks competing with one another for limited personnel and resources and financial measures designed to make workers careful about costs. These measures, too, failed to solve the problems. Production lagged, and costs continued to rise. The party returned to using pay as an incentive, adopting sharply stratified pay schedules in an effort to reward the skilled, productive worker in a managerial position. However, although the policy increased workers' pay packages, it did not reduce production costs, particularly in construction, where costs were dependent on many variables of which productivity was only one, and one of the hardest to measure because of the nature of the work. Further, this appeal to materialistic desires did not drive workers to work more; there was little enough for them to buy. The needs of the population were barely met, and there was no extra food, housing, or consumer goods to offer as incentives.

Ultimately, as the economy failed to meet planned targets, the party leadership became more directly involved in administration. Party groups at every official level investigated and reported on management and labor. Whether it was the Worker-Peasant Inspection Committee or the cell nucleus in Dneprostroi's mechanical workshop, the party entities had to investigate and activate managers and workers. Increasingly, the party members were called on to command and coach others at work. They were held responsible for production shortfalls. Their inability to offer workers positive incentives made them rely increasingly on negative incentives, the denial of access to the already limited food, goods, and housing; choice of work; and freedom of movement.

As the party leaders turned to the rank and file of the organization for the execution of the industrial plan and management of the work force, they began a far-reaching administrative purge of those who worked badly or questioned the party line. Unproductive officials and any who, citing "objective conditions," tried to reduce the tempo were fired. To hone the party organization as a tool, the leadership ceased to accept new members in December 1932 and expelled more than a million over the next two years. Dropouts thinned party ranks by another million. With these purges (and later with the Terror), the party strove to ensure that the membership was loyal to the central leadership, accepted its guidance in the setting of all policies, and abjured criticism and the suggestion of alternatives.

7

Building Socialism

Our Debt to the Ukraine

Where, with burning vodka,
　　　　with daring,
　　　　　even with blood,
The Zaporozhskaia Sech'
　　　　seethed,
Taming the Dnepr
　　　　with a bridle of wires.
They'll force
　　　　the Dnepr
　　　　to flow across turbines
And the Dnipro
　　　　through wire whiskers
　　　　will flow through the blocks
As electricity. . . .

Vladimir Maiakovskii,
Dolq Ukraine, 1926

The history of Dneprostroi brings to life the difficulties of translating the ill-defined goals of "building socialism" into reality. The first Five-Year Plan was designed to carry forward Lenin's electrification plan and, ultimately, establish a modern industrial state in the largely traditional, rural, and agricultural society of the Soviet Union. Nevertheless, the planners who debated the construction of the Dnepr dam did not, could not, start with a completely new, ideologically based plan. Economists, engineers, and political leaders who had won their leadership in a variety of noneconomic careers worked with plans based largely on work done in the prerevolutionary era. They bargained among themselves as well as with representatives of different regions and institutions who argued vehemently about the allocation of funds, claiming past injustice, economic rationality, national strategic need, and a host of lesser causes. As we saw in their decision to proceed with Dneprostroi, the party planners with final say had to weigh project choices when no one could accurately estimate construction costs, time, availability of resources, or the relative social and economic value of the projects under consideration—yet all those elements were called for in the decision-making process.

Even as the process of planning was compromised in the beginning, it became even more so as the first Five-Year Plan began. Local enterprise chiefs, such as Vinter at Dneprostroi and later his counterparts at Magnitostroi, Kuznetskstroi, and others, claimed that they could build more extensively and faster than planned if given more credit and priority ratings. They enlarged their projects with support from the super-industrializers in the party, creating further demands for labor, supplies, and food—not to mention credit, foreign machinery, housing, and transportation. The stepped-up tempo was equally crucial in agriculture, where collectivization devastated food production. The party-state entered into a state of near war with the peasants. Many in the villages became hostile. Food and goods became scarce and expensive.

Collectivization compounded the problems of industry and compromised the future of Soviet economic development. Short of food for the workers, agricultural cash crops, and the imported foreign materials that agricultural exports supported, on top of its own problems, industrial production fell far short of targets in 1930. As a result, party leaders extended the operative fiscal year by three months, moving to the calendar year to give planners, producers, and fiscal agents an opportunity to draw up new plans.

As they struggled to fulfill their targets, Vinter and other enterprise administrators competed with the center for control over their own domains in financing, personnel, supplies, and labor. Vinter played a role—or interfered, their officials claimed—in town affairs and communal organizations in addition to managing Dneprostroi. Soviet enterprise managers had many ancillary tasks, as Vinter pointedly complained, comparing his work to that of an American construction engineer. He tried with limited success to make his own labor agreements, to find his own supplies and credits. Moreover, he tried, again with limited success, to shed responsibility for onsite family housing, education, medicine, and cultural activities. The party leaders' idea of transforming the social context of work coincided with the patriarchal legacy of providing extensively for the workers, but such provision hampered the work of managers who were short of money, time, and expertise. As the party leaders came to stress production targets above all, the managers gave their best efforts to fulfilling those targets and let their social obligations slide. The methods used by managers in pursuit of production successes contributed to the accelerating decline of working and living standards. Vinter's substitution of men for machines was followed everywhere. The cost and delays in ordering labor-saving machinery, the shortage of skilled operators and managers experienced in their use, and the absence of service and spare parts pushed mechanization into the future. In the meantime, it appeared that labor was available and cheap. Marxism-Leninism taught that the living-working environment shaped the person's social psychology, so it was preferable ideologically to have workers in the public and industrial sector rather than in the private and agricultural sector.

However, the rapid, unexpected inflation of the demand for labor in the expanding industrial sector created new problems for long-term Bolshevik goals and the central plan. There were never enough workers. New workers' demands for housing, food, services, and training could not be met. Enterprises drew down their reserves trying to meet labor's minimal needs when their schedules and budgets were already overdrawn. In the long run, the chief costs of accelerated industrial development were paid by the recruits to the labor force and their families in the form of an extremely low standard of living.

The social upheaval caused by the forced pace of collectivization and industrialization changed the character of the growing work force. There were more peasants, more young people and women, and a smaller ratio of skilled or experienced workers. Age-old patterns of migrant (*otkhod*) labor changed, upset first by the threat and then by the reality of collectivization. Moreover, before the end of the Five-Year Plan, the character of construction work changed. A working family could find year-round work as construction became less dependent on the weather and as sites developed alternative factory jobs. On Dneprostroi, technological sophistication increased the length of the working season. It became possible to pour concrete during freezing weather and to protect it as it set. Better coffer dams, reusable framing pieces, and prefabricated sections contributed to the extension of the construction season. In addition, many *stroiki* workers were learning new skills in the training courses. They began mounting machinery inside as work progressed and went into the factories when the construction was finished. The expansion of the scope of work made it possible for enterprises such as Dneprostroi, Magnitostroi, and others to offer year-round jobs and to aim for a largely "permanent" work force. In spite of the variety of working opportunities, however, many construction workers continued to leave *stroiki* jobs and move on, even though some factories charged for the training they provided before allowing a worker to leave officially. The party hope that the promise of a regular work would promote the development of a permanent work force by contributing to labor stability was dashed.

The party-state tried to manage the development of the labor force, hiring urban workers preferentially, but soon had to give that up and hire workers wherever possible. It tried to organize recruitment, but enterprises overran controls in their competition for labor. Workers, too, bypassed state controls, while industrial expansion was unchecked. They moved from job to job often and relatively easily. Moreover, although records are unreliable, it would appear that skilled workers moved as often as unskilled workers did. Harsh laws forbidding movement could not be applied while demand for labor was high. Sometimes particular factors impeded movement—such as the lack of saleable skills or family obligations, as, for instance, when two earners worked at one place and both incomes were needed for the family's survival. Evidence from Dneprostroi suggests that the two most important factors contributing to the high rate of turnover were the desire to improve living conditions by trying some new place and the choice, once a new skill was mastered, to earn a higher wage by moving out of construction (or mining, timbering, etc.) into better-paid, higher-status factory work.

Under these conditions, what chance did the party leaders have of advancing productivity? Mechanization was expensive and hard to implement. Skilled operators and maintenance personnel were few in number. Faced by the conflict of their own expanded production targets and the workers' demands for better living and working conditions before they took an interest in improving productivity, the party and enterprise managers implemented a broad range of measures. They introduced "new, socialist forms" of work—socialist competition and shock work—trying to excite and exploit the pride of workers in their own or their groups' work in competition with others for the benefit of the country. Party leaders appealed to workers on behalf of their own, unique, proletarian republic, surrounded by hostile capitalists. Patriotism, the rights of future generations, and anger at foreigners figured in their slogans. They capitalized on workers' fear of public scorn and dismissal. The party bureau at Dneprostroi introduced one campaign after another on how to plan ahead, find necessary materials and machines, and use time efficiently. Fearful of losing control over costs, the party demanded that workers become responsible for meeting fiscal targets in their daily work. Thinking that they could divide labor into active producers and slothful workers, they introduced new pay schedules which workers and managers alike evaded as being against their best interests.

Mobilization campaigns contributed less and less toward the realization of production goals while costing more in food and other rewards as workers learned to join up for appearances. The campaigns did not serve to improve work habits, encouraging reliance on drastic emergency efforts rather than long-term planning, balanced use of resources, and the development of administrative and managerial skills. Shock brigades and socialist competition campaigns contributed significantly to irrational administration.

The mobilization campaigns failed to serve party purposes in another way. They had been used to tap the energy and enhance the work of enthusiasts. Participants were viewed as potential recruits for the unions and the party. But, distressingly for the party in 1931 and thereafter, shock workers often were not interested in the trade unions or the party. Equally distressing, many party members were not leaders in shock work. Desperate to keep up the industrialization momentum and to stay in touch with the expanding work force, the party organization hurriedly recruited new members in late 1931. Conscious of the mixed quality of these members, it then prepared to rid itself of undutiful or questioning ones through a cleansing or purge.

Discouraged by party discipline from making suggestions that were in any way critical of the headlong pace of development, party members and specialists outside the party alike could offer only hurrahs to the system if they wanted to speak out, or confine criticisms to individual shortcomings. Comments or experiments designed to improve quality, working conditions, speed, design, safety, or almost any other aspect, if they compromised immediate production totals, made the commentator or innovator subject to suspicion of plan sabotage. The very limited criticisms permitted meant that the grave, systemic problems were not addressed.

For the Western reader acquainted with the continued problems of Soviet development, particularly its cumbersome economic system, the history of Dneprostroi reflects the chaotic nature of Soviet industrialization—the tossing out of already exaggeratedly optimistic plans in favor of ad hoc expansion catering to regional and local interests. Schedules went awry. Shortages became characteristic of the economy, as did competition for financial, material, and labor resources, with disequilibrium and waste.

The history of Dneprostroi reflects as well the exploitation of the workers, their suffering, and that of the peasants. But the story of Dneprostroi is more than that. It is also the story of those thousands of individuals who shared in the pride of the successful harnessing of the broad, powerful river. They created what I. G. Aleksandrov called the beating heart of the Ukraine. Dneprostroi's story is that of P. I. Orlov, who spent hundreds of hours underwater; Zhenia Roman'ko pouring concrete; and F. K. Loginov, who learned his trade as a young man on the site and returned to rebuild the dam after World War II. A middle-aged man remembered thirty years later the closeness of the barracks, where everyone shared the joys and sorrows of neighbors, where birthdays were a community event, a far cry from the anonymity of his life in a modern Zaporozh'e apartment. Dneprostroi's story is the story of those workers from the countryside, young and old, who sacrificed their health and sometimes their lives in this battle for production. Many earned experience "diplomas" there which enabled them to go to jobs across the Soviet Union and share their expertise. Many later took pride in the part they played in the Soviet Union's struggle for great power status. The generation that emerged supplied the middle managers during World War II and, later, the Khrushchevs and Brezhnevs. Dneprostroi and the enterprises of the first Five-Year Plan tempered its graduates, who became the new generation of power in the mature Stalinist system.

Epilogue

Dneprostroi was the symbol of the success of the first Five-Year Plan. The workers' conquest of the great river and their victory over construction problems in the face of their own lack of knowledge became the themes of poems, songs, symphonies, paintings, and children's books. The battles to master the environment and to create a new psychology were subjects of Dovchenko's great silent film *Ivan* and F. Gladkov's full-length novel *Energiia*. Art celebrated the heroism of those who worked with pick and shovel, buckets of concrete, derricks, cranes, and, finally, giant generators and miles of cable, harnessing nature's power and directing it to serve society.

The work of construction had continued through the years of the first Five-Year Plan at an uneven pace. The most important task, closing the dam, was completed on March 28, 1932. It was done just in time before the annual spring flood. Very little work had been accomplished on the dam in the winter of 1930–31, partly because of inclement weather and ice formation. Work was further delayed because of the very high flood in May 1931. The river surpassed a fifty-year record when its rate of flow reached a maximum of about 835,000 second-feet (normally 6300 to 720,000 second-feet). The flood did little damage, however, and work continued soon on the dam, powerhouse steel framing, and the assembly of the turbines and traveling cranes which were to be used for the mounting of the spillway gates. The first stage of the plant construction, the installation of five generators, was completed in October 1932.

By opening day, 3.5 million cubic meters of earth and rock had been excavated, and more than one million cubic meters of concrete had been poured in the dam, powerhouse, and lock structures. Forty-seven sluice gates were mounted between piers; nine turbines and generators were put in place. With the installation of the ninth generator in 1939, generating capacity reached 560,000 kilowatts. During the years before the German invasion of 1941, the power station produced 16.7 billion kilowatts of electric power. The first instrumental steel was produced in 1932, a steel factory began to operate in 1933, and a coke factory, iron works, and aluminum complex were added in rapid succession. The Dnepr-Don transmission line, a pet project of Stalin's, was not finished until 1941. The population of Zaporozh'e grew from 56,000 in 1926 to 289,000 in 1939.[1]

The Germans invaded the Ukraine in 1941. The great dam was destroyed by the retreating Soviet army and rebuilt by the Germans, as were the power station, locks, and factories. It was destroyed a second time by the Germans in retreat. In view of its importance, Dneprostroi was one of the first enterprises rebuilt after the war. Much of the work was done by German prisoners of war. Work was started in 1944, and the last unit was in place in 1950. It is now one of six power dams on the Dnepr and part of an electrical network that supplies industry in Dnepropetrovsk, the Don Basin, Krivoi Rog, Nikopol, and Zaporozh'e itself. The old central administration building of Dneprostroi is now the administrative headquarters of this power network. Dneprostroi itself doubled in power capacity in 1977, its fiftieth birthday, and its locks were likewise doubled in 1980.

Dneprostroi, its client factories in the Dneprostroi combine, and the many thousands of other projects of the first Five-Year Plan provided the foundation for the further development of heavy industry. The completion of the power station, the first of the great regional hydroelectric stations, was a landmark in the execution of the GOELRO plan.

NOTES

Introduction

1. A. Vinter, chief engineer, at the May Day ceremonies, May 1, 1932. *Pravda*, 1 May 1932.

2. V. M. Mikhailov, deputy chief of Dneprostroi, at the opening ceremonies, 11 October 1932.

3. A. Khublarov, *Trud*, 1 May 1932.

4. I. S. Korniienko, *Kino sovetskoi Ukrainy* (Moscow, 1975), pp. 101–2. One of the best-known directors was A. Medvedvin, who produced documentaries on Krivoi Rog, Dneprostroi, Sverdlovsk, and others. Jay Leyda, *Kino* (London, 1960), pp. 286–89.

5. Louis Puls, "Dnieprostroy," unpaged typescript, 1932.

6. Alexander Erlich, *The Soviet Industrialization Debate 1924–1928* (Cambridge, Mass., 1967); E. H. Carr, *Socialism in One Country* (Baltimore, Md.: Penguin Books, 1970), Vols. 1 and 2.

7. Stephen F. Cohen, *Bukharin and the Bolshevik Revolution* (New York, 1973); Moshe Lewin, *Political Undercurrents in Soviet Economic Debates* (Princeton, 1974).

8. Roy Medvedev, trans. by Ellen de Kadt, *On Stalin and Stalinism* (Oxford, 1979).

9. Robert Conquest, *Industrial Workers in the USSR* (New York, 1967); Solomon Schwarz, *Labor in the Soviet Union* (New York, 1952).

10. Theodore Von Laue, *Why Lenin, Why Stalin?* (Philadelphia, 1964).

11. Roger Pethybridge, *The Social Prelude to Stalinism* (New York, 1974).

12. This is particularly true of the essays published in Sheila Fitzpatrick, ed., *Cultural Revolution in Russia, 1928–1932* (Bloomington, Ind., 1973).

13. Moshe Lewin, "Society and the Stalinist State in the Period of the Five-Year Plans," *Social History* 1, no. 2 pp. 139–75 (1976); "Society, State and Ideology during the First Five-Year Plan," in Fitzpatrick, *Cultural Revolution*, pp. 41–77; "The Social Background to Stalinism," in Robert C. Tucker, ed., *Stalinism; Essays in Historical Interpretation* (New York, 1977), pp. 111–36.

14. John Barber is the author of numerous studies distributed by the Center for Russian and East European Studies in Birmingham.

15. Kendall Bailes, *Technology and Society under Lenin and Stalin* (Princeton, 1978).

16. Nicholas Werth, *Etre communiste en URSS sous Staline* (Paris, 1981).

17. Sheila Fitzpatrick, *The Russian Revolution* (Oxford, 1982).

18. Puls, "Dnieprostroy," unpaged.

19. Ibid.

Chapter 1. *"Electrification Is the Second Party Plan"*

1. V. I. Lenin, "Report on the Work of the Central Executive Committee and Council of People's Commissars to the III All-Russian Congress of Soviets," 22 December 1920, *Polnoe Sobranie Sochineniia* 42 (5th ed., Moscow, 1958–1965): 155–61.

2. Nikolai I. Bukharin and Evgeni A. Preobrazhenski, *The ABC of Communism* (Ann Arbor, Mich:, Ann Arbor Paperback ed., 1967).

3. V. I. Lenin, "Speech to the Moscow Party Provincial Conference," 21 November 1920, *PSS* 42: 30.

4. From the 1927 dedication tablet at the Vladimir Il'ich Lenin Dam across the Dnepr.

5. A letter from Stalin to Lenin indicated he did not read it until March 1921. *Pravda*, 22 December 1930, included in *Krasnyi arkhiv*, Vol. 4, no. 94, pp. 9–10.

6. V. I. Lenin, "Agrarnyi vopros i kritika Marksa," June–September 1901, *PSS* 5: 139.

7. Ibid.

8. The speech by V. A. Rzhevskii, "Electricity in Agriculture" (in Russian), published in *Torgovo-Promyshlennaia Gazeta*, no. 6 (1902), was cited by Lenin in a revised edition of his "Razvitie kapitalizma v Rossii," 1899, *PSS* 3: 218.

9. V. I. Lenin, "Odna iz velikikh pobed tekhniki," 21 April 1913, *PSS* 23: 93–95.

10. Ibid.

11. *Plan elektrifikatsii RSFSR*, 2nd ed. (Moscow, 1955), introduction.

12. V. I. Lenin, "Report to the Central Executive Committee, VII Sozyv," 2 February 1920, *PSS* 40: 107–10.

13. Lenin, "Report on the work of the Central Executive Committee," pp. 158–61.

14. Ibid.

15. Ibid.

16. Lenin, "Speech to the Moscow Party Provincial Conference," p. 30.

17. Lenin "Report on the work of the Central Executive Committee," pp. 158–161.

18. Lenin, "Speech to the Moscow Party Provincial Conference," p. 30.

19. Ibid.

20. Henry Adams, *The Education of Henry Adams* (New York, 1931) p. 380.

21. "To the housewife Giant Power means the comforts not only of electric lighting, but of electric cooking and other aids to housework as well. To the farmer it means not only the safety and convenience of electric light, but electric power for milking, feed-cutting, woodsawing, and a thousand other tasks on the farm. To the traveling public it means the speed and cleanliness of electric transportation. To the dwellers in industrial cities it means the freedom from the smoke nuisance and the ash nuisance. To the consumer it means better service at cheaper rates. To every worker it means a higher standard of living, more leisure, and better pay." American Academy of Political and Social Science, *Annals* 98, no. 207 (March 1925): viii.

22. K. Marx and F. Engels, *Collected Works*, Vol. 23, p. 188, as cited in Iu. S. Meleshchenko and S. V. Shukhardin, *Lenin i nauchno-tekhnicheskii progress* (Leningrad, 1969), p. 13.

23. K. Marx, *Capital* (English ed., 1887), as cited in Robert Tucker, ed., *The Marx-Engels Reader* (New York, 1972), pp. 301, 322.

24. F. Engels, "On the Division of Labour in Production," from *Anti-Duhring*, as cited in Tucker, *The Marx-Engels Reader*, pp. 325–26.

25. V. Iu. Steklov, *V. I. Lenin i elektrifikatsiia* (Moscow, 1970), p. 12.

26. F. Engels, "Speech at the Graveside of Karl Marx," as cited in Tucker, *The Marx-Engels Reader*, p. 604.

27. W. Liebknecht, in *Vospominanie o Markse i Engel'se* (Moscow, 1956), p. 91.

28. Steklov, *V. I. Lenin i elektrifikatsiia*, p. 14.

29. Iu. S. Meleshchenko and S. V. Shukhardin, *Lenin i nauchno-tekhnicheskii progress* (Leningrad, 1969), p. 25.

30. V. I. Lenin, "Luchshe men'she, da luchshe," 2 March 1923, *PSS* 45: 404, 405.

31. Lenin, "Report on the Work of the Central Executive Committee," pp. 158–61.

32. Ibid.

33. E. H. Carr, *The Bolshevik Revolution*, Vol. 2 (Middlesex, Eng.: Penguin Books, 1971) Chap. 17, esp. p. 198.

34. G. M. Krzhizhanovskii was a longtime colleague of Lenin's and had shared Siberian exile with him.

35. G. M. Krzhizhanovskii had published "Oblastnye elektricheskie stantsii na torfe i ikh znachenie dlia Tsentral'nogo promyshlennogo raiona Rossii," *Trudy soveshchanii po podmoskovnomu ugliu i torfu* (Moscow, 1915).

36. V. I. Lenin, letter to G. M. Krzhizhanovskii, 26 December 1919, *PSS* 51: 105.

37. V. I. Lenin, letter to G. M. Krzhizhanovskii, 23 January 1920, *PSS* 40: 62, 63.

38. V. I. Lenin, "Report to the Central Executive Committee, VII Sozyv," pp. 107–10.

39. *Krasnyi arkhiv*, Vol. 4, no. 95, p. 31, 31n.

40. I. A. Gladkov, *Ocherki stroitel'stva sovetskogo planovogo khoziaistva 1917–1918* (Moscow, 1950), pp. 176–80, cited in Eugene Zaleski, *Planning for Economic Growth in the Soviet Union, 1918–1932*, trans. by M. C. MacAndrew and G. W. Nutter (Chapel Hill, N.C., 1971), p. 37.

41. "Vserossiiskii elektrotekhnicheskii s'ezd," *Trudy 8 vserossiiskogo elektrotekhnicheskogo s'ezda* (Moscow, 1921), pp. 1–10.

42. *Krasnyi arkhiv*, Vol. 4, no. 95, pp. 13, 14.

43. Ibid., p. 41.

44. I. I. Verhovtsev, ed., *Svet nad Rossiei* (Moscow, 1960), pp. 25–27.

45. *Krasnyi arkhiv*, Vol. 4, no. 95, p. 41.

46. V. Iu. Steklov, *V. I. Lenin i elektrifikatsiia*, 2nd ed. (Moscow, 1975), pp. 185, 186.

47. P. S. Neporozhnii, ed., *50 let leninskogo plana GOELRO* (Moscow, 1970), p. 88.

48. N. V. Valentinov, "Memoirs," Chap. 1, p. 43, unpublished, cited in Naum Jasny, "Essay VI, Soviet 'Perspective' Planning," *Essays on the Soviet Economy* (New York, 1962), p. 188.

49. *Krasnyi arkhiv*, Vol. 4, no. 95, pp. 47–50.

50. I. M. Bichuk, *Istoriia pokoreniia Dnepra* (Zaporozh'e, 1970), p. 12; Ester Bentsionovna Kartsovnik, "Leninskii plan elektrifikatsii i bor'ba partii za sooruzhenie Dneprovskoi gidroelektrostantsii imeni V. I. Lenina," candidate diss. (Kiev, 1964), p. 31; V. E. Timonov, "7ième question: Les cataractes du Dniepre," *VIe Congrès International de Navigation Intérieure* (St. Petersburg, 1894), p. 74.

51. John N. Westwood, *A History of Russian Railways* (London, 1964), p. 19.

52. R. A. Roosa, "The Association of Industry and Trade, 1906–1914," Ph.D. diss. (Columbia University, 1967), I, p. 133; also II, chap. 11.

53. Ibid., II, p. 348; N. S. Avdakov, "Nashi vodnye i shosseinye puti," *Promyshlennost' i torgovlia* 16 (15 August 1913).

54. Deviaty; Ocherdnoi S'ezd Predstavitelei Promyshlennosti i Torgovli, "Vnutrennie vodnye puti," *Doklad Soveta S'ezdov o merakh k razvitiiu proizvoditel'nykh sil Rossii* (Petrograd, 1915), p. 301.

55. In 1900, Russia had the capacity of 80,000 kw. By 1910, this rose to 1.1 million kw., and production reached 1.9 billion kw-hrs. Verkhovtsev, ed., *Svet nad Rossiei*, pp. 12, 13. By 1913, production reached 2 billion kw-hrs., after an industrial boom which began in 1909. Heiko Haumann, *Beginn der Planwirtschaft* (Dusseldorf, 1974), pp. 14–18. The electrical journals of Europe and the United States regularly reported on the great Russian interest in the development of power generation and use and the equally great shortage of investment money.

56. Boris Kushner, *Revoliutsiia i elektrifikatsiia* (Peterburg, 1920). Factories and mines were compared in terms of the amount of mechanical energy they used per worker. A measure of Russia's relative backwardness was that for every 100 persons the United States produced 25 hp; England, 24; Germany, 13; and Russia, 1.6. In industry, Russia ranked relatively higher. P. I. Liashchenko, trans. by L. M. Herman, *History of the National Russian Economy* (New York, 1949), pp. 672, 673.

57. Z. O. Bukhgeim, *K ekonomicheskomu osvobozhdeniiu Rossii* (Moscow, 1915), pp. 10–15; G. M. Krzhizhanovskii, in *Myslitel' i revoliutsioner* (Moscow, 1971), mentions Bukhgeim as one of the authors who influenced Lenin in his views on electricity.

58. Bichuk, *Istoriia pokoreniia Dnepra*, p. 26.

59. B. A. Bakhmetiev, *K voprosu o shliuzovanii i ispol'zovanii vodnykh sil' Dneprovskikh porogov* (St. Petersburg, 1914), p. 1 n. *The Electrical Engineer* (London), 27 April 1900, p. 579, noted that an English company sought a

concession to develop the Dnepr. The company proposed to supply the capital of 4.75 million, while the Russian government guaranteed three percent interest. The company hoped to exploit the electrical lease for eighty years, although the Russian government was to have the option of purchasing it after thirty years.

60. Chicago *Daily News*, as cited in *Electrical World and Engineer* 36, no. 8, 25 August 1900, p. 278.

61. Bichuk, *Istoriia pokoreniia Dnepra*, p. 26. Upravlenie Vnutrennikh Vodnykh Putei i Shosseinykh Dorog, *Razbor proektov gg. Defossa i Rukteshelia o provedenii morskogo kanala ot Rigi do Khersona* (St. Petersburg, 1905), introduction.

62. Upravlenie Vnutrennikh Vodnykh Putei i Shosseinykh Dorog, *Razbor proektov gg. Defossa i Rukteshelia.*

63. Ibid.

64. V. Malyshev, "Istoriia problemy ispol'zovaniia porozhistoi chasti Dnepra," *Gosudarstvennoe Dneprovskoe stroitel'stvo*, Vol. 2 (Moscow, 1925), pp. 99, 100.

65. Ministerstvo Putei Soobshcheniia, Inzhenernyi Sovet, *Kratkii istoricheskii ocherk* (Petrograd, 1917), p. 35; Malyshev, "Istoriia problemy," p. 103.

66. N. M. (no further identification), "Shliuzovanie Dneprovskikh porogov," *PiT*, no. 9 (1 May 1914).

67. Gosudarstvennyi Sovet, Soedinennaia Komissiia Finansovaia i Ekonomicheskaia, *Doklad po delu ob otpuske iz gosudarstvennogo kaznacheistva sredstv na raboty v porozhistoi chasti reki Dnepra* (Petrograd, 1916), no. 32.

68. Gosudarstvennyi Sovet, *Stenograficheskii otchet*, Sessiia IX, zasedaniia 54, 18 June 1914 (Petrograd, 1914), col. 2885; Sessiia XII, zasedaniia 23, 16 May 1916 (Petrograd, 1916), cols. 1323–26; 4 Sozyv, Sessiia VII, zasedaniia 59, 18 June 1916 (Petrograd, 1916), Cols. 5659, 5743–44, 5813–14; Bakhmetiev, *K voprosu o shliuzovanii*, p. 3; Malyshev, "Istoriia problemy," pp. 124–27; Ministerstvo Putei Soobshcheniia, Inzhenernyi Sovet, *Kratkii*, p. 31.

69. Leon Smolinski, "Grinevetskii and Soviet Industrialization," *Survey* 67 (April 1968): 102 n, in his paraphrase of an article by V. I. Grinevetskii, "Tekhniko-obshchestvennye zadachi v sfere promyshlennosti v sviazi s voinoi," *Vestnik inzhenerov* 1 (1915).

70. V. I. Grinevetskii, *Poslevoennye perspektivy russkoi promyshlennosti*, 2nd ed. (Moscow, 1922).

71. See, for example, Imperatorskoe Russkoe Tekhnicheskoe Obshchestvo, *Zapiski* (St. Petersburg), nos. 7–8, p. 1904; idem, VI Otdel, *Obshchaia svodka perepisi utilizirovannykh vodnykh sil Rossii po ankete 1912–13*, as cited in P. S. Neporozhnii, ed., *50 let Leninskogo plana GOELRO* (Moscow, 1970), pp. 147, 153; Trudy VII Vserossiiskogo elektrotekhnicheskogo s'ezda (St. Petersburg, 1913), as cited in G. M. Krzhizhanovskii, *Izbrannoe* (Moscow, 1957), p. 9.

72. Grinevetskii, *Poslevoennye perspektivy*, p. 53.

73. *Trudy GOELRO* (Moscow, 1960), p. 94, cited by Steklov, *V. I. Lenin i elektrifikatsiia*, p. 244.

74. Verkhovtsev, ed., *Svet nad Rossiei*, pp. 40, 42. This suggestion was included in a recommendation passed by the All-Russian Council of Congresses, 1921.

75. V. I. Lenin, letter to G. M. Krzhizhanovskii, December 1920, *PSS* 52: 39–40. It is ironic to read of electric lights being referred to as being the tsar's: "There was electric lighting in the village—it had already been extended from Shatury in the twenties. At the time, the newspapers wrote about 'little Il'ich [Lenin] lamps' and the peasants, their eyes goggling, called them 'Tsar Fire!.'" Aleksander Solzhenitsyn, *Matrenin dvor* (London, 1965), p. 12.

76. I. I. Skvortsov-Stepanov, *Elektrifikatsiia R.S.F.S.R. v sviazi s perekhodnoi fazoi mirovogo khoziaistva*, introductory remarks by V. I. Lenin and G. M. Krzhizhanovskii (Moscow and Petrograd, 1923), chap. 1.

77. Ibid., chap. 7, esp. p. 189.

78. V. I. Lenin, letter to I. I. Skvortsov-Stepanov, 19 March 1922, *PSS* 54: 210.

79. V. I. Lenin, Predislovie k knige I. I. Skvortsov-Stepanova "Elektrifikatsiia RSFSR v sviazi s perekhodnoi fazoi mirovogo khoziaistva," *PSS* 45: 51–52.

80. Ibid.

81. *Ekonomicheskaia zhizn'* 14, 23 December 1920; 9, 16, 19, 20 February 1921.

82. V. Miliutin, "O metodakh razrabotki edinogo khoziaistvennogo plana," cited by Steklov, *V. I. Lenin i elektrifikatsiia*, 2nd ed., p. 275.

83. *Leninskii sbornik*, Vol. 20 (Moscow, 1932), p. III. Trotsky questioned the viability of the plan; Steklov, *V. I. Lenin i elektrifikatsiia*, 2nd ed., p. 274.

84. *Leninskii sbornik*, Vol. 20, pp. 19–23.

85. V. I. Lenin, "Ob edinom khoziaistvennom plane," published in *Pravda*, 22 February 1921; *PSS* 42: 339–34. Lenin complained that Rykov was bureaucratic and bookish, Miliutin was bureaucratic, and the others were wrong.

86. Ibid.

87. This meeting took place on the same day as he published the *Pravda* article. Carr, *The Bolshevik Revolution*, Vol. 2, p. 373.

88. Ibid. Lenin tried to exclude Larin from Gosplan, according to Carr.

89. *Leninskii sbornik*, Vol. 20, pp. 23–24.

90. According to Jasny, only the construction of thirty electric power stations was approved. Ten to fifteen years was the time span allotted. Jasny, "Essay VI," p. 191.

91. Carr, *The Bolshevik Revolution*, Vol. 2, chaps. 18, 19; Stephen F. Cohen, *Bukharin and the Bolshevik Revolution* (New York, 1973), p. 106; Lewin, *Political Undercurrents*, pp. 84–96.

92. V. I. Lenin, "Luchshe men'she, da luchshe," 2 March 1923, cited in Tucker, *The Marx-Engels Reader*, p. 745.

93. Cohen, *Bukharin and the Bolshevik Revolution*, pp. 163–65; Alexander Erlich, *The Industrialization Debate, 1924–1926* (Cambridge, Mass., 1967).

94. Boris Kushner, *Revoliutsiia i elektrifikatsiia* (Petrograd, 1920), p. 8.

Chapter 2. The Decision

1. E. H. Carr, *The Bolshevik Revolution 1917–1923*, Vol. 2 (Middlesex, Eng.: Penguin Books, 1971), pp. 151–268.

2. Ibid., pp. 280–357.

3. The classic study of this debate is Alexander Erlich, *The Soviet Industrialization Debate 1924–1928* (Cambridge, Mass., 1967). Other important works include E. H. Carr, *Socialism in One Country*, Vols. 1 and 2 (Baltimore, Md.: Penguin Books, 1970); Nicholas Spulber, *Soviet Strategy for Economic Growth* (Bloomington, Ind., 1964); and appropriate chapters in Stephen F. Cohen, *Bukharin and the Bolshevik Revolution* (New York, 1973), and Moshe Lewin, *Political Undercurrents in Soviet Economic Debates* (Princeton, 1974). A useful summary is Alec Nove, *An Economic History of the USSR* (Middlesex, Eng: Penguin Books, 1969).

4. Erlich, *The Soviet Industrialization Debate*, p. 64; Kuibyshev was particularly outspoken about the importance of improved transportation. I. A. Gladkov, ed., *Razvitie elektrifikatsii Sovetskoi strany 1921–1925* (Moscow, 1956).

5. Lewin, *Political Undercurrents*, p. 51.

6. *Vestnik Kommunisticheskoi Akademii* 8 (1924): 58–59, cited in Carr, *Socialism in One Country*, Vol. 1, p. 220.

7. Ibid., p. 222.

8. Erlich, *The Soviet Industrialization Debate*, pp. 332–59.

9. Cohen, *Bukharin and the Bolshevik Revolution*, p. 176.

10. Ibid., p. 179.

11. Ibid., p. 200.

12. A good introduction to this period in Ukrainian history is John Sullivant, *Soviet Politics and the Ukraine, 1917–1957* (New York, 1962).

13. The work was done by the Commission for the Electrification of the Ukraine (KEU). D. Egorov, "Elektrifikatsiia ugol'noi promyshlennosti v plane GOELRO," *Energetika narodnogo khoziaistva v plane GOELRO* (Moscow, 1966), pp. 35–36.

14. Gosudarstvennaia Planovaia Komissiia pri Ukrainskom Ekonomicheskom Soveshchanii, *Ukrogosplan za tri goda* (Khar'kov, 1924), pp. 1–2, 113–114.

15. Nove, *An Economic History*, p. 93; Carr, *The Bolshevik Revolution*, Vol. 2, pp. 315–16.

16. The closing of the inefficient Iugostal' factory had been discussed, but it would have meant that three thousand workers would lose their jobs. There had been discussion of closing the inefficient Putilov factory, but it had been deemed politically unwise. S. S. Khromov, *F. E. Dzerzhinskii na khoziaistvennom fronte* (Moscow, 1977), p. 110.

17. P. S. Neporozhnii, ed., *50 let Leninskogo plana GOELRO* (Moscow, 1970), pp. 327–28.

18. Gladkov, *Razvitie*, Vol. 1, pp. 316, 317, 321, 322, 326, 336; Vol. 2, p. 384, 385; A. F. Nozhkin, "Ispol'zovanie porozhistoi chasti Dnepra" and "Nastoiashchee i budushchee elektricheskikh stantsii obshchestvennogo pol'zovaniia zaporozhskoi gubernii," *Khoziaistvo Zaporozh'ia* 3/4 (1922), pp. 48–67; P. O. Sidorenko, *Lenins'kyi plan GOELRO* (Khar'kov, 1973), p. 88.

19. Gladkov, *Razvitie*, Vol. 1, pp. 323, 325.

20. Ukrogosplan, *Ukrogosplan za tri goda*, pp. 113–14.

21. Rezoliustsiia VIII Ekaterinoslavskogo gubernskogo s'ezda soveta o Dne-prostroe KP(b) Ekaterinoslava, 10 January 1924; from *Zvezda*, 11 January 1924, cited in Gladkov, *Razvitie*, Vol. 1, p. 505.

22. V. Z. Drobizhev and N. V. Dumova, *Ia. Chubar* (Moscow, 1963).

23. Ibid., pp. 11–12, 49.

24. N. P. Bogdanov, "Nasha gordost', nasha slava, Dneproges," *Byli indus-trial'nye* (Moscow, 1973), p. 316.

25. V. E. Sproge, "Zapiski inzhenera iz SSSR," typescript (Zurich, 1963), pp. 106–8. *Ekonomicheskaia zhizn'* is the daily newspaper of Gosplan.

26. Sidorenko, *Lenins'kyi plan GOELRO*, p. 88.

27. Ukrains'ka Akademiia Nauk, Institut ekonomiki, *Ocherki razvitiia narod-nogo khoziaistva Ukrainskoi SSR* (Moscow, 1954), p. 220.

28. A. S. Gordon, "Budget Financing of Popular Economy," in Gregory So-kolnikov et al., trans. by Elena Varneck, ed. by Lincoln Hutchinson and Carl C. Plehn, *Soviet Policy in Public Finance 1917–1928* (Stanford, 1931), p. 369.

29. Gosudarstvennaia Komissia po Elektrifikatsii Rossii, *Biulleten'* 1 (Moscow, 1920): 11.

30. E. H. Carr and R. W. Davies, *Foundations of a Planned Economy*, Vol. 1. (New York, 1969), p. 899.

31. *Promyshlennost' i rabochii klass Ukrainskoi SSR v periode postroeniia fundamenta sotsialisticheskoi ekonomiki (1926–1932)*, Vol. 1. Sbornik dokumen-tov i materialov (Kiev, 1966), pp. 148–49.

32. Gladkov, *Razvitie*, Vol. 1, p. 332.

33. The estimate was made by Ukrogosplan on 10 July 1924. *Promyshlennost'*, p. 174. It was based on work done by the first All-Union Conference on Electric Supplies, 8–14 June 1924. It was given to the Council of Labor and Defense by Ukrogosplan on 12 July 1924. Gladkov, *Razvitie*, Vol. 1, p. 330.

34. Ibid., p. 332

35. Letter to Politburo members, dated 16 July 1924, cited in S. S. Khromov, *F. E. Dzerzhinskii vo glave metallopromyshlennosti* (Moscow, 1966), p. 121, n. 200; see also idem, *F. E. Dzerzhinskii na khoziaistvennom fronte*, pp. 141, 142.

36. *Promyshlennost'*, p. 360.

37. Carr, *Socialism in One Country*, Vol. 1, p. 360.

38. Khromov, *F. E. Dzerzhinskii vo glave metallopromyshlennosti*, pp. 176–229. The value of metal manufacturing to be produced was raised by 26% over earlier estimates to 362.1 million rubles; ibid., p. 225.

39. Ibid., p. 185.

40. Kommunisticheskaia partiia Ukrainy, *Deviatyi s'ezd Kommunisticheskoi partii bol'shevikov Ukrainy. Stenograficheskii otchet* (Khar'kov,1926), 218, 219, 252.

41. Ibid., p. 361.

42. *Promyshlennost'*, p. 225.

43. III S'ezd Sovetov SSSR, *Stenograficheskii otchet* (Moscow, 1925), p. 104.

44. Ibid., pp. 104–6; *Promyshlennost'*, p. 178.

45. III S'ezd Sovetov SSSR, "Rezoliutsii," *Stenograficheskii otchet*, p. 30.

46. Nove, *An Economic History*, p. 132.

47. *Torgovo-Promyshlennaia Gazeta*, 19, 27 February 1925; *Ekonomicheskaia zhizn'*, 19, 24 February 1925.

48. *TPG*, 22 January 1925.

49. Gladkov, *Razvitie*, Vol. 1, pp. 333–36; *TPG*, 4 February 1925.

50. *TPG*, 19, 27 February, 9 March 1925; *Ekzh*, 18 June 1925.

51. *Promyshlennost'*, p. 225.

52. *Ekzh*, 2 July 1925, reporting the meeting which took place on 30 June.

53. Ibid., 15 July 1925; *TPG*, 17 July 1925.

54. *Ekzh*, 23 July 1925; *TPG*, 23, 25 July 1925; Lev Trotsky, *Voprosy elektropromyshlennosti i elektrifikatsii. Rezoliutsii soveshchaniia pri Glavelektro 17–20 iiunia 1925* (Moscow, 1925).

55. Trotsky wrote that his efforts to act in technical matters were misinterpreted and obstructed by those who gave them political significance. Lev Trotsky, *My Life* (New York, 1936), p. 519. His association with Dneprostroi pleased the Ukrainian Gosplan members who learned only later that he had lost influence. Sproge, "Zapiski inzhenera iz SSSR," p. 109.

56. *Ekzh*, 18, 19, 20 June 1925; *TPG*, 18, 21, 24, 25 June 1925. The numbers differ from those usually given. The 8.3 million do not apparently include the 2.6 million required in valuta for purchases abroad.

57. Trotsky, *Voprosy elektropromyshlennosti*.

58. *Ekzh*, 28 July 1925.

59. Ibid., 22 July 1925.

60. Ibid., 28 August 1925.

61. *TPG*, 1 September 1925.

62. Ibid., 1, 2, 4 September 1925.

63. *Ekzh*, 8 September 1925.

64. Ibid.

65. III S'ezd Sovetov SSSR, *Stenograficheskii otchet*, pp. 426, 437.

66. A. Potebnia, "Problema Dneprostroia," *Khoziaistvo Ukrainy*, no. 10 (1925): 80–86.

67. *TPG*, 13 September 1925. The paper was edited at that time by M. A. Savel'ev.

68. Ibid., 20 September 1925; *Ekzh*, 5 November 1925.

69. *TPG*, 23 September 1925.

70. Ibid., 25 September 1925.

71. Ibid., 27 September 1925; *Ekzh*, 19, 25, 27 September 1925.

72. *Ekzh*, 27 September 1925; *TPG*, 27 September 1925.

73. *TPG*, 4 October 1925.

74. Manganese deposits were then being developed by Harriman (USA) in accordance with a concession agreement made in 1925.

75. *TPG*, 5 October 1925.

76. Ibid., 7 October 1925. Hinting at the enormous complexity of a rational evaluation of the project, Shaposhnikov said that the construction of a seaway

and the production of energy should be analyzed separately but that the technical and economic analysis should be an organic whole.

77. *TPG,* 13 October 1925.

78. *Ekzh,* 5 November 1925.

79. *TPG,* 20 October 1925. There was no mention of funds for Dneprostroi at the fourteenth Party Congress.

80. Kommunisticheskaia partiia Ukrainy, *Deviatyi s'ezd Kommunisticheskoi partii bol'shevikov Ukrainy,* p. 33.

81. Ibid., pp. 218, 219.

82. Ibid., pp. 219, 252.

83. G. F. Grin'ko, "Planovye problemy ukrainskoi ekonomiki," *Planovoe khoziaistvo* 6 (1926): 179–93. Published for discussion, being Grin'ko's speech to the first All-Union S'ezd Gosplanov, February 1926.

84. Trotsky resigned from the committee, and Rukhimovich became its chairman.

85. *Ekzh,* 6 April 1926. Cooper saw the plans and bid on them. He expected to get the contract in May 1926 and go to Russia in August. Frances Cooper, diary entry for 24 May 1926.

86. Sproge, "Zapiski inzhenera iz SSSR," pp. 123–25.

87. *TPG,* 5 August, 10, 16 September 1926; *Ekzh,* 7, 16 September 1926. Cooper changed the composition of the dam. Engineer S. A. Kukel-Kraevskii estimated the time for construction at four and a half or five years rather than seven. *Ekzh,* 8 October 1926.

88. A. Rykov, *Itogi plenuma TsK VKP (b)* (Moscow-Leningrad, 1926), pp. 1–13.

89. *Biulleten' oppozitsii* (Paris) nos. 29-30 (September 1932): 34; also no. 19 (March 1931): 16, 17.

90. Khromov, *F. E. Dzerzhinskii vo glave metallopromyshlennosti,* pp. 269, 275. In addition to nationalization, economy, and strict observation of the plan, Dzerzhinskii argued (p. 292) that *smychka* was necessary.

91. Carr and Davies, *Foundations,* Vol. 1, pp. 5–6, 279, 288.

92. Khromov, *F. E. Dzerzhinskii na khoziaistvennom fronte,* p. 301.

93. The control figures, published by the Supreme Economic Council immediately after Dzerzhinskii's death, had been rejected by him as too high. Carr and Davies, *Foundations,* Vol. 1, p. 282.

94. P. Berezov, *Valerian Vladimirovich Kuibyshev, 1888–1935* (Moscow, 1958); Kafedra istorii KPSS, Tomsk University, *V. V. Kuibyshev, vydaiushchiisia proletarskii revoliutsioner i myslitel'* (Tomsk, 1963); M. P. Evseev, *Voprosy sotsialisticheskoi ekonomiki v rabotakh V. V. Kuibysheva* (Tomsk, 1967).

95. Kuibyshev spoke about electrification as the only basis for a socialist society, the means of raising culture, and the rationalizer which would make possible the internal accumulation of investment capital. Speech, 1 November 1924. Gladkov, *Razvitie,* Vol. 1, pp. 24, 564.

96. *TPG,* 12 August 1926, cited in Carr and Davies, *Foundations,* Vol. 1, p. 742.

97. Cooper suggested a number of changes. He recommended concrete construction rather than rubble and estimated that this change would save two years of construction time. He relocated the powerhouse, setting it closer to the dam, changing its axis and location. These alterations permitted economies in material because of the new shape and because an island could be used to anchor a section of the dam. He also reduced the size of the sluices and increased their number to permit the use of a standard sluice gate. Cooper reduced the number and size of the locks, saving construction time and operating time as well. He recommended against the planned work on the Samar River and against ice protection. All of these suggestions were followed. Finally, he recommended the placement of the railroad on the dam instead of the construction of a separate railroad bridge, but, because this would have added time to the construction period while saving in material costs, this one recommendation was turned down. Louis Puls, "Dnieprostroi," typescript draft report; V. Malyshev, "Etapy proekta Dneprostroia," *Dneprostroi*, no. 1 (November 1927): 45–52; VSNKh, Tsentral'nyi elektrotekhnicheskii sovet, *Predvaritel'naia ekspertiza proekta Dneprovskoi gidro-elektricheskoi stantsii. Prilozhenie XIII. Materialy po ekspertize Amerikanskoi firmy Kh'iu L. Kuper i Ko.* (Leningrad, 1926).

98. A. F. Khavin, *U rulia industrii* (Moscow, 1968), pp. 47–52.

99. Carr and Davies, *Foundations*, Vol. 1, pp. 426–28, 427 n.

100. Ibid., p. 429.

101. Ibid., p. 286.

102. Sproge, "Zapiski inzhenera iz SSSR," pp. 122–25.

103. Ibid., p. 128.

104. As described above in note 97.

105. Sproge, "Zapiski inzhenera iz SSSR," pp. 122–24. Cooper went to the Crimea to speak to Rykov and Krzhizhanovskii, and Sproge went as the interpreter. See also *TPG*, 16 September 1926; 7, 8, October, 18 November 1926; *Ekzh*, 28 October, 7 November 1926.

106. *TPG*, 18 November 1926.

107. Berezov, *Valerian Vladimirovich Kuibyshev*, p. 243.

108. *TPG*, 7 October 1926.

109. *Ekzh*, 8 October 1926.

110. *TPG*, 8 October 1926.

111. *Ekzh*, 8 October 1926.

112. *TPG*, 10 October 1926.

113. Ibid., 12 October 1926; *Ekzh*, 10 October 1926.

114. O. Borzakivs'syy, "Dniprel'stan," *Zhyttia i revoliutsyia*, no. 11 (1926): 78–81; N. Iu. Kostrytsia, *Komunistychna partiia-orhanizator vsenarodnoi borot'by za zdiysnennia lenins'kykh idey elektryfikatsii na Ukraini* (Kiev, 1967), p. 44. Efremov, another member later expelled, agreed with him, quoting Stuart, an American consultant who had stressed the project's costs. M. D. Oliinychenko, *Lenins'ki nakreslennia v zhittia. KPRS-orhanizator budivytstva Dniprovs'koho kaskadu hidroelektrostantsii 1927–1970* (Kiev, 1970), p. 37.

115. Oliinychenko, *Lenins'ki nakreslennia v zhittia*, p. 38.

116. *Kommunisticheskaia Partiia Ukrainy v rezoliutsiiakh i resheniiakh s'ezdov i konferentsii 1918–1956* (Kiev, 1958), p. 361.

117. *TPG*, 28 October 1926; *Ekzh*, 28 October 1926; *Dniprel'stan, stenograficheskii otchet*, 27 October 1926 (Khar'kov, 1926).

118. *Dniprel'stan.*

119. Ibid.

120. Ibid.

121. Ibid.

122. Vsesoiuznaia Kommunisticheskaia Partiia (bol'shevikov) XV Konferentsiia 26 oktiabria–3 noiabra 1926 g., *Stenograficheskii otchet* (Moscow, 1927), pp. 148–49.

123. Ibid., p. 262.

124. *Resheniia partii i pravitel'stva po khoziaistvennym voprosam 1917–1967*, Vol. 1 (Moscow, 1967), pp. 545–47. Although much emphasis has been placed on the resolve to achieve independence of foreign manufactures, at this time it was only one of a number of goals. The undue importance which has been given to the struggle for immediate self-sufficiency stems from the Stalinist historiographical tradition which began as early as the 1930s.

125. Carr and Davies, *Foundations*, Vol. 1, pp. 904–5.

126. *TPG*, 9 November 1926.

127. V. V. Kuibyshev, Speech given 9 November 1926. Document 1, "V. V. Kuibyshev i sotsial'isticheskaia industrializatsiia SSSR," *Istoricheskii arkhiv*, no. 3 (May/June 1958): 44.

128. Ibid., pp. 44–45.

129. *TPG*, 11 November 1926.

130. *Resheniia partii i pravitel'sta po khoziaistvennym voprosam, 1917–1967*, Vol. 1 (Moscow, 1967), p. 561; Oliinychenko, *Lenins'ki nakreslennia v zhittia*, p. 40.

131. *Ekzh*, 3, 10, December 1926.

132. *TPG*, 4 December 1926.

133. *Pravda*, 22 December 1930. The letter is included in *Krasnyi arkhiv*, Vol. 4, no. 94, pp. 9–10. It is not included in most histories of electrification, presumably because it suggests how uninvolved Stalin was in one of Lenin's favorite projects.

Chapter 3. Management Policy

1. *Krasnoe Zaporozh'e*, 27 January 1927.

2. V. I. Lenin, *PSS*, 38, p. 55; 44, pp. 350–51.

3. V. L. Butkovskii, *Inostrannye kontsessii v narodnom khoziaistve SSSR* (Moscow, 1928); J. Watstein, "Soviet Economic Concessions: The Agony and the Promise," *ACES Bulletin* 16, no. 1 (Spring 1974); E. V. Iufereva, *Leninskoe uchenie o goskapitalizme v perekhodnyi period k sotsializmu* (Moscow, 1969); V. I. Kas'ianenko et al., "Iz istorii kontsessionnoi politiki sovetskogo gosudarstva," *Istoriia SSSR* 4, (1959).

4. *KZ*, 27 January 1927.

5. *TPG*, 9, 18 November 1926.

6. Bailes, *Technology and Society*, p. 37.

7. Cooper belonged to the American-Russian Chamber of Commerce and frequently visited Washington to promote Russian-American trade. On his special role as a self-taught engineer, see *New York Times*, 26 June 1937, p. 16.

8. H. L. Cooper, letter to his wife, 31 May 1927.

9. *KZ*, 2 February 1927; *TPG*, 2 February 1927; *Ekzh*, 2 February 1927.

10. *KZ*, 17 February 1927.

11. *TPG*, 2 February 1927.

12. This view was expressed strongly by the Democratic and Workers' Opposition.

13. Richard Day, *Leon Trotsky and the Politics of Economic Isolation* (Cambridge, 1973), p. 130.

14. Robert C. Tucker, *Stalin as a Revolutionary* (New York, 1973), chap. 10.

15. Sofia Vinogradskaia, *Inzhener nashei epokhi* (Moscow, 1934), pp. 30, 35; B. S. Baskov, "Memuary B. S. Baskova," *Voprosy istorii* 41, no. 3 (March 1966): 97.

16. *Ekzh*, 15 February 1927.

17. *TPG*, 15 February 1927.

18. Sproge, "Zapiski inzhenera iz SSSR," pp. 130–40.

19. *KZ*, 27 February 1927; *TPG*, 27 February 1927.

20. Nikita Khrushchev spoke of the good relations shared by the Americans and the Dneprostroi administration. V. Kas' ianenko, *Kak byla zavoevana tekhniko-ekonomicheskaia samostoiatel'nost' SSSR* (Moscow, 1964), p. 200. Sproge wrote of the good working relations he had with one of Cooper's engineers and of the technical experience he gained thereby, in "Zapiski inzhenera iz SSSR," p. 139.

21. Decree of the Council of Labor and Defense, 22 December 1926, *Sobranie zakonov i rasporiazhenii raboche-krest'ianskogo pravitel'stva Soiuza Sovetskikh sotsialisticheskikh Respublik*, Otdel pervyi (Moscow, 1927), pp. 47–48; *KZ*, 15 January, 27 February 1927; *Ekzh*, 1 January, 17 February 1927.

22. *TPG*, 8 October 1926.

23. B. Lewytzkyj, *The Stalinist Terror in the Thirties* (Stanford, 1974), p. 268.

24. *TPG*, 8 February 1927.

25. Ibid., 10 February, 7 March 1927; *Ekzh*, 17 February 1927. Only the Central Executive Committee, the Council of Commissars, the Council of Labor and Defense, and a special committee of the Supreme Economic Council could hold the board accountable and bring it to court.

26. Aleksandrov's pleasure in the life of Moscow is reflected in Sproge, "Zapiski inzhenera iz SSSR," pp. 141, 156, 165–67.

27. *TPG*, 2 December 1927.

28. Institut zur Erforschung der UdSSR, *Who Was Who in the USSR*, ed. H. E. Schulz et al. (Metuchen, N.J., 1972), p. 211. In spite of his foreign name, Graftio was a native-born Russian.

29. *TPG*, 12 February 1927; Vinogradskaia, *Inzhener nashei epokhi*, passim; Steklov, *V. I. Lenin i elektrifikatsiia* (1975), pp. 182, 183.

30. Baskov, "Memuary B. S. Baskova," p. 97.

31. Sproge, "Zapiski inzhenera iz SSSR," pp. 128–29.

32. *TPG*, 12 February 1927. Vedeneev became deputy head of the Volga Construction Trust in 1932 and deputy head of the Ministry of Heavy Industry. He was prominent thereafter in administration and science.

33. *TPG*, 12 February 1927.

34. Ibid., 20 February 1927.

35. Ibid., 22 February 1927.

36. *Ekzh*, 15, 19 April 1927.

37. *TPG*, 10 February 1927. Kviring's choice of words, "faith in the engineer," reflects the ongoing argument between those who were willing to work with "bourgeois specialists" and give them authority and high salaries and those who wanted to use specialists only under conditions of strict supervision and control by Communists.

38. Ibid., 21 April 1927; *Ekzh*, 3 March 1927; *KZ*, 22 April 1927.

39. *KZ*, 22 February, 4, 8 March, 14 July 1927; *TPG*, 18 February 1927.

40. *Ekzh*, 27 March 1927.

41. *KZ*, 16 April 1927.

42. Ibid., 27 April, 4 May 1927.

43. Ibid., 9 June 1927.

44. Sproge, "Zapiski inzhenera iz SSSR," p. 136.

45. *Ekzh*, 17 March 1927; *KZ*, 22 April 1927.

46. *Ekzh*, 16 March 1927.

47. *TPG*, 5 April 1927.

48. *Ekzh*, 11, 25 June 1927.

49. Vinter went to Europe and the United States in April and May and again to Europe in July. Aleksandrov went to the United States in June.

50. *TPG*, 7, 8 June 1927.

51. *Ekzh*, 8 June 1927.

52. Ibid., 11 June 1927; *KZ*, 11 June 1927; *TPG*, 11, 17 June 1927.

53. *KZ*, 30 November 1927.

54. *Ekzh*, 29 January 1928.

55. Ibid., 2, 15, 17 July 1927; *TPG*, 17 July 1927.

56. *TPG*, 10, 20 September 1927.

57. Sproge, "Zapiski inzhenera iz SSSR," p. 132.

58. Ibid., p. 134; *KZ*, 23 November 1927.

59. Sproge, "Zapiski inzhenera iz SSSR," p. 134.

60. *KZ*, 30 December 1927.

61. *TPG*, 6 January 1928.

62. Ibid., 2, 15, 17 July 1927; *Ekzh*, 29 January 1928.

63. *Ekzh*, 29 January 1928.

64. *Informatsionnyi listok Dneprostroia*, no. 5 (July 1929): 536–71.

65. N. Uskov and P. Shinder, *Dneprostroi kak shkola sovetskogo stroitel'stva* (Moscow and Leningrad, 1931).

66. *KZ*, 25 January 1928.

67. Ibid.

68. Ibid., 28 January 1928.

69. Ibid., 10, 12 May, 9 July, 30 November, 19 December 1928.

70. "Polozhenie o Gosudarstvennom Dneprovskom Stroitel'stve-Dneprostroi," dated 14 May 1928, signed by representatives of the Council of Labor and Defense and the Council of People's Commissars. *Sobranie zakonov*, no. 286, pp. 614–19; *Postroika*, 3 June 1928.

71. *Ekzh*, 28 January, 23 March 1927.

72. *KZ*, 29 January 1928.

73. *Ekzh*, 28 January, 7, 21 February 1928; *KZ*, 25, 27 March 1928; Akademiia nauk SSSR, Institut ekonomiki, *Elektrifikatsiia SSSR: Sbornik dokumentov i materialov 1926–1930 gg.* (Moscow, 1966), p. 70.

74. *Ekzh*, 23 March 1928.

75. Ibid., 28 March 1928. Chubar announced that the goal of Dneprostroi was not just to help the Donbass but to provide the basis for an integrated industrial combine. Ibid., 28 January 1928; *KZ*, 29 January 1928.

76. *Ekzh*, 26 April 1928.

77. Ibid., 9 June 1928.

78. N. Osinskii's speech is in Trotsky's archives, T 1834, cited in Carr and Davies, *Foundations*, Vol. 1, pp. 76–77.

79. N. Mikhailov in *Rabochaia gazeta*, 9 June 1928, quoted in *KZ*, 16 June 1928, and again in *Rabochaia gazeta*, 19 November 1928, quoted in *KZ*, 9 December 1928. Mikhailov argued that cost estimates could not stand serious criticism and therefore that the arguments over the factories could not be based on the presumption of cheap energy. Another antagonist was Shatunovskii, author of "Delo Dneprogesa," a memorandum sent to M. I. Kalinin which I have not been able to obtain but which is mentioned by P. B. Zhibarev in *Lenin i elektrifikatsiia Sovetskoi strany* (Moscow, 1960), p. 181.

80. N. Sazonov, "O stoimosti elektroenergii raionnykh gidrotsentralei," *Puti industrializatsii*, nos. 23-24 (1928); and its rebuttal, S. A. Kukel-Kraevskii, "Zabluzhdeniia i istina v voprose o stoimosti elektroenergii raionnykh gidrotsentralei," *Puti industrializatsii*, no. 2 (1929).

81. This was regularly pointed out in the frequent discussions of the building of a new factory complex.

82. This complaint was voiced earlier by Shumskii, cited in Oliinychenko, *Lenins'ki nakreslennia v zhyttia*, p. 38; M. Volobuev, "Do problemy Ukrainsk'koi ekonomiky," *Bil'shovyk Ukrainy*, 1928, no. 2, pp. 46–72; no. 3, pp. 43–63; and the rebuttal, A. Richysts'kii, "Do problemy likvidatsii perekoloniial'nosty ta natsionalizmu," *Bil'shovyk Ukrainy*, 1928, no. 2, pp. 73–93; no. 3, pp. 64–84.

83. Notes sent to members of the Supreme Economic Council, Glavelektro, and Dneprostroi's Technical Council in Akademiia Nauk SSSR. Institut ekonomiki,

Elektrifikatsiia SSSR: Sbornik dokumentov i materialov 1926–1930 gg. (Moscow, 1966), pp. 70–73.

84. *TPG*, 9, 16 December 1928; *Ekzh*, 2, 9, 11, 26 December 1928; *KZ*, 5, 9 December 1928.

85. Vinter regularly provided for emergencies by stockpiling materials, buying abroad, and making substitutions. He felt he did not need foreign consultants and tried to ignore them, to circumvent their suggestions, and, in 1930, to send them home. Memoirs breathe the same self-confidence in Vsesoiuznyi institut po proektirovaniiu organizatsii energeticheskogo stroitel'stva, Orgenergostroi, *Sdelaem Rossiiu elektricheskoi, Sbornik vospominanii uchastnikov komissii: GOELRO i stroitelei pervykh elektrostantsii* (Moscow and Leningrad, 1961).

86. *Ekzh*, 2, 9, 26 December 1928.

87. Carr and Davies, *Foundations*, Vol. 1, pp. 911–12.

88. Cohen, *Bukharin and the Bolshevik Revolution*, pp. 245–47.

89. Ibid.

90. Ibid., pp. 280–86.

91. This committee had been created in 1926 to promote the project's all-union approval and continued in existence after approval to provide republican support at the highest level.

92. "Iz otcheta o rabote partiinoi iacheiki Dneprostroia s maia 1927 g. po le ianvaria 1928 g.," 27 January 1928. Document 40, *Pervenets industrializatsii strany-Dneproges: Sbornik dokumentov* (Zaporozh'e, 1960), pp. 56–65.

93. Ibid., 10 August 1927.

94. Werth, *Etre communist en URSS sous Staline*, p. 59.

95. "Iz doklada sekretaria partbiuro o rabote partiinoi organizatsii Dneprostroia," 3 September 1927. Document 30, *Pervenets*, p. 41; Ester B. Kartsovnik, "Partiinaia organizatsiia Dneprovskogo stroitel'stva v bor'be za osushchestvlenie reshenii partii o sooruzhenii Dneproges im. V. I. Lenina," candidate diss. Zaporozh'e, 1951.

96. *KZ*, 21 May 1927.

97. Merle Fainsod, *How Russia Is Ruled* (Cambridge, Mass. 1955), p. 196.

98. KP(b)Uk Zaporozhskii Okrug Komitet, *Otchet Zaporozhskogo Okruzhkoma KP(b)Uk k XII Okrpartkonferentsii* (Zaporozh'e, 1927), p. 23; *KZ*, 18 August 1927.

99. *KZ*, 10 August 1927.

100. Ibid.

101. Document 30, *Pervenets*, p. 41.

102. Document 40, *Pervenets*, p. 58.

103. "Rezoliutsiia Orgbiuro Tsk KP(b)Uk po dokladu o rabote partiinoi organizatsii Dneprostroi," 25 January 1928. Document 39, *Pervenets*, pp. 54–55.

104. Document 39, *Pervenets*, p. 56; Document 40, *Pervenets*, p. 56.

105. Document 40, *Pervenets*, p. 59.

106. *KZ*, 13 February 1929; *Dneprostroi*, 5 July 1929.

107. Document 30, *Pervenets*, p. 42; *KZ*, 29 June 1928.

108. *KZ*, 29 June 1928.

109. Ibid., 15 July, 1 October 1927, 31 March 1928; Document 40, *Pervenets*, p. 62.

110. By 1 January 1929, there were still only 18 engineering-technical personnel in the party, and of the 226 in administration only 26 had positions of any authority. "Iz dokladnoi zapiski v Tsk KP(b)Uk Zaporozhskogo Okruzhkoma partii i sostoianii partiinoi raboty na stroitel'stve Dneprogesa," 25 July 1929. Document 63, *Pervenets*, p. 112.

111. Document 40, *Pervenets*, p. 56.

112. Ibid.

113. Later there was also founded a branch of the Pioneer organization for children.

114. "Iz dokladnoi zapiski Zaporozhskogo okruzhkoma LKSMUk v okruzhnuiu organizatsiu s 1 ianvaria po 1 sentiabria 1927 g.," 4 September 1927. Document 31, *Pervenets*, p. 44.

115. The numbers dropped to 202 in February.

116. Document 31, *Pervenets*, pp. 44–45; Document 40, *Pervenets*, p. 64.

117. "Rezoliutsiia pervoi Dneprostroevskoi raionnoi partiinoi konferentsii, priniataia po otchetu raikoma KP(b)Uk," 24 November 1928. Document 46, *Pervenets*, pp. 80–81.

118. Rabochkom stroitelei Dneprostroi, *Otchet* (Zaporozhe, 1927), pp. 1–2.

119. One hundred workers, two hundred research personnel.

120. *KZ*, 20 April 1927.

121. *Postroika*, 1 May 1927; *KZ*, 4 May 1927.

122. *KZ*, 13 May 1927.

123. Ibid.

124. Originally, anyone who regularly worked for a wage could join a union. Criteria for membership became more restrictive, however, at Dneprostroi in August 1928. *KZ*, 11 August 1928.

125. Document 30, *Pervenets*, p. 41.

126. Ibid.

127. Ibid., 25 August 1927.

128. *KZ*, 31 May, 25 August 1927.

129. "Iz doklada rabochego komiteta profsoiuza Dneprostroia o rabote za period s 1 maia po sentiabr' 1927," 20 September 1927. Document 32, *Pervenets*, pp. 45–47.

130. Rabochkom stroitelei Dneprostroia, *Otchet*, p. 1.

131. KP(b)Uk, *Materialy k rabote delegatskikh sobranii rabotnits i selianok, 1925–1926* (n.p., 1925), p. 36.

132. At the end of 1927, there were 791. Thirty were in the Rabochkom. Forty-nine were members of the seven-sector *profburo*.

133. Rabochkom stroitelei Dneprostroia, *Otchet*, p. 1.

134. *KZ*, 12 February, 12 April 1927.

135. Ibid., 16 April, 4 May, 21 June 1927; *Postroika*, 2 July 1927.

136. *KZ*, 21 June 1927.

137. *Postroika*, 6 October 1927.

138. Rabochkom stroitelei Dneprostroia, *Otchet*; *KZ*, 22 July 1927.

139. *KZ*, 7 October 1927.

140. The party defined the production information meeting as the vehicle through which the trade union "might consciously and decisively turn to the task of instructing workers and all laborers in directing the economy, creating the cultural environment conducive to labor discipline, and improving productivity; knowing that this would require sustained activity over a long period of time." *KPSS v rezoliutsiiakh i resheniiakh s'ezdov, konferentsii i plenumov TsK* (Moscow, 1954), Vol. 1, pp. 608–9; Vol. 2, p. 219. The first such production conference had been held in Leningrad in 1923; the XIV S'ezd, in 1925, said they were the preferred form for drawing the masses into productive work.

141. Rabochkom stroitelei Dneprostroia, *Otchet*, p. 2.

142. Ibid.

143. *Postroika*, 6 October 1927.

144. Rabochkom stroitelei Dneprostroia, *Otchet*, p. 2.

145. *Postroika*, 10 September 1927.

146. Document 32, *Pervenets*, pp. 45–47.

147. *KZ*, 17, 24 December 1927.

148. Bailes, *Technology and Society*, pp. 44–66.

149. Stalin's role in the charade of the Shakhti trial is not proven by documentary evidence, but it is clear that the trial itself was not based on real crimes. The style of the trial makes it likely that it was authored by Stalin. Stalin had also attacked Trotsky earlier for using military specialists trained before the revolution.

150. Bailes, *Technology and Society*, chap. 3.

151. Sproge, "Zapiski inzhenera iz SSSR," p. 133. According to Sproge, one felt fine at work, surrounded by well-educated people, well paid, and able to tolerate the sense of impending destruction by not thinking about it. On the street, he was pushed and accused of parasitism, incidents also described by another Dneprostroi engineer, Interview 5.

152. *KZ*, 3 April 1929; *Chervone Zaporizhzhe*, 3 October 1929, accused the young, newly qualified engineers of this as well; *Dneprostroi*, 22 March 1930; *Za industrializatsiiu*, 10 February 1931. Engineers not only sat in their offices, but some refused to leave the big cities. A law was passed requiring them to accept their assignments and permitting certain incentives. *Industrializatsiia SSSR 1926–1928 gg.: Dokumenty i materialy* (Moscow, 1969), p. 364.

153. James H. Pierce, "Assisting the Soviet Coal Industry," *Economic Review of the Soviet Union* 6, no. 6 (March 1931): 136; Paul Scheffer, "An der Baustelle des Dnjepr Staudamus," *Berlines Tagesblatt*, October 1928, cited in Paul Scheffer, *Augenzeuge im Staate Lenins* (Munich, 1972), p. 100; *KZ*, 26 September 1928.

154. Already in January 1928, the Ukrainian Central Committee had warned against specialist-baiting. Document 39, *Pervenets*, p. 54. In Document 46, *Per-*

venets, p. 79, the party warned the Rabochkom not to enculpate all engineering and technical personnel for the mistakes of a few.

155. *KZ*, 4 April 1928.

156. Ibid., 3, 8 March, 4 April 1928.

157. Ibid., 11 April 1928.

158. *Postroika*, 30 August 1928; *KZ*, 27 June 1928. Sheila Fitzpatrick, "Stalin and the Making of a New Elite, 1928–1939," *Slavic Review* 38, no. 3 (September 1979): 377–402, suggests that Stalin played an important role in *vydvizhenie*. Evidence from Dneprostroi suggests that it was a constant theme in Bolshevik policy that became associated with Stalin in relation to the changes precipitated by collectivization.

159. V. I. Lenin, *State and Revolution* (1917), especially chap. 5, part 4, in Robert Tucker, ed., *The Lenin Anthology* (New York, 1975), pp. 382–84.

160. The administration was more successful in finding workers to promote than were the trade unions. *KZ*, 2 April 1929.

161. Ibid., 15 November 1928.

162. Ibid., 19 September 1928.

163. KP(b)Uk Zaporozhskii Okruzhnoi Komitet, *Otchet*, p. 71.

164. *KZ*, 30 May 1928.

165. Ibid., 25 April 1928.

166. Ibid., 16, 19, 21, 26, 30 May 1928. There were also many articles on this subject in *Ekzh* in April and May; see esp. 1 April, 6, 10, 27 May 1928. See also Bailes, *Technology and Society*, chap. 2.

167. KP(b)Uk Zaporozhskii Okruzhnoi Komitet, *Otchet*, p. 23.

168. *KZ*, 30 May 1928.

169. Ibid., 25 April 1928.

170. Ibid., 19 September 1928.

171. Ibid., 11 April 1928.

172. Rabochkom stroitelei Dneprostroia, *Otchet*, p. 2.

Chapter 4. The Labor Force and Labor Policy

1. *Narodnoe khoziaistvo SSSR 1922–1972gg.* (Moscow, 1972), p. 345. Of these, 4.4 million were in heavy industry, including mining, transport, and military industrial enterprises. G. A. Arutiunov, *Rabochee dvizhenie v Rossii v period novogo revoliutsionnogo pod'ema 1910–1914 gg.* (Moscow, 1975), p. 29. In 1927, this number had grown to 15 million; with employees, 18.5 million. L. S. Gaponenko, *Rabochii klass Rossii v 1917 godu* (Moscow, 1970), p. 72, cited in A. I. Vdovin and V. Z. Drobizhev, *Rost rabochego klassa SSSR 1917–1940* (Moscow, 1976), pp. 68–69; "Materialy perepisi 1917 goda," *Istoriia SSSR*, no. 6 (1961): 104.

2. *Narodnoe khoziaistvo SSSR 1922–1972 gg.*, p. 345.

3. G. Zinoviev in his address to the Eleventh Party Congress, March 1922, cited in Anatole V. Baikaloff, *The Land of the Communist Dictatorship* (London, 1929), p. 20.

4. Ibid., p. 21.

5. Vdovin and Drobizhev, *Rost rabochego klassa*, p. 96; *Trud v SSSR* (Moscow, 1968), p. 22; A. A. Matiugin, *Rabochii klass v godu vostanovitel'nogo perioda* (Moscow, 1962), p. 71; O. I. Shkaratan, *Problemy sotsial'noi struktury rabochego klassa* (Moscow, 1970), p. 254.

6. Zaleski, *Planning*, p. 317.

7. I. M. Nekrasova, *Leninskie idei elektrifikatsii* (Moscow, 1960), p. 100.

8. *TPG*, 27 March 1927; *Ekzh*, 27 March 1927.

9. Many émigré Dneprostroevtsi recall they went to the site in response to letters from family members already there.

10. *KZ*, 9, 16 December 1926, 6 January, 20 March, 13, 16 April 1927; *Postroika*, 12 February, 16 March 1927.

11. *KZ*, 16 February, 28 April, 25 May 1929.

12. Baikaloff, *The Land of the Communist Dictatorship*, pp. 98, 99. Workers were taken out of turn, according to the local press.

13. *KZ*, 13 July 1927.

14. *Moskovskaia pravda*, 21 December 1967.

15. *KZ*, 16 February, 3, 25 November 1927.

16. Ibid., 9 March, 11 October 1927.

17. Carr and Davies, *Foundations*, Vol. 1, chap. 17.

18. The majority of these stories were confided in private conversations and letters. Most of those interviewed had emigrated from the USSR. It was not possible to interview many Dneprostroevtsi in the USSR in spite of the fact that many were still living. Most serious is the lack of interviews with party personnel. The chief party personnel died in the purges in the late 1930s. It was not possible to locate the other officials.

19. This woman lost her job when her husband went back to the United States. She supported herself with unskilled work until she received an exit visa. Interview 1.

20. Interview 2. Other workers corroborated that peasants were the lowest class on site; only carters who lived apart with their horses held a lower social position.

21. Interview 3.

22. Statement by Heinrich Rempel, included in a report from the Riga Consulate to State Department, 13 November 1927. U.S. State Department, microfilm 861.5017, Living Conditions/109.

23. Construction workers in the Soviet Union numbered 557,153 in 1925–26; 582,257 in 1926–27; 754,350 in 1927–28; 936,313 in 1928–29, according to V. P. Danilov, "Krest'ianskii otkhod na promysly v 1920-kh godakh," *Istoricheskie zapiski* 94 (1974): 80. Most seasonal workers worked for six to eight months, coming home for the harvest and when it was too cold to work outside.

24. *Ekzh*, 16 October 1927.

25. Ibid., 9 August 1928.

26. Danilov, "Krestianskii otkhod," pp. 108–11; cited by R. W. Davies, *The Industrialization of Soviet Russia, 1: The Socialist Offensive* (Cambridge, 1980), p. 48 n.

27. *KZ*, 18 February, 30 July, 2 September 1927.

28. *Inf. listok*, no. 6 (November 1929): 79; *KZ*, 1 January 1932, in *Pervenets industrializatsii strany—Dneproges* (Zaporozhe, 1969), p. 215. Mistakes in labor planning and the need to learn from them were discussed in the party press. See, for example, *Za industrializatsiiu*, 2 February 1930.

29. *Za industrializatsiiu* regularly carried pleas by enterprises for more workers to dig, break up rocks, and carry loads. Memoirs mention how, in the absence of machines, men worked together as a living conveyor.

30. Carr and Davies, *Foundations*, Vol. 1, pp. 464–65. The plan had foreseen a twenty percent increase in the labor force in "ten or fifteen years." There was a thirty percent increase by 1931 and a one hundred percent increase by 1934. Zaleski, *Planning*, p. 39 n.

31. Cited in Zaleski, *Planning*, p. 342.

32. "Dokladnaia zapiska presedatelia soveta narodnykh komissarov UkSSR v TsK KP(b) o neobkhodimosti bezotlagetel'no reshit' vopros o Dneprostroe," 12 October 1926. Document 2, *Pervenets*, p. 18.

33. *KZ*, 12 April 1927.

34. Ibid., 16 April, 4 May, 21 June 1927; *Postroika*, 2 July 1927.

35. *KZ*, 13 May 1927; about events of 30 April.

36. Ibid., 21 June 1927.

37. Ibid.

38. *Postroika*, 6 October 1927.

39. *Inf. listok*, no. 1 (December 1928): 61–65.

40. *KZ*, 26, 29, 30 July 1927.

41. *Inf. listok*, no. 6 (November 1929): 778–110; nos. 8–9 (June 1930): 549–57; Louis Puls, "Dnieprostroi," unpaged manuscript.

42. *Postroika*, 3 June 1928.

43. *KZ*, 23 August 1928.

44. *Postroika*, 31 January 1928; *KZ*, 8 March 1928, 6 June 1929.

45. *Postroika*, 3 June 1928.

46. *KZ*, 2 June 1928.

47. *Postroika*, 3 June 1928.

48. *KZ*, 2 June 1928; *Postroika*, 3 June 1928.

49. *KZ*, 16 February, 11 June, 30 July 1927.

50. *Inf. listok*, no. 5 (July 1929): 536–74.

51. Ibid.

52. *KZ*, 28 June 1929.

53. Ibid., 22 May 1927.

54. N. Uskov and P. Shinder, "Dneprostroi," *Promyshlennost'. Sbornik statei po materialam TsKK VKP(b)—NKI RKI*, ed. by A. P. Rozengol'ts (Moscow and Leningrad, 1930), pp. 239–41.

55. Housing problems were regularly discussed in all the local newspapers and in VKK and RKI investigations. See, for example, *KZ*, 10 March, 11 June, 17

November, and esp. 10 October 1929 for a contemporary description and the RKI report of Uskov and Shinder, "Dneprostroi."

56. Stealing was also often discussed in the local press. See, for example, *KZ*, 10, 28 February, 10 October 1928.

57. Ibid., 11 June 1927.

58. Ibid., 23 August 1928. "The beds were ranged along the walls with tables in the center, where, between five and six o'clock, workers play chess and checkers or read. The elders lay on the beds (with clean feet) and the literate read aloud, of politics, industry, and Dneprostroi."

59. Ibid., 24 March 1929.

60. Paul Scheffer, "An der Baustelle des Dnjepr Staudamus," *Berlines Tagesblatt* (October 1928), cited in Paul Scheffer, *Augenzeuge im Staate Lenins* (Munich, 1972), p. 100.

61. *KZ*, 28 June 1929; *Postroika*, no. 181, 1929.

62. The first large cafeteria was not built until mid-1928 and never lived up to expectations.

63. *Sed'moi S'ezd professional'nykh soiuzov SSSR* (1927), pp. 148–49, 200, 372; cited in Carr and Davies, *Foundations*, Vol. 1, p. 614.

64. *Obzor deiatel'nosti NKT SSSR za 1927–1928 gg.* (1928), p. 165, cited in Carr and Davies, *Foundations*, Vol. 1, p. 615.

65. *TPG*, 23 April 1929.

66. *KZ*, 12 April 1927. Dinner cost eighty-five kopecks and left the worker "half-starved."

67. Ibid., 30 April 1927.

68. Three were promised, then two. *Postroika*, 2 July, 4 August 1927.

69. Ibid., 7 June, 14 August 1927; *KZ*, 22 May, 15 October 1927.

70. *KZ*, 11 October 1927.

71. Ibid., 19 June 1927.

72. *Postroika*, 12 July 1929.

73. Ibid., 20 June 1929; *Dneprostroi*, 21 June 1929.

74. *KZ*, 20 September 1928.

75. Ibid., 16 February 1929.

76. Carr and Davies, *Foundations*, Vol. 1, pp. 689–96.

77. James Millar and Alec Nove, "Was Stalin Really Necessary? A Debate on Collectivization," *Problems of Communism* 25 (July–August 1976): 49–66.

78. Davies, *The Socialist Offensive*, p. 56.

79. The head of the factory kitchen was fired largely as a result of *rabkor* attacks. *KZ*, 20 September 1928.

80. Ibid., 7 July 1928.

81. *Postroika*, 11 August 1927; *KZ*, 1, 3 January 1928. At the all-site conference in January, workers ironically asked the trade union committee what it was doing for them.

82. So little progress was achieved that the party threatened to call in the all-Ukrainian antialcohol commission.

83. *Postroika*, 2 December 1927.

84. Ibid.

85. But the party recognized that it was widely sold. As much was spent on vodka "as on a whole city budget." *KZ*, 28 January 1928. Money spent on vodka "could pay for seven Dneprostroi." *Postroika*, 7 April 1929.

86. Its sale was forbidden in the clubs, but it was increased in the cooperative stores. *KZ*, 8, 9 May 1929.

87. Ibid., 16 February, 31 March, 16 May, 30 July, 5 August 1927.

88. *Dneprostroi*, 26 September 1929.

89. Ibid., 12 January 1929.

90. *Inf. listok*, no. 2 (February 1929): 94.

91. *KZ*, 10 July 1929.

92. *Inf. listok*, no. 2 (February 1929): 94.

93. Marcel Anstett, *La formation de la main-d'oeuvre qualifiée en Union Sovietique* (Paris, 1958), pp. 77–84. The depth and scope of training for workers stirred much controversy in the latter half of the 1920s, but the principal importance of mechanization and a trained labor force were never questioned. Carr and Davies, *Foundations*, Vol. 1, pp. 475–82.

94. *Ekzh*, 28 April 1928; *KZ*, 3 April 1929. Bailes, *Technology and Society*, explores Lenin's support of technology and that expressed by other political leaders; chap. 1, 2, 13, esp. pp. 345–46.

95. *Ekzh*, 9 August 1928.

96. Hugh L. Cooper, "Address before the Society of American Military Engineers at the Engineers' Club, Philadelphia, February 25, 1931," *Engineers and Engineering* 48, no. 4 (April 1931): 76.

97. IX Z'izdovi KP(b)Uk ta XVI z'izdovi VKP(b), *Raport budivnykiv Dniprobudu* (Khar'kov, 1930). In discussing the problems of waste and spoilage of materials and the lack of effect of fines, one worker suggested lower norms and better tools. No follow-up was published. *Dneprostroi*, 29 March 1929.

98. *Dneprostroi*, 20 June 1930.

99. *KZ*, 2 February 1928.

100. Ibid., 20 June, 9 July, 23 October 1927.

101. *Instruktsiia dlia dumpkar'shchikov* (Kichkas, 1930).

102. The daily press noted a need for literacy classes and then noted, six months later, that they were going badly. *KZ*, 28 June, 17 December 1927. The trade union reported five circles and plans for eight more. An evening literacy school for 130 adults was formed, and 250 students studied on their own. Document 40, *Pervenets*, p. 64.

103. *Postroika*, 26 June, 6 October 1928.

104. Ibid., 16 August 1929; *KZ*, 17 August 1929.

105. There were 600 illiterates on the site; more circles were needed. *KZ*, 10 January 1929. By March 1929, there were seven circles. The number reported in

August was 200 illiterates; by fall there were 320 in eighteen circles. Ibid., 10 March, 17 August, 10 October 1929.

106. *KZ*, 31 August 1928.
107. Ibid.
108. Ibid., 28 December 1928.
109. Ibid., 17 August 1929.
110. Ibid., 23 December 1928.
111. Ibid., 4 April, 30 May 1928.
112. Ibid., 5 February 1928.
113. Interview 3.
114. *Dneprostroi*, 22 May 1930.
115. *KZ*, 23 August 1928.
116. Ibid., 16 August 1929.
117. *Dneprostroi*, 4 January 1930.
118. *Postroika*, 18 August 1929.
119. *KZ*, 29 June 1929.
120. Ibid., 18 January 1929; *Proletar Dniprobudu*, 6 January 1932.
121. See above, chap. 3.
122. *Ekzh*, 1 January 1930; *Za indus.*, 20 July 1930.
123. *KPSS v rezoliutsiiakh i resheniiakh s'ezdov, konferentsii i plenumov TsK*, (Moscow, 1954), Vol. 1, pp. 608–9; Vol. 2, p. 219. The first such production conference had been held in Leningrad in 1923; the XIV S'ezd, in 1925, said they were the preferred form for drawing the masses into production work.
124. *Postroika*, 3 June, 30 August, 13, 19 September 1928.
125. *KZ*, 19 September 1928; *Dneprostroi*, 30 June 1928.
126. See above, Chapter 3.
127. *KZ*, November 1927.
128. Document 40, *Pervenets*, p. 55.
129. *KZ*, 24, 29 June 1928.
130. Ibid., 11 April, 22 June 1928.
131. Ibid., 22 April 1928.
132. Ibid., 5 September 1928.
133. Ibid., 14 January, 10, 29 February, 28 April, 17 May, 24 June 1928.
134. Ibid., 10 June, 18 July, 11 August, 2 October 1928.
135. Document 40, *Pervenets*, p. 58.
136. *KZ*, 29 June 1928.
137. Ibid., 24 June 1928.
138. Ibid., 30 September 1928. The local party discussed the need for *raion* status in June. Ibid., 29 June 1928.
139. Ibid., 12, 14, 30 September 1928.
140. Document 46, *Pervenets*, pp. 78–81; *KZ*, 21 November 1928.
141. Document 46, *Pervenets*, pp. 78–81.
142. *KZ*, 19 December 1928.
143. Ibid., 20 December 1928.

144. The speeches emphasized the necessity of mastering technical and political questions and the place of Dneprostroi as the school for the masses in both these areas.

145. This was done to accelerate the production of manufactured goods for sale to the peasants in exchange for grain. Carr and Davies, *Foundations*, Vol. 1, p. 504.

146. Ibid.

147. *KZ*, 9 July 1929; Arzhanov and Mikhalevich, *Dneprostroi k XVI S'ezdu VKP(b)* (Moscow, 1930), pp. 20–24.

148. *KZ*, 18 January 1929.

149. Ibid., 27 March 1929.

150. Ibid., 16 February, 15, 28 March, 15, 18 April 1929.

151. Ibid., 14, 15 March 1929.

152. Ibid., 10 March 1929.

153. Puls, "Dnieprostroi."

154. *Inf. listok*, no. 6 (November 1929): 87.

155. Davies, *The Socialist Offensive*, pp. 44–46.

156. *Dneprostroi*, 22 March 1929.

157. It was responding to a directive from the all-union Central Committee secretariat which demanded improved tempo and quality in construction, lower costs, and better labor discipline, as well as to the obvious problems on the site. "Iz dokladnoi zapiski sekretaria Dneprostroevskogo raikoma KP(b)Uk Zaporozhskomu okruzhnomu komitetu partii 'O vypolnenii resheniia sekretariata TsK VKP(b) po Dneprostroiu ot 25 ianvaria 1929,'" 7 July 1929. Document 61, *Pervenets*, pp. 103–5. This directive was not published at the time, either indicating a sensitivity to local sentiments of independence or concealing the degree of interference by the secretariat in local affairs.

158. *Dneprostroi*, 22 March 1929.

159. "Pravila," *Inf. listok*, no. 5 (July 1929): 635–42.

160. *Postroika*, 14 July 1929.

161. Carr and Davies, *Foundations*, Vol. 1, p. 514.

162. Ibid., p. 515.

163. Lenin, *PSS* 26: 367. "Our task now that the socialist government is in power is to organize socialist competition." The first contest was on 5 March 1929 in Leningrad.

164. *KZ*, 1 June 1929.

165. *Dneprostroi*, 30 August 1929.

166. Ibid., 10 January, 21 June, 30 August 1929; *TPG*, 8 October 1929.

167. *Dneprostroi*, 14 June 1929.

168. *KZ*, 30 June, 4 July, 20 September 1929; *Dneprostroi*, 30 August 1929; *Postroika*, 10 July 1929.

169. *Postroika*, 18 September 1929.

170. *Dneprostroi*, 14 June 1929.

171. *Inf. listok*, no. 6 (November 1929): 231, for example.

172. *TPG*, 23 April 1929.

173. *KZ*, 5 July 1929. The district council asked peevishly, what is the chief engineer supposed to be occupied with—construction of Dneprostroi or giving permission for an abortion?

174. *KZ*, 5 June 1929; *Dneprostroi*, 8 June 1929.

175. *KZ*, 30 July 1929.

176. Ibid., 10, 30 July 1929; *Dneprostroi*, 12 July 1929; *Raport budivnikov Dniprobudu*; *PD*, 1 March 1932.

177. Uskov and Shinder, "Dneprostroi," p. 250; *Ekzh*, 31 July 1929.

178. Interview 5; Scheffer, "An der Baustelle des Dnjepr Staudamus," pp. 100–104. An antagonism to the German influence was still evident in the memoirs of N. A. Filimonov, "Tri stroiki—tri etapa," Vsesoiuznyi institut po proektirovaniiu organizatsii energeticheskogo stroitel'stva, Orgenergostroi. *Sdelaem Rossiiu elektricheskoi. Sbornik vospominanii uchastnikov komissii GOELRO i stroitelei pervykh elektrostantsii* (Moscow and Leningrad, 1961).

179. *KZ*, 30 July 1929; *Ekzh*, 31 July, 7 August 1929; *TPG*, 8 July, 21 December 1929; a financial estimate was worked out by the administration with the assistance of the RKI, *Inf. listok*, no. 7 (April 1930): 361.

180. Uskov and Shinder, "Dneprostroi," p. 250; A. N. Epshtein, *Robitnyky Ukrainy v borot'bi za stvorennia material'no-tekhnichnoi bazy sotsializmu* (Khar'kov, 1969), p. 108.

181. *KZ*, 12 January 1928.

182. *KZ*, 12, 16 January, 1, 21, 23 February, 5 June 1929.

183. *Pravda*, 31 March 1929, cited in T. H. Rigby, *Communist Party Membership in the U.S.S.R., 1917–1967* (Princeton, 1968), p. 178.

184. Rigby, *Communist Party Membership*, pp. 176–96.

185. Ibid., pp. 176–77. "Verification and purge of organizations of alien elements and of corrupt and bureaucratized people, etc., must be carried out far more determinedly and more systematically. . . . A bold new impetus must be given to the promotion of new party cadres drawn from the workers, to all branches of the work of the state."

186. *KZ*, 4 July 1929. Honest, good-hearted workers (among party members) had nothing to fear, the party press reported. The purge was supposed to encourage economy and rationalization but also eliminate anti-Soviet bureaucrats, class aliens, and wreckers.

187. Ibid., June and July 1929, *passim*.

188. *Postroika*, 30 July, 2 August 1929.

189. *KZ*, 27 June 1929.

190. Ibid.

191. Party members were expelled for drunkeness, breaking labor discipline, belonging to a church, leaving one wife and family unsupported and marrying another, stealing and speculation, or any proven ties to White, Petlura, or anarchist forces.

192. Antagonism to grain collection or to industrial loans, sympathy for the

kulak, support for equalization of wages, or questioning of the party line on industrialization constituted support for the Right Opposition.

193. The purge was covered regularly in *KZ* throughout July, August, and September.

194. *KZ*, 1, 5, 8, 10 October 1929; *Kommunist*, 1 October 1929.

195. *KZ*, 1 October 1929.

196. Uskov and Shinder, "Dneprostroi," p. 250; Epshtein, *Robitnyky Ukrainy*, p. 108.

197. E. B. Kartsovnik "Leninskii plan elektrifikatsii i bor'ba partii za sooruzhenie Dneprovskoi gidroelektrostantsii imeni V. I. Lenina," candidate diss. (Kiev, 1964). Other appointments included that of Evsei Grigor'evich Makar as the district *raikom* secretary. Makar had previously served in East Asia and had recently been secretary of the Sevastopol party organization. He replaced Tumanov and served as secretary from December 1929 through February 1931. *Dneprostroi*, 4 January 1930. Numerous district party officials who served at Dneprostroi stayed on as well, including Arkadev, who served as an *agitprop*, or propagandist and as secretary of the cell in the electromechanical workshop, and M. L. Leibenzon, president of the district Control Commission and member and later secretary of the Dneprostroi *raikom*. *Zaporozhskii industrial'nyi kompleks* (Dnepropetrovsk, 1975), p. 21.

198. Robert C. Tucker, *Stalin as a Revolutionary*, p. 219. V. M. Mikhailov (1894–1939) joined the VKP(b) in 1915.

199. Mikhailov has also been considered a member of the Right Opposition.

200. For example, Sokol'nikov was sent to London.

201. *Chervone Zaporizhzhia*, 20 October 1929.

202. *Zaporozhskii industrial'nyi kompleks*, p. 24.

Chapter 5. The Expansion of the Work Force

1. I. G. Turovski, *Ekonomicheskoe obozrenie*, no. 9, 1929, summed up in Zaleski, *Planning*, 76 n.

2. Zaleski, *Planning*, p. 84.

3. Machine building, for example, grew faster (34 percent growth) than did the supply of necessary constituent materials such as ferrous metals (17.2 percent growth). Ibid., 88.

4. Ibid., p. 94.

5. Investment in state and collective farms was raised 182.6 percent and 56.8 percent respectively, but that for privately owned farms was reduced by 11.4 percent. Ibid.

6. I. V. Stalin, *Voprosy Leninizma*, 11th ed. (Moscow, 1947), pp. 264–74. The number of collective farms had risen from 33,000 to 57,000 between 1 June 1928 and 1 June 1929, embracing respectively 417,000 households.

7. Moshe Lewin, *Russian Peasants and Soviet Power*, trans. by Irene Nove (Evanston, Ill., 1968), pp. 446–520, esp. p. 514; Robert W. Davies, *The Indus-*

trialization of Russia—The Socialist Offensive: The Collectivization of Soviet Agriculture, 1929–1930 (Cambridge, Mass., 1980), pp. 260–61.

8. Davies, *The Industrialization of Russia*, pp. 377–81.

9. Zaleski, *Planning*, statistical appendix, Table A-2, no. 188, pp. 342–43.

10. *Za industrializatsiiu*, 2 February 1930.

11. Ibid.

12. *KZ*, 29 October 1928; 28 November 1929; *Dneprostroi*, 10 October 1930; *Inf. listok*, nos. 8–9 (June 1930): 530.

13. In the same month, *Za industrializatsiiu* compared Dneprostroi, Magnitostroi, and Kuznetskstroi, and argued that Dneprostroi had the best labor supply; the others were all claiming even greater shortages.

14. Ibid., 18 July 1930.

15. See *TsIK SSSR*, 10 January 1931, cited in *Na Trudovom Fronte*, no. 3 (1931): 16; see also *NTF*, no. 2 (1931): 12.

16. A. M. Panfilova, *Formirovanie rabochego klassa SSSR v gody pervoi piatiletki* (Moscow, 1964), p. 107, citing TsGAOR 5515; *Trud*, 8 December 1931.

17. *Kh. D.*, no. 11 (January 1931): 31.

18. U.S. State Department documents on film, no. 861.50 FYP/218. The dispatch from Riga cites a resolution of the TsIK of the Sovnarkom, 30 June 1931, in *Izvestiia* of Narkomtrud, no. 29 (1931): 562; the Joint Instruction of the Committee for Labor, VSNKh, 18 June 1931, ibid., p. 568; the Resolution of the Kolkhoztsentr of the USSR and RSFSR, 9 July 1931, ibid., p. 570; the Resolution of the TsKKK of RKI, 28 August 1931, ibid., p. 572; L. Ginzburg, "Bol'nye voprosy organizovannogo nabora rabochei sily," *VT*, no. 7 (1932): 3–21; S. Klivanskii, "Otkhodnichestvo v SSSR v 1928/29–1931 gg.," *VT*, no. 10 (1932): 66–68; Eduard Ianovich Iakubovskii, *Vovlechenie kolkhoznikov v promyshlennost'* (Moscow, 1931).

19. Ginzburg, p. 19.

20. Ibid.

21. Zatonskii, Commissar for the RKI in the Ukraine, in *NTF*, no. 3 (1931): 5.

22. Speech by Zatonskii, reported in ibid., p. 6.

23. *NTF*, no. 10 (1931): 8.

24. Interview 4.

25. *NTF*, nos. 26–27 (1931): 3.

26. Ginzburg, "Bol'nye voprosy organizovannogo," pp. 16–19.

27. Ibid., p. 18.

28. Klivanskii, "Otkhodnichestvo v SSSR," pp. 66–73; Ginzburg, "Bol'nye voprosy organizovannogo," pp. 16–17; N. Aristov, "Novye zadachi organizatsii otkhodnichestva iz kolkhozov," *VT*, no. 6 (1933): 21; U.S. State Department microfilm, Narkomtrud, *Izvestia*, pp. 562, 564, 568, 570, 572. Panfilova, *Formirovanie, rabochego klassa SSSR*, pp. 24–28.

29. Ginzburg, "Bol'nye voprosy organizovannogo," pp. 3–4.

30. *NTF*, no. 16 (1931): 17.

31. Ibid., pp. 16–17.

32. Panfilova, *Formirovanie rabochego klassa SSSR*, pp. 24–28; Ginzburg, "Bol'nye voprosy organizovannogo," pp. 16–19.

33. *Inf. listok*, nos. 10–11 (1931): 212.

34. Ibid., p. 213.

35. Ibid.

36. Ibid., nos. 8–9 (1930): 681.

37. M. Arzhanov, "Robitnytsvo Dniprobudu," *Bylshovyk Ukrainu*, no. 1 (1931): 51.

38. *NTF*, no. 1 (1931): 4; no. 7 (1931): 12; no. 22 (1931): 9.

39. Ibid., no. 22 (1931): 9.

40. Interview 8.

41. *PD*, 1 March 1933.

42. The target number of women in relation to men for FZU recruitment grew from 30.2 percent in 1930 to 47 percent or 329,000 in 1931. *NTF*, nos. 4–5 (1931): 6.

43. Georg: Serebrennikov, *Zhenskii trud v SSSR* (Moscow and Leningrad, 1934), p. 67. S. Ginzburg, "Stroitel'naia industriia SSSR," *Planovoe khoziaistvo*, no. 8 (1934): 46–63, suggests that the percentage rose even higher during 1933, to 18 percent.

44. M. T. Gol'tsman, "Sostav stroitel'nykh rabochikh SSSR v gody pervoi piatiletki," *Izmeneniia v chislennosti i sostave sovetskogo rabochego klassa* (Moscow, 1961), pp. 176–78. The ages fell in the construction work force from 38.8 in 1929 to 29.9 in 1933, according to Ginzburg, "Stroitel'naia industriia."

45. *Dneprostroi*, 27 August 1930.

46. *Postroika*, 8 March 1931; *PD*, 6 January 1932.

47. *PD*, 8 March 1932.

48. Liudmilla D. Vitruk, *Zhinky trudivnytsi v period sotsialistychnoi industrializatsii* (Kiev, 1973), pp. 51–75.

49. Gol'tsman, "Sostav stroitel'nykh," p. 178.

50. Vitruk, *Zhinky trudivnytsi*, p. 62.

51. *Postroika*, 8 March 1931.

52. Serebrennikov, *Zhenskii trud*, p. 78.

53. A. Mokhson, "Trud v chernoi metallurgi v 1931," *VT*, no. 3 (1932): 3–11.

54. *PD*, 8 March 1933.

55. Ibid.

56. Ibid.

57. Ibid.

58. Ibid., 6 July 1932.

59. "Kharakteristika na Komsomol'tsev—geroev truda, rekomenduemykh TsK LKSMU dlia nagrazhdeniia ordenom Lenina," Document 48, *Promyshlennost' i rabochii klass Ukrainskoi SSR, 1933–1941*, Vol. 1 (Kiev, 1977), pp. 101–2.

60. Interview 12.

61. V. D. Iastrebova, "Ot Volkhova k Dneprogesu," Vsesoiuznyi institut po proektirovaniiu organizatsii energeticheskogo stroitel'stva, Orgenergostroi, *Sdelaem*

Rossiiu elektricheskoi. Sbornik vospominanii uchastnikov kommissii GOELRO i stroitelei pervykh elektrostantsii (Moscow and Leningrad, 1961), pp. 325–32.

62. Sh. A. Zil'bershtein, "Dneprovskaia imeni Lenina," *Sdelaem Rossiiu elektricheskoi*, pp. 347–53.

63. In the western oblasts, "almost no results," for example, and in the northern Caucasus, "2%–60% of plan." *NTF*, nos. 23–24 (1931): 12.

64. There were also eighteen deputies, thirteen managers of production, three hall managers, three inspectors, and more than three hundred cooks. *PD*, 8 March 1933.

65. *NTF*, no. 18 (1931): 4.

66. Ibid.

67. Ibid., nos. 4–5 (1931): 7.

68. *PD*, 8 March 1933. In 1932, when there were more than 7000 women workers out of 36,000 total, there were 310 women in the party. In April, out of 4937, there were 418 party members. *Pervenets*, p. 227. Of the 8159 members of the Komsomol, 2584 were women in 1933. There had been 1842 women in the Komsomol in 1932. *PD*, 8, 10 March 1933.

69. *Dneprostroi*, 6 December 1929.

70. *PD*, 8 March 1933.

71. Ibid., 6 March 1933.

72. G. Datsuk and A. Margolin, "O nekotorykh voprosakh balansa truda Severokavkaznogo kraia," *VT*, nos. 5–6 (1932): 117–22.

73. A. Vladimirov, "Zarabotnaia plata rabochikh SSSR za 15 let," *VT*, nos. 11–12 (1932): 33; Serebrennikov, *Zhenskii trud*, p. 69.

74. *KZ*, 10 July 1929. Average industrial housing of two cubic meters was reported in *NTF*, no. 10 (1930): 16.

75. *Postroika*, 28 January 1930.

76. Ibid., 20 March 1930.

77. Ibid., 20 March, 16 April 1930.

78. Ibid., 11, 19, 23 June, 2 August 1930.

79. *Dneprostroi*, 18 June 1930.

80. Ibid., 20 August 1930.

81. *Chervone Zaporizhzhe*, 8 October 1929. On 12 March 1930, the same paper reported, "There is no bread in the villages."

82. *Kh.D.*, no. 17 (1931): 43.

83. Ibid., no. 19 (1931): 41.

84. *PD*, 11 March 1933.

85. Ibid., 24 March 1932.

86. Ibid., 11, 15 February 1932.

87. Ibid., 5 February 1932.

88. Ibid., 1 March 1932.

89. Ibid., 8 March 1932, 12, 14 March 1933.

90. Ibid., 11 March 1933.

91. Ibid., 4 January 1933.

92. Ibid., 6 March 1933, for example.
93. *Trud*, 14 February 1931.
94. Ibid.

Chapter 6. Production and Productivity

1. Zaleski, *Planning*, pp. 67, 248–50.
2. Ibid., pp. 249–51.
3. *Dneprostroi*, 17 January 1930; *Za indus.*, 7 February 1930; *Postroika*, 8 February 1930.
4. N. Uskov and P. Shinder, *Dneprostroi kak shkola sovetskogo stroitel'stva* (Moscow and Leningrad, 1931), p. 34.
5. See above, chapter 4.
6. *Postroika*, 3 January 1930.
7. See above, Chapter 4.
8. Of the students, 61.9 percent were male, 38.1 percent female. A significant number had been brought up in children's homes and reformatories. Simonna Shulman, "Dneprostroi v bor'be za kadry," *Za promyshlennye kadry*, no. 1, (1931): 19.
9. *Postroika*, 13 January 1931.
10. *Za prom. kadry*, no. 1, (1931): 55–56.
11. *Postroika*, 21 October 1930.
12. Bailes, *Technology and Society*, pp. 161–76.
13. *Postroika*, 17 October, 16 November 1931.
14. Shulman, "Dneprostroi v bor'be za kadry," pp. 15–20.
15. P. Pronin, "Bol'she vnimania voprosam podgotovki rabochikh kadrov," *VT*, nos. 5–6 (1932): 90.
16. Shulman, "Dneprostroi v bor'be za kadry," p. 17.
17. Ibid.
18. Ibid., p. 17.
19. "Na bor'bu s otsevom v shkolakh FZU," *Za prom. kadry*, no. 10 (1932): 49.
20. *Za prom. kadry*, no 10 (1932): 32, nos. 11–12 (1932): 40.
21. Shulman, "Dneprostroi v bor'be za kadry," p. 20.
22. Ibid.
23. For example, at Dneprostroi. *PD*, 16 January, 21, 27 February 1932.
24. P. Pronin and N. Arenkov, "Magnitostroi gotovit kadry," *NTF*, no. 6 (February 1932): 13.
25. See, for example, *PD*, 6 January 1932.
26. Pronin and Arenkov, "Magnitostroi gotovit kadry," p. 13.
27. *PD*, 3 March 1932.
28. Ibid.
29. *Za indus.*, 24 April, 14 May 1930.
30. Ibid., 18 May 1930.
31. *Dneprostroi*, 17 January 1930.

32. *Postroika*, 30 December 1930.

33. *Za indus.*, 10 January 1930; *Dneprostroi*, June *passim*, 1, 11 October 1930; *Postroika*, 29 July 1930.

34. *Za indus.*, 3 June 1930.

35. Ibid.

36. *Kh. D.*, no. 5 (August 1930).

37. Makar reporting in *Za indus.*, 1 August 1930.

38. *Postroika*, 6 June 1930.

39. Ibid., 18 July 1931.

40. A. Kuznetsov, *Za stroitel'nuiu industriiu* (Moscow, 1931), p. 22.

41. *NTF*, no. 1 (1931): 3–4.

42. In construction alone, investment in machines had grown from 39 million rubles to 200 million. P. Ogiev, I. Giberman, E. Gol'dberg, "Perspektivy proizvoditel'nosti truda stroitel'nykh rabochikh vo vtoroi piatiletke," *VT*, no. 7 (1933): 6, citing Gosplan figures.

43. N. Zavodskii, "Trud v stroitel'stve," *Nashe stroitel'stvo*, nos. 15–16 (1931): 997–1001.

44. Ibid., p. 1000.

45. Ibid.

46. *Dneprostroi*, 29 February 1932.

47. "Vnimanie na fronte stroitel'stva," *NTF*, no. 10 (1932): 4; no. 16 (1932): 9–11.

48. *Za indus.*, 22 July 1930.

49. *NTF*, no. 14 (1931): 18. This approach was annually rediscovered. The campaign to increase productivity by guaranteeing the presence of support personnel culminated in the well-known Stakhanovite movement which started in mining in 1934 and was carried throughout industry.

50. Ogiev et al., "Perspektivy proizvoditel'nosti," p. 17.

51. For example, *PD*, 26 February 1932.

52. *NTF*, no. 23 (1932): 5.

53. Ogiev et al., "Perspektivy proizvoditel'nosti," p. 18.

54. Ibid., p. 17.

55. M. Avirom, "Tekhnicheskoe rukovodstvo i kadry ITR chernoi metallurgii," *VT*, no. 5 (1932): 28, 48.

56. *Za indus.*, 17 July 1930.

57. Ibid. Such tugboat brigades were also being used in collectivization.

58. Bailes, *Technology and Society*, pp. 363–64.

59. *Dneprostroi*, 14 August 1930.

60. Ibid., 16 October 1930.

61. Ibid.

62. *NTF*, no. 9 (1931): 8.

63. Ibid.

64. *PD*, 12 March 1932.

65. *NTF*, no. 7 (1931): 12.

66. F. Zil'berbrod, I. Dobzhinskii, E. Kochetovskaia, Tselmin, "Za nemedlennuiu realizatsiiu vtorogo ukazaniia t. Stalina na novostroikakh," *VT*, nos. 2–3 (1933): 2–3.

67. Ibid., p. 6.

68. Ibid.

69. Ibid.; *NTF*, nos. 26–27 (1932): 7.

70. Zil'berbrod et al., "Za nemedlennuiu," pp. 9, 11–12.

71. Zaleski, *Planning*, pp. 124–25.

72. *Chervone Zaporizhzhe*, 22 February 1930. Sixty workers from Dneprostroi and Zaporozh'e went to Korostishivs'kii raion. Lynne Viola, *The Best Sons of the Fatherland* (New York, 1987).

73. *Dneprostroi*, 1, 4 January, 13 April, 16 May 1930.

74. *Za indus.*, 17 January 1930.

75. *Cher. Zap.*, 13 February 1930; *Postroika*, 2 February 1930.

76. *Postroika*, 11 June 1930.

77. *Dneprostroi*, 14 August 1930.

78. Ibid., 25 May, 8, 11 June, 8, 14 October 1930.

79. Ibid., 25 May, 8, 20 June, 6 July 1930.

80. M. Rozental', "K voprosu o sotsialisticheskikh formakh truda," *Pod znamenem marksizma*, nos. 9–10 (1931): 219–21; G. Novikov, *Marksistsko-Leninskoe vospitanie na Dneprovskom stroitel'stve* (Moscow, 1932), pp. 11–12.

81. Interviews.

82. *Istoriia VLKSM i vsesoiuznoi pionerskoi organizatsii imeni V. I. Lenina* (Moscow, 1983), pp. 142–46.

83. *Raport Komsomola Dniprobudu VIII z'izdovi LKSMUk IX z'izdovi VLKSM* (Moscow, 1931), pp. 5–16.

84. Ibid., p. 32.

85. Ibid., p. 39.

86. *Dneprostroi*, 4 January 1930.

87. Ibid., 10 September 1930.

88. Ibid., 4 January 1930.

89. Ibid.

90. *Postroika*, 6 June 1930.

91. Ibid., 21 August 1930.

92. Ibid.

93. S. I. Syrtsov and V. V. Lominadze were among those who spoke out. Syrtsov also wrote a pamphlet protesting the too rapid industrial construction. Roy Medvedev, *Let History Judge: The Origins and Consequences of Stalinism*, trans. Colleen Taylor, ed. David Joravsky and George Haupt (New York, 1972), p. 142.

94. *Dneprostroi*, 17 June 1930.

95. Ibid., 14 October 1930.

96. Ibid., 20 April 1930.

97. *Za indus.*, 20 June 1930.

98. *Postroika*, 29 July 1930.
99. Ibid., 12 January 1931; Novikov, *Marksistsko-Leninskoe vospitanie*, p. 13.
100. He was invited back for opening ceremonies in 1932 and was awarded a Banner of Labor.
101. *Postroika*, 21 February 1931.
102. *Dneprostroi*, 3 August 1930.
103. Ibid., 13 April 1930.
104. Novikov, *Marksistsko-Leninskoe vospitanie*, p. 15.
105. *Dneprostroi*, 23 October 1930.
106. Ibid.
107. Novikov, *Marksistsko-Leninskoe vospitanie*, pp. 15–19, 34, 41.
108. Ibid., p. 18.
109. Ibid., p. 20.
110. Ibid., p. 29.
111. *Dneprostroi*, 18 March 1930. In January 1929, the party had numbered 629 and candidates 202, 9.9 percent of the 8440 on the site. Only four of these had joined before 1917; more than two thirds joined between 1924 and 1928. Of the members, 599 were of worker origins, the others not identified; 385 were Ukrainian, 311 Russian, 59 Jewish, and 74 of other nationalities. The number of women was so insignificant as to be unmentioned. Document 63, *Pervenets*, p. 110.
112. The number varies slightly in different sources. *Dneprostroi*, 22 May 1930; *Postroika*, 29 May, 9 June 1930.
113. *Postroika*, 9 June 1930.
114. Ibid. The numbers in the table are compiled from a number of sources. They sometimes vary between sources by as much as 100 for a given month but tend to even out. Two sources contradict each other concerning the third quarter of 1931. Whereas Novikov claims zero growth, the local party report, dated 14 April 1932, claims a growth of 546 (433 in the first quarter, 335 in the second, 546 in the third, and 663 in the fourth). The absence of growth in the third quarter of 1930, the tone of the daily paper *Proletar Dniprobudu*, and the acknowledged problems of the party in 1931 suggest that Novikov reported correctly and that the official party report averaged the numbers so that the record would look more consistent. Sources include newspapers (*Postroika*, 28 May 1930; *Dneprostroi*, 13 May, 10 October 1930; *Proletar Dniprobudu*, 11 October 1932); party reports (Documents 63, 82, 133, *Pervenets*, pp. 109, 145, 225); Novikov, *Marksistsko-Leninskoe vospitanie*; Kartsovnik, "Leninskii plan elektrifikatsii"; P. I. Shcherbak, *Partiyna orhanizatsiia Dniprobody-kerivna syla v bort'bi za dostrokovyy pusk hidroelektrostantsii. Pratsi Odes'kogo derzhavnogo universytetu im. I. I. Mechnikova* 97, Vol. 150, Vypusk V, 1961; *Ot fevralia k oktiab'riu iz anket uchastnikov Velikoi Oktiabr'skoi sotsialisticheskoi revoliutsii* (Moscow, 1957).
115. Document 133, *Pervenets*, p. 225.
116. Novikov, *Marksistsko-Leninskoe vospitanie*, p. 81.

117. Ibid., pp. 10, 12.
118. *PD*, 4 February 1932.
119. Ibid., 6 January 1932.
120. Ibid., 4 March 1932.
121. Ibid., 18 March 1932.
122. Ibid., 12, 14, 20 March 1932; 23, 27 April, 24 August 1933.
123. Ibid., 1 March 1932; 20, 31 January, 9 February 1933.
124. Rigby, *Communist Party Membership*, pp. 200–205.
125. *PD*, 20 January, 8, 10 February 1933.
126. Ibid., 12 March 1933.
127. M. Solomonov, "Problema truda v stroitel'stve," *VT*, no. 5 (1933): 53.

Epilogue

1. *Istoriia mist i sil Ukrains'koi RSR Zaporiz'ka oblast'* (Kiev, 1970), p. 45; *KZ*, 30 July 1927.

BIBLIOGRAPHY

Unpublished Primary Sources

Cook, J. E. Letter to his employer, 15 July 1930. Ohio Locomotive Crane Co., Bucyrus, Ohio. Company archives.

Cooper, Frances. Personal diary in three volumes, covering the years 1922 to 1935, with a few lines for each day. These volumes are currently in possession of the author.

Cooper, H. L. Letters to his wife, Frances Cooper, 1926–32. These letters are currently in possession of the author.

Interviews and correspondence with former Dneprostroevtsi.

Puls, Louis. "Dnieprostroy." Draft report, typewritten.

Sproge, V. E. "Zapiski inzhenera iz SSSR." Zurich, 1963. Typescript.

Contemporary Newspapers

Dneprostroi, 1927–29; *Proletar Dniprobudu* (*PD*), 1929–32.

Ekonomicheskaia zhizn' (*Ekzh*), 1924–32.

Kommunist.

Krasnoye Zaporozh'e (*KZ*), 1925–29; *Chervone Zaporizhzhe* (*Cher. Zap.*), 1929–33.

Moskovskaia pravda.

Postroika, 1927–33.

Pravda.

Torgovo-promyshlennaia gazeta (*TPG*), 1925–29; *Za industrializatsiiu* (*Za indus.*), 1930–32.

Trud.

Contemporary Journals

Dneprostroi.

The Economic Review of the Soviet Union.

The Electrical Engineer, London.

Electrical World and Engineer.

Elektrichestvo.

Engineering News Record.

The G.E. Monogram.

Informatsionnyi listok Dneprostroia (*Inf. listok*).

Khoziaistvo Ukrainy.
Khronika Dneprostroia (Kh.D.).
Komsomol i elektrifikatsiia.
Na fronte industrializatsii.
Na trudovom fronte (NTF).
Promyshlennost' i torgovlia. (PiT)
Voprosy truda.
Za promyshlennye kadry.

Published Primary Sources

Adams, Henry. *The Education of Henry Adams.* New York: Modern Library, 1931.

Akademiia Nauk SSSR, Institut ekonomiki. *Elektrifikatsiia SSSR. Sbornik dokumentov i materialov 1926–1930 gg.* Moscow, 1966.

Akademiia Nauk SSSR, Institut istorii. *Istoriia natsional'no-gosudarstvennogo stroitel'stva v SSSR 1917–36.* Moscow, 1968.

———. *Materialy po istorii SSSR,* VII. Moscow, 1959.

Akademiia Nauk SSSR, Institut istorii SSSR. *Industrializatsiia SSSR 1926–1928 gg.* Moscow, 1969.

Akademiia Nauk URSR. *Kompleksna ekspedytsiia v raioni Dniprel' stanu.* Kiev, 1931.

Akademiia Nauk URSR, Institut istorii. *Promyshlennost' i rabochii klass Ukrainskoi SSR v period postroeniia fundamenta sotsialisticheskoi ekonomiki, 1926–1932. Sbornik dokumentov i materialov.* 2 vols. Kiev, 1966.

———. *Promyshlennost' i rabochii klass Ukrainskoi SSR, 1933–1941.* 2 vols, Kiev, 1977.

Aleksandrov, I. G. *Dneprostroi. Razvitie iuzhnogo gorno-promyshlennogo raiona i Dneprovskoe stroitel'stvo.* Moscow, 1927.

———. *Dneprovskoe stroitel'stvo i ego ekonomicheskoe znachenie.* Khar'kov, 1925.

———. *Elektrifikatsiia Dnepra.* Moscow, 1925.

———. "Materialy GOELRO po iuzhnomu raionu." *Trudy gosudarstvennoi komissii po elektrifikatsii Rossii, GOELRO.* Moscow, 1925.

American-Russian Chamber of Commerce. *Economic Handbook of the Soviet Union.* New York, 1931.

Anov, N. I. *Dneprostroi.* Moscow, 1931.

Arzhanov, M. "Robitnystvo Dniprobudu." *Bil'shovyk Ukrainy,* no. 1 (1931).

Arzhanov, M., and Mikhalevich. *Dneprostroi k XIV s'ezdu VKP(b).* Moscow, 1930.

Avdakov, N. S. "Nashi vodnye i shosseinye puti." *Promyshlennost' i torgovlia,* no. 16, 15 August 1913.

———. "O nashikh vodnykh putiakh." *Promyshlennost' i torgovlia,* no. 10, 15 May 1910.

Bakhmetiev, B. A. *K voprosu o shliuzovanii i ispol'zovanii vodnykh sil Dneprovskikh porogov.* St. Petersburg, 1914.

Baskov, B. S. "Memuary B. S. Baskova." *Voprosy istorii* 41, no. 3 (March 1966).

Biulleten' oppozitsii (Paris), no. 19 (March 1931) and nos. 29-30 (September 1932).

Bogdanov, N. P. "Nasha gordost', nasha slava—Dneproges." *Byli industrial'nye.* Moscow, 1973.

————. "Pervye opyty po ratsionalizatsii stroitel'stva na Dneprostroe." *Dneprostroi,* nos. 2-3 (1928).

Borzakivs'kyy, O. "Dniprel'stan." *Zhyttia i revoliutsyia,* no. 11 (1926).

Bublikov, A. "Kak uluchshit' nashi vodnye puti." *Promyshlennost' i torgovlia,* no. 22, 15 November 1908.

Budil'nik, no. 21 (1887).

Bukharin, Nikolai I., and Eugene A. Preobrazhenskii. *The ABC of Communism.* Ann Arbor, Mich.: Ann Arbor Paperback ed., 1967.

Bukhgeim, Z. O. *K ekonomicheskomu osvobozhdeniiu Rossii.* Moscow, 1915.

Butkovskii, V. L. *Inostrannye kontsessii v narodnom khoziaistve SSSR.* Moscow, 1928.

Byli industrial'nye; ocherki i vospominaniia, 2nd ed. Moscow, 1973.

Chaplinskii, V. S. *Ratsionalizatorstvo i izobretatel'stvo na Dneprostroe.* Moscow, 1932.

Chubar, V. Ia. *Vybrani statti i promovy.* Kiev, 1972.

Cooper, Hugh L. "Address before the Society of American Military Engineers at the Engineers' Club, Philadelphia, February 25, 1931."*Engineers and Engineering* 48, no. 4 (April 1931).

Dneproges. Kak stroilas' plotina, gidrostantsiia i shliuz. Khar'kov, 1932.

Dneprostroi, *Instruktsiia dlia dumpkar'shchikov.* Kichkas, 1930.

Dneprovskaia gidroelektricheskaia stantsiia i ispol'zovanie ee energii. Materialy komissii po razrabotke general'nogo plana potrebitelei Dneprovskoi energii pri prezidiume VSNKh SSSR. Moscow, 1929.

Dniprel'stan; stenograficheskii otchet, 27 October 1926. Khar'kov, 1926.

Dreier, L. *Zadachi razvitiia elektrotekhniki.* Moscow, 1919.

Elektrifikatsiia SSSR. Sbornik dokumentov i materialov, 1926-1932. Moscow, 1966.

Energeticheskoe stroitel'stvo SSSR za 40 let, 1917-1957. Sbornik statei. Moscow and Leningrad, 1958.

Energetika narodnogo khoziaistva v plane GOELRO. Moscow, 1966.

Filimonov, N. A. *Vstrechi v puti.* Moscow, 1963.

Fridman, D. "Sostoianie elektrotekhnicheskoi promyshlennosti k nachalu 1928 goda i perspektivy ee razvitiia." In *Elektrokhoziaistvo SSSR k nachalu 1927-29 goda,* ed. Iuri N. Flakserman. Moscow, 1929.

Gavrilov, A. M., and I. V. Popov. *Dnepr idet v step'.* Leningrad, 1931.

Ginzburg, S. "Stroitel'naia industriia SSSR." *Planovoe khoziaistvo* 8 (1934).

Gladkov, Fedor. *Energiia.* Moscow, 1932.

Gladkov, Ivan A. *Ocherki sovetskoi ekonomiki 1917–1929.* Moscow, 1956.

———. *Ocherki stroitel'stva sovetskogo planovogo khoziaistva 1917–1918.* Moscow, 1950.

———. *Ot plana GOELRO k planu shestoi piatiletki.* Moscow, 1956.

———, ed. *Razvitie elektrifikatsii Sovetskoi strany, 1921–1925. Sbornik dokumentov i materialov.* Moscow, 1956.

Gordon, A. S. "Budget Financing of Popular Economy." In *Soviet Policy in Public Finance, 1917–1928,* ed. Gregory Y. Sokolnikov et al., trans. Elena Varneck, trans. ed. Lincoln Hutchinson and Carl C. Plehn. Stanford, Calif.: Stanford University Press, 1931.

Gosudarstvennaia Duma. *Stenograficheskii otchet.* 4 sozyv, sessia VII, zasedaniia 59, 18 June 1916. Petrograd, 1916.

Gosudarstvennaia komissia po elektrifikatsii Rossii. *Biulleten* 1. Moscow, 1920.

Gosudarstvennaia planovaia komissia pri Ukrainskom ekonomicheskom soveshchanii. *Ukrogosplan za tri goda.* Khar'kov, 1924.

Gosudarstvennoe Dneprovskoe stroitel'stvo. *Materialy k proektu prof. I. G. Aleksandrova.* 3 vols. Moscow, 1925. Reissued with added materials, 5 vols. Moscow, 1929–35.

Gosudarstvennoe Dneprovskoe stroitel'stvo, Tekhnicheskii sovet. *Opyt stroitel'stva gidroelektricheskikh stantsii SSR; materialy rasshirennoi sessii Tekhnicheskogo Soveta Dneprostroia v Kichkasa s 31-go oktiabria po 2-oe noiabria 1929 g.* Moscow, 1930.

Gosudarstvennyi institut po proektirovaniiu novykh metallicheskikh zavodov. *Dneprovskii kombinat. Materialy k proektu.* Leningrad, 1929.

Gosudarstvennyi Sovet. *Stenograficheskii otchet.* Sessia IX, zasedaniia 54, 18 June 1914. Petrograd, 1914.

———. *Stenograficheskii otchet.* Sessia XII, zasedaniia 23, 16 May 1916. Petrograd, 1916.

Gosudarstvennyi Sovet, Soedinennaia Komissia Finansovaia i Ekonomicheskaia. *Doklad po delu ob otpuske iz gosudarstvennogo kaznacheistva sredstv na raboty v porozhistoi chasti reki Dnepra,* no. 32. Petrograd, 1916.

Grinevetskii, V. I. *Poslevoennye perspektivy russkoi promyshlennosti,* 2nd ed. Moscow, 1922.

———. "Tekhniko-obshchestvennye zadachi v sfere promyshlennosti v sviazi s voinoi." *Vestnik inzhenerov,* no. 1 (1915).

Grin'ko, G. F. "Planovye problemy Ukrainskoi ekonomiki." *Planovoe Khoziaistvo* VI (1926).

Hryshko, W. I. "An Interloper in the Komsomol." *Soviet Youth: Twelve Komsomol Histories.* In *Issledovaniia i materialy* (Munich), series I, no. 51 (July 1959). Published by the Institut zur Erforschung der UdSSR.

Iakubovskii, Eduard Ianovich. *Vovlechenie kolkhoznikov v promyshlennost'.* Moscow, 1931.

Iantarov, S. *Dnepr rabotaet na sotsializm.* Moscow, 1933.

———. *Velikoe istoricheskoe stroitel'stvo.* Moscow, 1934.

Ibatulin, I., and M. Rubin, *Ot Dneprostroia k Dneprogesu.* Khar'kov, 1932.

Imperatorskoe Russkoe Tekhnicheskoe Obshchestvo, St Petersburg. *Zapiski.* St. Petersburg, 1901–17.

Imperatorskoe Russkoe Tekhnicheskoe Obshchestvo, Kievskii otdel. *Zapiski.* Kiev, 1912.

Imperatorskoe Russkoe Tekhnicheskoe Obshchestvo, VI otdel. *Zapiski 1912–13.*

Industrializatsiia SSSR, 1926–1928 gg. Sbornik. Moscow, 1969.

Industrializatsiia SSSR, 1929–1932 gg. Sbornik. Moscow, 1970.

Industrializatsiia SSSR, 1933–1937 gg. Sbornik. Moscow, 1971.

K istorii plana elektrifikatsii Sovetskoi strany, 1918–1920 gg. Dokumenty i materialy. Moscow, 1952.

Kovalevskii, A. A. *Dneprovskaia gidroelektricheskaia stantsiia.* Moscow and Leningrad, 1932.

Kommunisticheskaia partiia Ukrainy. *Deviatyi s'ezd Kommunisticheskoi partii bol'shevikov Ukrainy. Stenograficheskii otchet.* Khar'kov, 1926.

Kommunisticheskaia partiia Ukrainy v rezoliutsiiakh i resheniiakh s'ezdov i konferentsii 1918–1956. Kiev, 1958.

Komsomol, shef elektrifikatsii. Moscow, 1931.

Komsomol'tsy Dneprostroia. Moscow, 1931.

Korotkyy zvit pro rabotu komitetu spriiannia Dniprel'stanovi pry Prezydii VUTSVKu. Khar'kov, 1929.

KP(b)Uk. *Materialy k rabote delegatskikh sobranii rabotnits i selianok, 1925–1926.* 1925.

KP(b)Uk Zaporozhskii Okrug Komitet. *Otchet Zaporozhskogo Okruzhkoma KP(b)Uk k XII Okrpartkonferentsii.* Zaporozh'e, 1927.

KPSS v rezoliutsiiakh i resheniiakh s'ezdov konferentsii i plenumov TsK. Moscow, 1954.

Kraevskii, I., and M. Bugaev. *Komsomol Dneprostroia v bor'be za tempy.* Moscow and Leningrad, 1931.

Krasnyi arkhiv.

Krzhizhanovskii, Gleb M. *Izbrannoe.* Moscow, 1957.

———. *Trudy soveshchanii po podmoskovnomu ugliu i torfu.* Moscow, 1915.

———, ed. *Voprosy ekonomicheskogo raionirovaniia SSSR: Sbornik materialov i statei, 1917–1929.* Moscow, 1957.

Kukel-Kraevskii, S. A. "Zabluzhdeniia i istina v voprose o stoimosti elektroenergii raionnykh gidrotsentralei." *Puti industrializatsii,* no. 2 (1929).

Kushner, Boris. *Revoliutsiia i elektrifikatsiia.* Petrograd, 1920.

Kuznetsov, A. *Za stroitel'nuiu industriiu.* Moscow and Leningrad, 1931.

Lavrukhin, P. "Finansirovanie rabot Dneprostroia." *Dneprostroi*, no. 5 (1928).
Lenin, V. I. *O kul'turnoi revoliutsii*, 2nd ed. Ed. G. G. Karpov. Moscow, 1971.
———. *Ob elektrifikatsii*, 2nd ed. Ed. V. Steklov and L. Fotieva. Moscow, 1964.
———. *Polnoe sobranie sochineniia*, 5th ed. Moscow, 1958–65.
Leninskii sbornik. Moscow, 1932.

Malyshev, V. "Etapy proekta Dneprostroia." *Dneprostroi*, no. 1 (November 1927).
———. "Istoriia problemy ispol'zovaniia porozhistoi chasti Dnepra." *Gosudarstvennoe Dneprovskoe stroitel'stvo* 2. Moscow, 1925.
Mazurin, V. *Kak rodilsia Dneprostroi*. Moscow, 1929.
Ministerstvo Putei Soobshcheniia. *Kratkii istoricheskii ocherk razvitiia vodianykh i sukhoputnykh soobshchenii i torgovykh portov v Rossii*. St. Petersburg, 1900.
Ministerstvo Putei Soobshcheniia, Inzhenernyi Sovet. *Kratkii istoricheskii ocherk*. Petrograd, 1917.
"Ministerstvo Putei Soobshcheniia o nuzhdakh vodnykh putei." *Promyshlennost' i torgovlia*, no. 19, 1 October 1908, pp. 334–36.
Ministry of Finance. *The Industries of Russia, Agriculture and Forestry* 4. Ed. John Martin Cleveland. St. Petersburg, 1893.
Mints, L. E. *Agrarnoe perenaselenie i rynok truda SSSR*. Moscow, 1929.
Mislavskii, N. P. *Dneprostroi*. Moscow and Leningrad, 1930.

N. M. "Shliuzovanie Dneprovskikh porogov." *Promyshlennost' i torgovlia*, no. 9, 1 May 1914.
Nabokov, M. *Iz derevni v promyshlennost' i stroitel'stvo zaverbuem 8 millionov rabochikh*. Moscow and Leningrad, 1931.
Neprozhnii, P. S., ed. *50 let Leninskogo plana GOELRO*. Moscow, 1970.
Novikov, G. *Marksistsko-leninskoe vospitanie na Dneprovskom stroitel'stve*. Moscow, 1932.
Nozhkin, A. F. "Ispol'zovanie porozhistoi chasti Dnepra." *Khoziaistvo Zaporozh'ia*, nos. 3–4 (1922).
———. "Nastoiashchee i budushchee elektricheskikh stantsii obshchestvennogo pol'zovaniia zaporozhskoi gubernii." *Khoziaistvo Zaporozh'ia*, nos. 3–4 (1922).

"Ocherednoi vopros." *Promyshlennost' i torgovlia*. 15 March 1909.
Ogiev, P., I. Giberman, and E. Gol'dberg. "Perspektivy proizvoditel'nosti truda stroitel'nykh rabochikh vo vtoroi piatiletke." *Voprosy truda*, no. 7 (1933).
Ot fevralia k oktiabriu iz anket uchastnikov Velikoi Oktiabr'skoi sotsialisticheskoi revoliutsii. Moscow, 1957.

Pervenets industrializatsii strany-Dneproges. Sbornik dokumentov. Zaporozh'e, 1960.

Pierce, James H. "Assisting the Soviet Coal Industry." *Economic Review of the Soviet Union* 6, no. 6 (March 1931).

Potebnia, A. "Problema Dneprostroia." *Khoziaistvo Ukrainy,* no. 10, 1925.

Deviatyi Ocherednoi S'ezd Predstavitelei Promyshlennosti i Torgovli. "Vnutrennie vodnye puti." *Doklad Soveta S'ezdov o merakh k razvitiiu proizvoditel'nykh sil Rossii.* Petrograd, 1915.

Predvaritel'naia ekspertiza proekta Dneprovskoi gidroelektricheskoi stantsii. Leningrad, 1926.

Prozhektor, no. 19. (15 October 1932).

Rabochkom stroiteli Dneprostroia. *Otchet.* Zaporzh'e, 1927.

Raport budivnykiv Dniprobudu XVI z"izdu VKP(b) i IX z"izdu KP(b)Uk. Khar'kov, 1930.

Raport Komsomolii Dniprobudu VIII z"izdovi LKSMUk IX z"izdovi VLKSM. Moscow, 1931.

Resheniia partii i pravitel'stva po khoziaistvennym voprosam 1917–1967. Moscow, 1967.

Richyts'kii, A. "Do problemy likvidatsii perekoloniial'nosty ta nationalizmu." *Bil'shovyk Ukrainy,* nos. 2, 3 (1928).

Romanov, M. *Organizatsiia otkhodnichestva na novom etape.* Moscow and Leningrad, 1931.

Rozental', M. M. "K voprosu o sotsialisticheskikh formakh truda." *Pod znamenem marksizma,* nos. 9–10 (1931).

Rozov, M. *Dniprovs'ke budivnytstvo i sil'ske hospodarstvo rayoniv zrosheniia.* Khar'kov, 1933.

The Russian Year Book, 1916. London: Eyre and Spottiswoode, 1916.

Rykov, A. *Itogi plenuma TsK VKP(b).* Moscow and Leningrad, 1926.

Sazonov, N. "O stoimosti elektroenergii raionykh gidrotsentralei." *Puti industrializatsii,* nos. 23–24 (1928).

Scheffer, Paul. *Augenzeuge im Staate Lenins.* Munich: R. Piper, 1972.

VII Vserossiiskii elektrotekhnicheskii s'ezd. *Trudy.* St. Petersburg, 1913.

Serebrennikov, Georgi. *Zhenskii trud v SSSR.* Moscow and Leningrad, 1934.

Shaposhnikov, N. "Proekt Dneprovskogo stroitel'stva i ego kritiki." *Khoziaistvo Ukrainy,* no. 2 (1927).

Shatunovskii, Ia. *Belyi ugol' i revoliutsionnyi Piter.* Moscow, 1921.

Shul'man, Simonna. "Dneprostroi v bor'be za kadry." *Za promyshlennye kadry,* no. 1 (1932).

Skvortsov-Stepanov, I.I. *Elektrifikatsiia R.S.F.S.R. v sviazi s perekhodnoi fazoi mirovogo khoziaistva.* Moscow and Petrograd, 1923.

Smith, Andrew. *I Was a Soviet Worker.* London: Hale, 1937.

Sobranie zakonov i rasporiazheniia raboche-krest'ianskogo pravitel'stva Soiuza sovetskikh sotsialisticheskikh Respublik. Moscow, 1927.

Solomonov, M. "Problema truda v stroitel'stve." *Voprosy truda*, no. 5 (1933).

Sotsialisticheskoe stroitel'stvo. Moscow, 1934.

Stalin, I. V. "Novaia obstanovka-novye zadachi khoziaistvennogo stroitel'stva, 23 June 1931." *Sochinenie* 13. Moscow, 1951.

———. *Voprosy Leninizma*, 11th ed. Moscow, 1947.

Tekhnika i Elektrichestvo, nos. 7–8, 1914.

Timonov, V. E. "7ième Question: Les Cataractes du Dnièpre." *VIe Congrès International de Navigation Interièure*. St. Petersburg, 1894.

III S'ezd Sovetov SSSR. *Stenograficheskii otchet*. Moscow, 1925.

Trotsky, Lev. *K sotsializmu ili k kapitalizmu*. Moscow, 1925.

———. *My life*. New York: Scribner, 1930.

———. *Voprosy elektropromyshlennosti i elektrifikatsii. Rezoliutsii soveshchaniia pri Glavelektro 17–20 iiunia 1925*. Moscow, 1925.

Trudy gosudarstvennoi komissii po elektrifikatsii. Moscow, 1960.

Trudy gosudarstvennoi komissii po elektrifikatsii RSFSR-GOELRO. Materialy po elektrifikatsii otdel'nykh raionov. Moscow, 1964.

Tucker, Robert C., ed. *The Lenin Anthology*. New York: Norton, 1975.

———. *The Marx-Engels Reader*. New York: Norton, 1972.

Ukrains'ka Akademiia Nauk, Institut ekonomiki. *Ocherki razvitiia narodnogo khoziaistva Ukrainskoi SSSR*. Moscow, 1954.

United States Department of State. *Records of the Department of State relating to Internal Affairs of Russia and the Soviet Union*. 1910–29 and 1930–39 (catalogue no. 861).

Upravlenie vnutrennikh vodnykh putei i shosseinykh dorog. *Ob assignovanii kredita na raboty po shliuzovaniiu porozhistoi chasti r. Dnepra mezhdu g.g. Ekaterinoslavom i Aleksandrovskom*. Petrograd, 1914.

———. *Razbor proektov gg. Defossa i Rukteshelia o provedenii morskogo kanala ot Rigi do Khersona*. St. Petersburg, 1905.

Upravlenie vnutrennikh vodnykh putei i shosseinykh dorog, Biuro issledovanii vodnykh putei. *Ob ustanovlenii plana stroitel'stva novykh vodnykh putei, ulushcheniia i razvitiia sushchestvuiushchikh i o potrebnykh na to assignovaniiakh*. Petrograd, 1917.

Uskov, N., and P. Shinder. "Dneprostroi." In *Promyshlennost'. Sbornik statei po meterialam TsKK VKP(b)—NKI RKI*, ed. A. P. Rosengolts. Moscow and Leningrad, 1930.

———. *Dneprostroi kak shkola sovetskogo stroitel'stva*. Moscow and Leningrad, 1931.

"V. V. Kuibyshev i sotsialisticheskaia industrializatsiia SSSR." *Istoricheskii arkhiv*, no. 3 (May–June 1958).

Viktorov, B. K. "Chomu treba negayno buduvaty Dniprel'stan." *Bil'shovyk Ukrainy*, nos. 4–5 (1926).

————. *Dneprostroi.* Khar'kov, 1926.

————. "K proektu Dneprovskogo stroitel'stva." *Khoziaistvo Ukrainy*, no. 10 (1926).

————. "Potrebiteli Dneprovskoi energii." *Khoziaistvo Ukrainy*, no. 4 (1928).

Virin, D. *Dnepr sluzhit delu sotsializma.* Khar'kov, 1932.

Volobuev, M. "Do problemy Ukrains'koi ekonomiky." *Bil'shovyk Ukrainy*, nos. 2 and 3 (1928).

VIII Vserossiiskii elektrotekhnicheskii s'ezd. *Biulleten' organizatsionogo komiteta*, no. 1, 26 August 1921.

————. *Trudy 8 Vserossiiskogo elektrotekhnicheskogo s'ezda.* Moscow, 1921.

Vospominaniia o Markse i Engel'se. Moscow, 1956.

Vsesoiuznaia Kommunisticheskaia Partiia (bol'shevikov) XV konferentsiia 26 oktiabria–3 noiabra 1926 g. *Stenograficheskii otchet.* Moscow, 1927.

Vsesoiuznyi institut po proektirovaniiu organizatsii energeticheskogo stroitel'stva, Orgenergostroi. *Sdelaem Rossiiu elektricheskoi. Sbornik vospominanii uchastnikov kommissii GOELRO i stroitelei pervykh elektrostantsii.* Moscow and Leningrad, 1961.

VSNKh, Tsentral'nyi elektrotekhnicheskii sovet. *Predvaritel'naia ekspertiza proekta Dneprovskoi gidro-elektricheskoi stantsii. Prilozhenie XIII. Materialy po ekspertize Amerikanskoi firmy Kh'iu L. Kuper I Ko.* Leningrad, 1926.

Zavodskii, N. "Trud v stroitel'stve." *Nashe stroitel'stvo* 15–16 (1931).

Zil'berbrod, F., I. Dobzhinskii, E. Kochetovskaia, and Tselmin. "Za nemedlennuiu realizatsiiu vtorogo ukazaniia t. Stalina na novostroikakh." *Voprosy truda*, nos. 2–3 (1933).

Unpublished Secondary Works

Anderson, Barbara A. "Internal Migration in a Modernizing Society: The Case of Late Nineteenth Century European Russia." Ph.D dissertation, Princeton University, 1974.

Kartsovnik, Ester Bentsionovna. "Leninskii plan elektrifikatsii i bor'ba partii za sooruzhenie Dneprovskoi gidroelektrostantsii imeni V. I. Lenina." Dissertation, Kiev, 1964.

————. "Partiinaia organizatsiia Dneprovskogo stroitel'stva v bor'be za osushchestvlenie reshenii partii o sooruzhenii Dneprogres im. V. I. Lenina." Dissertation, Zaporozh'e, 1951.

Kolodiazhnii, I. I. "Istoriia stroitel'stva Dneprogesa im. V. I. Lenina, 1927–1932." Dissertation, Kiev, 1953. Summary published in Donets'skii derzhavnii pedinstytut, *Naukovi zapysky*, vyp. VII, 1959.

Kreshtapov, A. D. "Bor'ba Kommunisticheskoi Partii za elektrifikatsiiu strany v pervoi stalinskoi piatiletke, 1928–1932." Dissertation, Moscow, 1953.

Roosa, Ruth Amende. "The Association of Industry and Trade, 1906–1914: An Examination of the Economic Views of Organized Industrialists in Prerevolutionary Russia." Ph.D. dissertation, Columbia University, 1970.

Shcherbak, P. I. "Partiina orhanizatsiia Dniprobudu-kerivna syla v borot'bi za dostrokoyi pusk hidroelektrostantsii." Dissertation, Odessa, 1961.

Published Secondary Works

Akademiia Nauk SSSR, Institut ekonomiki. *Istoriia sotsialisticheskoi ekonomiki SSSR.* 5 vols. Moscow, 1976–79.

Akademiia Nauk URSR, Biblioteka. *Rozvytov elektryfikatsii Ukrainskoi RSR; bibliohrafichnyi pokazhchyk.* Kiev, 1962.

Akademiia Nauk URSR, Institut ekonomiki. *Ocherki razvitiia narodnogo khoziaistva Ukrainskoi SSR.* Moscow, 1954.

Anstett, Marcel. *La formation de la main-d'oeuvre qualifiée en Union Soviétique de 1917 à 1924.* Paris: Rivière, 1958.

Arutinov, G. A. *Rabochee dvizhenie v Rossii v period novogo revoliutsionnogo pod'ema.* Moscow, 1975.

Baikaloff, Anatole V. *The Land of the Communist Dictatorship.* London: J. Cape, 1929.

Bailes, Kendall E. *Technology and Society under Lenin and Stalin.* Princeton, N.J.: Princeton University Press, 1978.

Bash, Iakiv. *Na beregakh Dniprovikh.* Kiev, 1965.

———. *Tvori.* 2 vols. Kiev, 1968.

Belianova, A. M. *O tempakh ekonomicheskogo razvitiia SSSR: Po materialam diskussii 20-kh godov.* Moscow, 1974.

Bel'kind, D. D. *Pavel Nikolaevich Iablochkov.* Moscow, 1950.

Berezov, P. *Valerian Vladimirovich Kuibyshev, 1888–1935.* Moscow, 1958.

Bichuk, Ivan M. *Istoriia pokoreniia Dnepra.* Zaporozh'e, 1970.

Bogdashkin, P. I. *Elektrifikatsiia sel'skogo khoziaistva SSSR.* Moscow, 1967.

Carr, E. H. *The Bolshevik Revolution, 1917–1923.* Vols. 1–3. Middlesex: Penguin Books, 1971.

———. *The Interregnum, 1923–1924.* Baltimore, Md.: Penguin Books, 1969.

———. *Socialism in One Country, 1924–1926.* Vols. 1–3. Baltimore, Md.: Penguin Books, 1970.

Carr, E. H., and R. W. Davies. *Foundations of a Planned Economy.* Vol. 1. New York: Macmillan, 1969.

Chamberlin, William Henry. *Russia's Iron Age.* London: Duckworth, 1935.

Cherniavskii, D. F. "Dniprel'stan ta bibliografiia pro n'oho." *Zhyttia y Revoliutsyia,* no. 9 (1927).

Cohen, Stephen F. *Bukharin and the Bolshevik Revolution.* New York: Knopf, 1973.

Conquest, Robert. *The Great Terror.* New York: Macmillan, 1968.
————. *Industrial Workers in the U.S.S.R.* New York: Praeger, 1967.

Danilevskii, V. V. *Russkaia tekhnika.* Leningrad, 1948.
Danilov, V. P. "Krest'ianskii otkhod na promysly v 1920-kh godakh." *Istoricheskie zapiski* 94 (1974).
Davies, R. W. "Aspects of Soviet Investment Policy in the 1920's." In *Socialism, Capitalism, and Economic Growth,* ed. C. H. Feinstein. London: Cambridge University Press, 1967.
————. *The Socialist Offensive.* Vol. 1 of *The Industrialization of Soviet Russia.* Cambridge, Mass.: Harvard University Press, 1980.
————. "Some Economic Controllers, I, II, III." *Soviet Studies* 11, no. 3 (January, 1960); 11, no. 4 (April 1960); and 12, no. 1 (July 1960).
Day, Richard B. *Leon Trotsky and the Politics of Economic Isolation.* Cambridge: Cambridge University Press, 1973.
Diakin, V. S. *Germanskie kapitaly v Rossii: Elektroindustriia i elektricheskii transport.* Leningrad, 1971.
Drobizhev, Vladimir Zinovevich, and N. V. Dumova. *Ia. Chubar.* Moscow, 1963.

Egorov, K. D. "Elektrifikatsiia ugol'noi promyshlennosti v plane GOELRO." *Energetika narodnogo khoziastva v plane GOELRO.* Moscow, 1966.
Epshtein, Arkadi I. *Robitnyky Ukrainy v borot'bi za stvorennia material'no-tekhnichnoi bazy sotsializmu, 1928–1932 rr.* Khar'kov, 1968.
Erlich, Alexander. *The Soviet Industrialization Debate, 1924–1928,* 2nd ed. Cambridge, Mass.: Harvard University Press, 1967.
Evseev, M. P. *Voprosy sotsialisticheskoi ekonomiki v rabotakh V. V. Kuibysheva.* Tomsk, 1967.

Fainboim, I. V. *Ivan Gavrilovich Aleksandrov.* Moscow, 1955.
Fainsod, Merle. *How Russia Is Ruled.* Cambridge, Mass.: Harvard University Press, 1955.
Finarov, A. P. *Bor'ba partii za sotsialisticheskuiu industrializatsiiu strany i podgotovku sploshnoi kollektivizatsii sel'skogo khoziaistva, 1926–1929.* Moscow, 1973.
Fitzpatrick, Sheila. *Cultural Revolution in Russia, 1928–1931.* Bloomington, Ind.: Indiana University Press, 1978.
————. *The Russian Revolution.* Oxford: Oxford University Press, 1982.
————. "Stalin and the Making of a New Elite, 1928–1939." *Slavic Review* 38, no. 3 (September 1979).
Friedman, E. *Russia in Transition: A Businessman's Appraisal.* New York: Viking, 1932.

Genkina, Esfir B. *Gosudarstvennaia deiatel'nost' V. I. Lenina, 1921–1923.* Moscow, 1969.

Gol'tsman, M. T. "Sostav stroitel'nykh rabochikh SSSR v gody pervoi piatiletki po materialam profsoiuznykh perepisei 1929 i 1932 gg." *Izmeneniia v chislennosti i sostave sovetskogo rabochego klassa.* Moscow, 1961.

Haumann, Heiko. *Beginn der Planwirtschaft: Elektrifizierung, Wirtschaftsplanung und gesellschaftliche Entwicklung Sowjetrusslands 1917–1921.* Dusseldorf: Bertelsmann, 1974.

Hunter, Holland, with Robert Campbell, Stephen F. Cohen, and Moshe Lewin. "The Overambitious First Five Year Plan." *Slavic Review* 32, no. 2 (June 1973).

Ikonnikov, S. N. *Sozdanie i deiatel'nost' ob"edinennykh organev TsKK-RKI v 1923–1934.* Moscow, 1971.

Institut zur Erforschung der UdSSR. *Who Was Who in the USSR.* Ed. H. E. Schulz et al. Metuchen, N.J.: Scarecrow Press, 1972.

Ipatieff, V. N. "Modern Science in Russia." *Russian Review* 2, no. 2 (Spring 1948).

Istoriia mist i sil Ukrains'koi RSR, Zaporiz'ka oblast'. Kiev, 1970.

Istoriia VLKSM i vsesoiuznoi pionerskoi organizatsii imeni V. I. Lenina. Moscow, 1983.

Iufereva, E. V. *Leninskoe uchenie o goskapitalizme v perekhodnyi period k sotsializmu.* Moscow, 1969.

Jasny, Naum. "Essay VI, Soviet 'Perspective' Planning." *Essays on the Soviet Economy.* New York: Praeger, 1962.

———. *Soviet Economists of the Twenties: Names to Be Remembered.* Cambridge: Cambridge University Press, 1972.

Kas'ianenko, V. I. *Kak byla zavoevana tekhniko-ekonomicheskaia samostoiatel'nost SSSR.* Moscow, 1964.

Kas'ianenko, V. I., et al. "Iz istorii kontsessionoi politiki sovetskogo gosudarstva." *Istoriia SSSR* 4 (1959).

Khavin, A. F. *U rulia industrii.* Moscow, 1968.

Khromov, S. S. *F. E. Dzerzhinskii na khoziaistvennom fronte.* Moscow, 1977.

———. *F. E. Dzerzhinskii vo glave metallopromyshlennosti.* Moscow, 1966.

Kirchner, Walter. "The Industrialization of Russia and the Siemens Firm, 1853–1890." *Jahrbücher für Geschichte Osteuropas* 22, no. 3 (1974).

Korniilenko, I. S. *Kino Sovetskoi Ukrainy.* Moscow, 1975.

Kostin, Kh. I. "Sredi pokoritelei Dnepra, Vospominaniia." *Voprosy istorii* 77 (November 1968).

Kostrytsia, N. Iu. *Komunistychna partiia-orhanizator vsenarodnoi borot'by za zdiysnennia lenins'skykh idey elektryfikatsii na Ukraini.* Kiev, 1967.

Krzhizhanovskii, Gleb M. *Myslitel' i revoliutsioner.* Moscow, 1971.

Lewin, Moshe. *Political Undercurrents in Soviet Economic Debates.* Princeton, N.J.: Princeton University Press, 1974.
———. "The Social Background to Stalinism." In *Stalinism: Essays in Historical Interpretation,* ed. Robert C. Tucker. New York: Norton, 1977.
———. "Society and the Stalinist State in the Period of the Five Year Plans." *Social History,* no. 2 (May 1976).
———. "Society, State and Ideology during the First Five-Year Plan." In *Cultural Revolution in Russia, 1928-1931,* ed. Sheila Fitzpatrick. Bloomington, Ind.: Indiana University Press, 1978.
Lewytzkyj, B. *The Stalinist Terror in the Thirties.* Stanford, Calif.: Hoover Institution Press, 1974.
Leyda, Jay. *Kino: A History of the Russian and Soviet Film.* London: Allen & Unwin, 1960.
Liashchenko, P. I. *History of the National Russian Economy.* Trans. L. M. Herman. New York: Macmillan, 1949.
———. *Istoriia narodnogo khoziaistva SSSR. Sotsializm.* Vol. 3. Moscow, 1956.

McKay, John. *Pioneers for Profit: Foreign Entrepreneurship and Russian Industrialization, 1885-1913.* Chicago: University of Chicago Press, 1970.
Mai, Joachim. *Das Deutsche Kapital in Russland, 1850-1894.* Berlin: Deutscher Verlag des Wissenschaften, 1970.
"Materialy perepisi 1917 goda." *Istoriia SSSR,* no. 6 (1961).
Matiugin, A. A. *Rabochii klass v godu vosstanovitel'nogo perioda.* Moscow, 1962.
Medvedev, Roy. *Let History Judge: The Origins and Consequences of Stalinism.* Trans. Colleen Taylor, ed. David Joravsky and Georges Haupt. New York: Random House, Vintage Books, 1972.
———. *On Stalin and Stalinism.* Trans. Ellen de Kadt. Oxford: Oxford University Press, 1979.
Meleshchenko, Iu. S., and S. V. Shukhardin. *Lenin i nauchno-tekhnicheskii progress.* Leningrad, 1969.
Millar, James R. "Mass Collectivization and the Contribution of Soviet Agriculture to the First Five Year Plan: A Review Article." *Slavic Review* 33, no. 4 (December 1975).
Millar, James R., and Alec Nove. "Was Stalin Really Necessary? A Debate on Collectivization." *Problems of Communism* 25 (July–August 1976).

Narodnoe khoziaistvo SSSR 1922-1927 gg. Moscow, 1972.
Narysy istorii Zaporiz'koi oblasnoi partyinoi orhanizatsii. Kiev, 1968.
Nekrasova, I. M. *Leninskii idei elektrifikatsii.* Moscow, 1960.
———. "Problemy elektrifikatsii SSSR v sovetskoi istoricheskoi nauke." *Voprosy istorii,* no. 8 (August 1969).
Nove, Alec. *An Economic History of the USSR.* Middlesex: Penguin Books, 1969.

Odom, William E. *The Soviet Volunteers: Modernization and Bureaucracy in a Public Mass Organization.* Princeton N.J.: Princeton University Press, 1973.
Oliinychenko, M. D. *Lenins'ki nakreslennia v zhittia. KPRS-orhanizator budivnytstva Dniprovs'koho kaskadu hidro-elektrostantsii 1927–1970.* Kiev, 1970.
Oppenheim, Samuel A. "The Supreme Economic Council 1917–1921." *Soviet Studies* 25, no. 1 (July 1973).

Padmore, George. *Pan-Africanism or Communism.* Garden City, N.Y.: Doubleday, 1972.
Panfilova, A. M. *Formirovanie rabochego klassa SSSR v gody pervoi piatiletki 1928–1932.* Moscow, 1964.
Pethybridge, Roger. *The Social Prelude to Stalinism.* New York: St. Martin's Press, 1974.
Plan elektrifikatsii RSFSR, 2nd ed. Moscow, 1955.
Pollock, Frederick. *Die planwirtschaftlichen Versuche in der Sowjetunion 1917–1927.* Leipzig: Hirschfield, 1929.

Rigby, T. H. *Communist Party Membership in the USSR, 1917–1967.* Princeton, N.J.: Princeton University Press, 1968.
Rogachevskaia, L. S. *Likvidatsiia bezrabotitsy v SSSR, 1917–1930 gg.* Moscow, 1973.

Schwarz, Solomon M. *Labor in the Soviet Union.* New York: Praeger, 1952.
Shatelen, M. A. *Russkie elektrotekhniki vtoroi poloviny XIX veka.* Moscow and Leningrad, 1950.
Shcherbak, P. I. *Partiyna orhanizatsiia Dniprobudu-kerivna syla v borot'bi za dostrokovyy pusk hidroelektrostantsii.* Pratsi Odes'kogo derzhavnogo universytetu im. I. I. Mechnikova, 97, Vol. 150, Vypusk V, 1961.
Shkaratan, O. I. *Problemy sotsial'noi struktury rabochego klassa.* Moscow, 1970.
Sidorenko, P. O. *Lenins'kyi plan GOELRO.* Khar'kov, 1973.
Slutskii, A. B. *Rabochii klass Ukrainy v bor'be za sozdanie fundamenta sotsialisticheskoi ekonomiki 1926–1932.* Kiev, 1963.
Smolinski, Leon. "Grinevetskii and Soviet Industrialization." *Survey,* no. 67 (April 1968).
Solzhenitsyn, Alexander I. *Matrenin dvor.* London: Flegon Press, 1965.
Spulber, Nicholas. *Soviet Strategy for Economic Growth.* Bloomington, Ind.: Indiana University Press, 1964.
Starr, S. Frederick. "Visionary Town Planning during the Cultural Revolution." In *Cultural Revolution in Russia, 1928–1931,* ed. Sheila Fitzpatrick. Bloomington, Ind.: Indiana University Press, 1978.
Steklov. V. Iu. *50 Let Leninskogo plana elektrifikatsii: Bibliograficheskii ukazatel'.* Moscow, 1970.
———. *V. I. Lenin i elektrifikatsiia.* Moscow, 1970.
———. *V. I. Lenin i elektrifikatsiia,* 2nd ed. Moscow, 1975.

————, et al., eds. *Gleb Makimilianovich Krzhizhanovskii; zhizn' i deiatel'nost'.* Moscow, 1974.

Sullivant, Robert S. *Soviet Politics and the Ukraine, 1917–1957.* New York: Columbia University Press, 1962.

Sutton, Anthony. *Western Technology and Soviet Economic Development.* 3 vols. Stanford, Calif.: Hoover Institution Press, 1968–73.

Tomsk, Universitet, Kafedra istorii KPSS. *V. V. Kuibyshev, vydaiushchiisia proletarskii revoliutsioner i myslitel'.* Tomsk, 1963.

Tucker, Robert C. *Stalin as Revolutionary, 1870–1929: A Study in History and Personality.* New York: Norton, 1973.

Vdovin, A. I., and V. Z. Drobizhev. *Rost rabochego klassa SSSR 1917–1940.* Moscow, 1976.

Verkhovtsev, I. I., ed. *Svet nad Rossiei.* Moscow, 1960.

Vilenskii, M. A. *Po Leninskomu puti sploshnoi elektrifikatsii.* Moscow, 1969.

Vinogradskaia, Sofia. *Inzhener nashei epokhi.* Moscow, 1934.

Viola, Lynne. *The Best Sons of the Fatherland.* New York: Oxford University Press, 1987.

Vitruk, Liudmilla D. *Zhinky trudivnytsi v period sotsialistychnoi industrializatsii.* Kiev, 1973.

Von Laue, Theodor. *Why Lenin? Why Stalin?* Philadelphia: Lippincott, 1964.

Watstein, J. "Soviet Economic Concessions; the Agony and the Promise." *ACES Bulletin* 16, no. 1 (Spring 1974).

Weitz, B. I., ed. *Electric Power Development in the USSR.* Trans. L. Mins. Moscow, 1936.

Werth, Nicholas. *Etre communiste en URSS sous Staline.* Paris: Gallimard/ Julliard, 1981.

Westwood, John N. *A History of Russian Railways.* London: G. Allen and Unwin, 1964.

Zaleski, Eugene. *Planning for Economic Growth in the Soviet Union 1918–1932.* Trans. M. C. MacAndrew and G. W. Nutter. Chapel Hill, N.C.: University of North Carolina Press, 1971.

Zaporozhskii industrial'nyi kompleks. Dnepropetrovsk, 1975.

Zelenetskaia, V. N. "Istoriia elektrifikatsii SSSR v dokumentakh." *Voprosy istorii,* no. 1 (January 1971).

Zhibarev, P. B. *Lenin i elektrifikatsii Sovetskoi strany.* Moscow, 1960.

Zhimerin, D. G. *Istoriia elektrifikatsii SSSR.* Moscow, 1962.

Zvorykin, A. A., et al. *Istorii tekhniki.* Moscow, 1962.

INDEX

DATE DUE
